Theodore Roosevelt
and the Assassin

ALSO BY GERARD HELFERICH

Humboldt's Cosmos: Alexander von Humboldt and the Latin American Journey That Changed the Way We See the World

High Cotton: Four Seasons in the Mississippi Delta

Stone of Kings: In Search of the Lost Jade of the Maya

THEODORE ROOSEVELT AND THE ASSASSIN

Madness, Vengeance, and the Campaign of 1912

GERARD HELFERICH

LYONS PRESS
Guilford, Connecticut
An imprint of Globe Pequot Press

Lyons Press is an imprint of Globe Pequot Press.

Photos on pages 196 and 198 are in the public domain. All other photos courtesy of the Library of Congress unless otherwise noted.

Map by Melissa Baker © Morris Book Publishing, LLC
Project editor: Meredith Dias
Layout artist: Sue Murray

Library of Congress Cataloging-in-Publication Data

Helferich, Gerard.
  Theodore Roosevelt and the assassin : madness, vengeance, and the campaign of 1912 / Gerard Helferich.
    pages cm
  Summary: "Rich with local color, period detail, and a fully realized historical and political backdrop, the forgotten story of the lone, fanatical assailant who stalked Theodore Roosevelt on the 1912 presidential campaign trail until the evening of October 14 in Milwaukee, when he shot the Bull Moose in the chest from ten feet away"—Provided by publisher.
  ISBN 978-0-7627-8299-4 (hardback)
  1. Roosevelt, Theodore, 1858-1919—Assassination attempt, 1912. 2. Schrank, John Flammang, 1876-1943. 3. Presidents—United States—Election—1912. I. Title.
  E765.H45 2013
  973.911092—dc23

                                                                    2013019156

Printed in the United States of America

10 9 8 7 6 5 4 3 2 1

With gratitude and love to my extended family of brothers and sisters—Bill and Carol, Marlene and Bob, Lisa and Joel, and Debbie and Jan

CONTENTS

The Travels of Theodore Roosevelt and John Schrank, September 21–October 14, 1912.

PROLOGUE
"Avenge My Death!"
Sunday, September 15, 1901

THE YOUNG, HEAVYSET MAN FOUND HIMSELF ALONE IN A CAVERNOUS room. Eerily quiet, the dim chamber was crowded with wreaths and sprays of flowers exuding an overpowering, syrupy odor. In the center of the room rested an open coffin of polished Santo Domingo mahogany. Inside the casket lay a portly, middle-aged man dressed in a black suit, a white shirt with a stiff collar, and a slender black bow tie. The man's thinning gray hair was oiled, revealing a high forehead, owlish brows, and a square, cleft chin. Even in death, the features wore a stolid but kindly expression, revealing no trace of malice, no hint of the suffering he'd endured. The young man recognized the face immediately. It belonged to President William McKinley, who had perished early the previous morning.

For the past week, the young man had pored over the newspapers, immersing himself in the details of the tragedy. The president had been attending the Pan-American Exposition in Buffalo, a lavish spectacle meant to showcase American prosperity at the dawn of the twentieth century, with fanciful lagoons and canals, a midway of rides and attractions, and massive exhibition halls dedicated to sciences such as agriculture and mining, all bathed in electric light from the newly harnessed power of Niagara Falls. But while Buffalo had begun to call itself "the City of Light," its exposition would forever after be linked with something dark and hideous.

The fair had opened in May, and President McKinley had planned to make an official visit in June. But when the First Lady had another of her "attacks," the trip was postponed until September.

The president finally arrived in Buffalo on Wednesday the fourth, and the following day delivered a fine speech on one of his pet themes, the need to expand overseas markets for American goods. On Friday, declared President's Day at the exposition, he boarded a train to view the spectacular Falls, twenty miles away, then returned to Buffalo and prepared to greet the public at the exposition's Temple of Music. Fearing for his chief's safety in the throng, McKinley's personal secretary had canceled the reception twice, but the president had insisted on attending. "No one would wish to hurt me," he'd scoffed. Besides, the president enjoyed meeting the public. "Everyone in that line has a smile and a cheery word," he said. "They bring no problems with them; only good will."

William McKinley had coasted to reelection less than a year before, on the slogan "Prosperity at Home and Prestige Abroad." The economy had finally recovered from the Panic of 1893, the worst financial depression the nation had ever seen. Thanks to its swift, seemingly effortless victory in the Spanish-American War, the country had won strategic possessions in the Caribbean and the Pacific and had joined the ranks of the world's great powers. By the time the Temple of Music's doors opened at 4:00 p.m., a queue had been waiting for hours to shake the popular president's hand.

The Temple was the exposition's principal auditorium, designed in the Italian Renaissance style and set beside the fair's central Fountain of Abundance. The exterior was painted soft yellow, trimmed with red and gold, and topped by a sky-blue dome. At each of the building's four corners opened a graceful arched doorway, surmounted by a plaster statue representing a different musical genre. Outside the east entrance this afternoon, waiting with the rest of the crowd under the warm September sun, stood a mill worker named Leon Czolgosz.

Born in Michigan, the son of Polish immigrants, the twenty-eight-year-old Czolgosz had lived most of his life in McKinley's home state of Ohio. He'd arrived in Buffalo the week before and had registered in a rooming house under the name Fred Nieman, saying he'd come to sell souvenirs at the fair, though none of the other boarders had noticed any evidence of mercantile activity. Keeping to himself, the newcomer seemed to spend most of his time hunched over the daily newspapers.

Several years ago, after losing his job during a strike at a Cleveland wire mill, Czolgosz had been drawn to the radical philosophy of anarchism. Dedicated to fomenting revolution and establishing an egalitarian and stateless society, anarchists subscribed to the "propaganda of the deed," the belief that the most potent way to advance their cause was through spectacular acts of violence such as bombings and assassinations. Over the past two decades, anarchists had orchestrated dozens of acts of terrorism, especially in Europe, where they had killed Russian Czar Alexander II, French President Marie François Sadi Carnot, Spanish Prime Minister Antonio Cánovas del Castillo, and, just the year before, King Umberto I of Italy.

The United States had also seen two presidents assassinated over the past thirty-six years. But the first, Abraham Lincoln, had been a casualty of civil war. And the other, James Garfield, had been shot by a lunatic named Charles Guiteau, who thought to claim the presidency for himself. Neither of these domestic assassins was an anarchist, wishing to abolish all government. Yet even as Americans celebrated the new century, the nation was deeply divided. Over the past several decades, as the country had grown more industrial, more urban, and more ethnically diverse, huge monopolistic "trusts" such as John D. Rockefeller's Standard Oil and J. P. Morgan's U.S. Steel had come to dominate the nation's commerce and, increasingly, its politics, until it seemed that the interests of the wealthy and powerful had eclipsed the needs of working people. And into this broken soil were sown the fertile seeds of anarchy.

William McKinley was a child of the middle class, but his election campaign had been underwritten by millionaires and corporations, and as president he had served those interests well. He advocated steep tariffs to protect American companies, even though the levies meant higher prices for consumers. And though he assured workers that they too would benefit from the expanding economy, the lion's share of the gains had gone to investors. Over the past few decades, as new machines had decreased the demand for labor and as waves of European immigrants had increased the supply, factory employees had watched their wages fall, even as their hours remained long and their working conditions hazardous. In case after case, the Supreme Court had ruled against workers and in favor of capitalists. And if employees dared to strike, they were apt to be brutalized by private security forces, the police, or the Army, and then discarded for new, even more desperate recruits willing to work for less. In the words of "the Great Commoner," William Jennings Bryan, who had run against McKinley in 1896, "The extremes of society, [were] being driven further and further apart."

Leon Czolgosz had felt labor injustice firsthand, and after hearing the anarchist Emma Goldman address a rally in Chicago, he had determined to act. The day before, when McKinley had delivered his speech at the Pan-American Exhibition, Czolgosz had been standing in the throng, but he hadn't been able to shoulder his way close to the president. Reading in one of his newspapers that McKinley would spend this morning at Niagara Falls, Czolgosz had shadowed him there, but again unable to get near, he had taken an early train back to Buffalo. That same afternoon, he was among the first in line outside the Temple of Music.

At four o'clock, when the doors opened, the president stood beneath the Temple's soaring dome, flanked by an enormous American flag and a display of potted plants, while a Bach sonata wafted from the new pipe organ. Then, as the public began filing past the cordon of soldiers, a dark-skinned, "foreign-looking" man attracted the suspicion of guards, who were on the alert for anarchists. Concern mounted when the man persisted in pumping the president's hand for an unseemly time before finally being led away. In the confusion, no one noticed Leon Czolgosz, with his right hand jammed into his coat pocket.

The line of greeters inched forward, and Czolgosz reached the president's side at 4:07. McKinley smiled, and the anarchist withdrew his hand, swathed in a white handkerchief. Inside was a silver-plated, .32-calibre Johnson revolver, the same model that had been used to kill Umberto I.

Two explosions shook the Temple's dome. Then a heavy silence descended. A look of confusion spread over McKinley's face, and a sudden pallor. He slumped but didn't collapse. Guards and bystanders began pummeling the shooter. But as the president was helped away, he said, "Don't let them hurt him."

"I done my duty," Czolgosz was heard to say.

With blood seeping onto his white shirt and vest, McKinley was carried by an electric ambulance to the exposition's hospital. Like most of the fair buildings, and even the spectacular Temple of Music, the low, mission-style hospital was a temporary construction of a plaster-like material called staff, destined to be demolished after the exhibition's six-month run. But whereas the public venues were bathed in brilliant light, the infirmary hadn't been fitted with electricity. To inspect the president's wound, doctors rigged a hospital pan to reflect the late-afternoon sun.

One slug had been deflected by the president's sternum. The other had entered the left side of his body, about five inches below the breast. Probing the wound with bare, unsterilized fingers, the doctors were unable to locate the bullet.

As it happened, Buffalo's leading expert on gunshot wounds had been called away to Niagara Falls on another case, so officials summoned a gynecological surgeon named Matthew Mann from a nearby barbershop where he was having his hair trimmed. Arriving at the fairgrounds with his head half shorn, Mann stitched the president together as best he could and decided not to risk removing the projectile.

As news of the shooting spread, the nation crowded into houses of worship to pray for its stricken leader. Newspapers reported that McKinley was resting comfortably at the home of exposition president John G. Milburn, and after four days he was pronounced out of danger. Reassured, Vice President Theodore Roosevelt, who'd been called to Buffalo, left for a family camping vacation in the Adirondacks.

Then, on the afternoon of September 12, McKinley's pulse abruptly weakened, and he began to drift in and out of consciousness. On the evening of the thirteenth, a telegram went out to Roosevelt: "The president appears to be dying and members of the cabinet in Buffalo think you should lose no time coming." And so the vice president began a headlong journey to Buffalo, thirteen hours away by buckboard and special train. En route, he muttered of Czolgosz, "If it had been I who had been shot, he wouldn't have got away so easily. . . . I'd have guzzled him first."

That night, the president glanced about his sickroom and murmured, "God's will be done, not ours." The First Lady leaned close and sang his favorite hymn, "Nearer, My God, to Thee." Then, at 2:15 on the morning of September 14, the fifty-eight-year-old McKinley expired. The autopsy showed that the bullet had sliced through his stomach, pancreas, and a kidney, before lodging deep in his back; the cause of death was gangrene.

Now, as the young man stood over McKinley's coffin, he saw the serene expression drain from the president's face. McKinley stirred in his casket and sat straight as a lamppost. He narrowed his sharp, dark eyes and extended a waxy finger toward a corner of the room. The young man followed the president's gaze. Against the wall, a shadowy figure was cowering in the coarse robes of a Catholic monk. The young man expected to see the lean features of poor Leon Czolgosz, still bruised from his beating. But this was an older face, wide and fierce, all spectacles and teeth.

The young man sat up in bed, his breathing ragged. At this hour, there was no clip-clop of horses' hooves from the Manhattan streets, no clang of church bells, no sound at all. Peering at his watch, he saw that it was nearly two o'clock.

Hours later, when the first thin, gray light seeped over the East River, the words the president had spoken still ricocheted through his brain: "This is my murderer and nobody else! Avenge my death!"

And he could still see the figure skulking in the shadows near the presidential casket: Gazing from beneath the monk's cowl had been the smirking face of Theodore Roosevelt.

PART ONE

ONE

"We Stand at Armageddon"
Wednesday, August 7, 1912

ON THIS COOL SUMMER MORNING, AN UNREMARKABLE FIGURE PAUSED at the corner of Elizabeth and Canal Streets in Lower Manhattan. Standing five feet four inches tall and weighing 160 pounds, he was dressed in a cheap suit and bowler. Beneath the hat, his face was moon-shaped, with a prominent nose and receding chin. His hair was dirty blond and his eyes blue-gray, their heavy lids lending him a slow, sleepy look that might prompt some to underestimate him. In his hand were three of the city's dogmatic dailies.

It was early, but already the stench was rising from the garbage in the gutter and the barrels of trash along the sidewalk. With no breeze to stir them, sheets of newsprint were draped on the pavement where they had fallen. Over the cobblestone roadway clattered double-decker buses and delivery trucks headed for the recently completed Manhattan Bridge. In just a few decades, New York had become the most modern city on earth, with electric lighting, telephone service, skyscrapers—every innovation that American ingenuity could devise

John Flammang Schrank.

3

and American enterprise could market. As the nation's business capital, New York was home to a third of the country's millionaires and two-thirds of its largest corporations. And as the nation's cultural capital, it boasted dozens of opera houses, concert halls, and museums, all vying for the patronage of the moneyed class.

Yet, just a few blocks from this corner festered one of the world's most notorious slums, the Lower East Side, where Jewish, Irish, and Italian immigrants were crowded so closely in wretched tenements that it was said to be the most densely populated place on earth. Newcomers and blue bloods, industrialists and laborers, political hacks and wild-eyed reformers—there was no contradiction too great for New York to admit. Encompassed in its five boroughs was the best and worst of American society, all the disparate elements the nation's expansive character could produce.

The White House Hotel, 156 Canal Street, New York City, where John Schrank began his cross-country stalking of Theodore Roosevelt.

Spying a break in the traffic, John Flammang Schrank gripped his newspapers and darted through the vehicles' exhaust. Across the street, he turned east, passing the plain brick storefronts of Abrahams's shoes, Peltz's fabrics, Kahn's hosiery, and an advertisement for Shapiro's sign shop, tucked up a flight of stairs. Then he slowed before 156 Canal, with its two tall shoeshine stands flanking the entrance. Bar & Lunch Room, read the gold lettering on the window. Overhead arched an ornate metal marquee touting George Ehret's Hell Gate Brewery, and above that rose a once-elegant, once-white marble façade barely wide enough to front three sooty windows. If one looked closely, above the second floor one could make out the legend The White House inscribed in a stone panel. On the third story, the architect's Beaux-Arts imagination had run rampant, producing a marble balustrade, three arched windows, a pediment, and, soaring over all, an American eagle, also carved in marble.

The White House Hotel's proprietor, Gustav Jost, had met John Schrank half a dozen years before, when the young man had taken to stopping at the saloon for a beer or two. Then, just this past spring, Schrank had applied for a job tending bar. Said he'd been in real estate and insurance but hadn't made a go of it. Jost didn't need a bartender and told him so. But Schrank must have found work somewhere, because right after their conversation he'd rented a room above the saloon, and in seven months had never missed paying his rent of two dollars a week.

To the left of the White House's façade, beyond the big plate-glass window, opened a narrow doorway with more gold lettering on the transom: Hotel/Transients. Leaning on the unlocked door, John Schrank passed through the vestibule and climbed the steep stairs to his room.

For most of his twenty-three years in America, Schrank had lived in a brick tenement over his aunt and uncle's saloon at 370 East Tenth Street, between Avenues B and C. Even now he remembered the interminable voyage to New York, the feeling, at once heady and terrifying, of a thirteen-year-old boy on his own in the world. Then, after a week in the cramped dankness of the ship's hold, had come the miraculous vision of the Statue of Liberty, the gruff scrutiny at Castle Island, the abrupt expulsion into the seething city, and the awkward embrace of his aunt and uncle, strangers to him in all but blood.

At first, as he luxuriated in the shocking comfort of his own bed, young Johann, as he was still known, would let his thoughts drift back to his farming village of Erding, Bavaria, and to the mother, brother, and sister he'd left behind. They said his father, Michael, had died of consumption; beside him in the family plot lay an infant brother and sister as well. At age three, Johann had gone to live with his grandparents. When he was nine, he'd moved back to the house of his mother, Catharine. Just four years later had come the envelope with the strange stamps and the postmark *New York, New York.*

In his new home, his aunt and uncle, Annie and Dominick Flammang, welcomed Johann with the pent-up affection of the childless. It wasn't long before he was calling them his "folks" and Bavaria receded even further than the four thousand miles on the map. He spoke no English at first, but as he wiped tables in the bar and lugged buckets of beer to nearby apartments, he found it no handicap here in *Kleindeutchland,* "Little Germany."

With more than a quarter million of its residents born in places such as Bavaria, Saxony, and Prussia, New York was home to more native German speakers than any city in the world except Berlin or Vienna. And the Germans had done well in New York. Arriving in great numbers beginning in the mid-1800s, they'd come with education and skills, opening small businesses and quickly earning a place in the city's middle class. They'd also brought an intense interest in politics, and a predilection toward unionism and socialism. Many had fought for the North in the Civil War, and in the bar, young Johann hung on their stories of patriotism and sacrifice.

In the winters, he attended night classes to supplement his five years of schooling in Erding. Though he'd never call himself well educated, his English became passable, then quite good, with just the hint of an accent. When he was fifteen, he discovered poetry and began writing verses in his acquired language. He read several newspapers a day, and after Andrew Carnegie erected one of his public libraries on East Tenth Street, just a block from the saloon, Johann could borrow books on the history of his adoptive country. George Washington became his special hero. On July 23, 1897, four months after reaching his twenty-first birthday, Johann Flammang Schrank, now known as John, took the oath of American citizenship.

—◦—

The great tragedy of John Schrank's life came on June 15, 1904, when he was twenty-eight years old. It was a Wednesday, as ordinary a day as can be found on the calendar. The morning broke sunny and humid, and at 9:40, the 250-foot steamboat *General Slocum* cast off from the Third Street Pier and chugged up the East River, its twin side wheels churning, the organ blasting "A Mighty Fortress Is Our God," and passengers waving gaily from the railings on all three decks. It was the annual Sunday-school picnic of St. Mark's Lutheran Church, and on board were fourteen hundred day-trippers from Little Germany, mostly women and children, bound for the Locust Grove Picnic Ground at Eaton's Neck, on Long Island's northern shore.

Among them was a seventeen-year-old factory worker named Elsie Ziegler. Elsie made her living by sewing men's caps, for which she earned three to ten cents a dozen, depending on the style. She labored ten hours a day, every day but Sunday, and netted five dollars a week after the deduction for her sewing machine, which she was buying from her employer on the installment plan. Like John Schrank and the Flammangs, Elsie lived at 370 East Tenth Street, sharing an apartment with her mother, Minnie, a dressmaker; and three siblings,

Edward, nineteen; Alfred, eleven; and Ellie, nine. Though none of their neighbors—the Kuhlins, the Pollacks, old lady Koch—was privy to the fact, John Schrank planned to marry Elsie Ziegler.

As the *General Slocum* slipped through the narrow Hell Gate, just off Astoria, Queens, a fire was discovered in a forward compartment, where it must have been burning for some time. With the rocky shore lined with lumberyards and oil tanks, Captain William Van Schaick decided to steam ahead and beach the ship on North Brother Island, where it would be easier for passengers to leap to safety. But the headwinds and forward motion only fed the flames. Although the *Slocum* had recently passed a safety inspection, the fire hoses were rotten, the lifeboats were inaccessible, and the cork in the life preservers had disintegrated.

"I never saw such a sight in my life and hope I shall never witness such a thing again," one observer told the *Brooklyn Daily Eagle*. "The stern seemed to be black with people, and men and women were frantically running along the deck. . . . The mass of humanity on the upper deck seemed to be in a constant action. Some were climbing over the railings in an effort to reach the water. The shrieks of the dying and panic stricken reached us in an awful chorus. As the boat swung around, showing her starboard side to those on the Manhattan shore, I noticed that a line of hawser running from the stern to the paddle box was fringed with women, boys and girls. They were hanging there like clothes on a Monday wash, below the lower deck line of the steamer. They had climbed over in an effort to escape from the flames, and clouds of smoke were sweeping over their heads. One by one, it seemed to me, they dropped into the water."

Tugboats, launches, even rowboats sped to pick the victims out of the river, but the swimmers were quickly dragged down by their heavy clothing. Other passengers were burned alive. Some were crushed when the top deck collapsed. Within fifteen minutes, the wooden paddle-wheeler was razed to the waterline.

Every available ambulance sped to the scene, and the injured were laid out row upon row on the shore of North Brother Island. In the end, more than a thousand people perished in the tragedy, the worst loss of life the city had ever seen. With no facility large enough to accommodate them, the victims were sent to mortuaries on Long Island and Manhattan, even to police stations. Among the thousands of loved ones stumbling from morgue to morgue was John Schrank; the burden of identifying Elsie's body fell to him.

The city was stunned by the disaster, which had turned a flawless, blue morning into a date that would never be forgotten. Two years later, the Sympathy Society of German Ladies erected a memorial to the *General Slocum's* victims in Tompkins Square Park, just down the street from Dominick Flammang's saloon. Carved from pink marble, the simple, nine-foot-tall fountain showed a boy and a girl gazing out to sea, with the inscription: THEY WERE EARTH'S PUREST CHILDREN, YOUNG AND OLD. John Schrank would sit beside the monument for hours, running his fingers over the cold stone and composing his poetry. He never had another girl. "That wouldn't be right to Elsie," he later said.

Little Germany never recovered from the disaster, either. In the coming years, John Schrank watched as many of his neighbors relocated uptown to the more prosperous German community of Yorkville, on the East River. As immigrants from the Lower East Side moved in to take their places, Italian and Yiddish became common on the sidewalks of *Kleindeutchland*. Before long, Schrank and the Flammangs joined the exodus. Uncle Dominick, now sixty-eight, retired from the liquor business, first renting the bar and later selling it outright. He and Aunt Annie bought a ten-unit brick tenement at 433 East Eighty-first Street, and the family moved into a first-floor apartment. If John missed Little Germany, he didn't let it show. To his new neighbors he seemed quiet and likeable.

Annie died in November 1907. Dominick passed away in February 1911, and John was left with no family at all, at least in America.

He hadn't kept up with his mother, brother, and sister in Germany, though as far as he knew they were still living. He had no friends, attended no church since falling away from the Catholicism of his youth. Nervous and distracted, he never returned to the funeral parlor to claim his uncle's ashes.

From his New York "folks," Schrank inherited the tenement in Yorkville and assumed its mortgage of $13,000. But in the fall of 1911 he moved out of his apartment there, and a stranger began appearing on the first of every month to collect the rents from the remaining tenants. Storing his belongings in a warehouse at Eightieth Street and Third Avenue, Schrank rented a room in the Homestead Hotel, at 148 Cooper Street in Brooklyn. He took to frequenting a coffee house near the Brooklyn Bridge, where he talked a bit about politics; but mostly he complained about his money problems. Even with the rents, it seemed he was barely able to meet his mortgage.

He got a job as a porter in a bar on Flushing Avenue, near the navy hospital, and was soon promoted to lunch man. But when he proved too slow, he was demoted to porter again. He quit, demanding his full week's wages of eleven dollars, and when the bar owners refused, he filed suit in Municipal Court. In the run-up to the trial, he would barge into the defense attorney's office three times a day, insisting on a settlement. The lawyer declined, and eventually the court found for the defendants.

A day or two after the verdict, Justice Jacob S. Strahl received an anonymous letter that began, "Judge—You have branded me as a man who lies. By not believing me under oath, I think you have done me a great, monstrous, and incorrectible injustice. I mean to avenge this. You are a Judge. As a Judge you ought to right the wrongs of the poor. You have decided for the rich people against the poor man. You have decided to be the plutocrats' friend, instead of that of the people who do the world's work. I have been appointed to see to it that you do not judge other cases." The letter was signed "An Avenger," and the judge believed it had come from John Schrank.

After his arrival at the White House Hotel in the spring of 1912, Schrank kept regular hours, leaving in the morning and returning in the evening, when he'd stop in the saloon and have half a dozen beers and maybe a cigar. Keeping to himself, he'd sit in the bar's back room, across from four black-framed photos on the wall, portraits of presidents Abraham Lincoln, Ulysses Grant, James Garfield, and Theodore Roosevelt.

After a while Schrank would ask for his key and go to his room. On the nights he had trouble sleeping, he would get up and work on his verses. Many days, he'd take long, solitary ambles through Lower Manhattan or over the bridge to Brooklyn, composing poetry and brooding over the political stories in the three newspapers he read faithfully: the German-language *Staats-Zeitung*; the *New York Herald,* though it was a bit conservative for his taste; and Joseph Pulitzer's more proletarian *World,* which was filled with sensational headlines and human-interest pieces.

On this pleasant August morning, with the rattle of traffic rising through the windows of his hotel room, John Schrank snapped open his newspapers. He already knew what he would find, but that didn't diminish his disgust on reading the reports for himself. They concerned the speech Theodore Roosevelt had made in Chicago the night before.

On leaving the presidency four years ago, Roosevelt had handpicked as his successor Secretary of War William Howard Taft, who had been elected by a comfortable margin in November 1908. But eventually Roosevelt had regretted his decision not to stand for a third term, and early this year had challenged President Taft for the Republican nomination. When the G.O.P. had spurned him in favor of the incumbent, Roosevelt had ginned up a new faction, the Progressives. The Bull Moose Party, it was calling itself, from Roosevelt's brag that he was "fit as a bull moose."

This week, the Progressives were convening in the Chicago Coliseum, and from the accounts in the newspapers, the assembly was more revival than political meeting. Though custom demanded that a candidate not attend his party's nominating convention, "Colonel" Roosevelt, as he styled himself since leaving the White House, had trampled on that tradition along with all the others. And so yesterday afternoon he had mounted the Coliseum's dais and addressed the faithful. With the band blasting "Onward Christian Soldiers" and "The Battle Hymn of the Republic," he had thrust out his barrel chest and grinned that ferocious grin as he waited for the crowd of more than ten thousand to quiet. But they only continued to acclaim him and to wave the red bandana that was the Progressive emblem.

John Schrank was still a boy in Bavaria when Theodore Roosevelt began his spectacular rise. Born to an old, moneyed New York family, the young "Teedie" had revealed his pugnacious tendencies early on, overcoming childhood asthma with weightlifting, boxing, and other virile pursuits. But the boy was also a voracious reader and a keen student of natural history. As a student at Harvard, he'd written *The Naval War of 1812*, an acknowledged classic in its genre and the first of his dozens of books, including the acclaimed *Winning of the West* and *African Game Trails*. After graduating from Harvard magna cum laude in 1880, he'd enrolled in Columbia Law School. It wasn't done for someone of his class to enter politics, but Theodore heard a call to public service. And so, leaving Columbia, he became active in the Republican Party, and in 1881 was elected to the New York assembly from Manhattan's twenty-first district.

Though he represented one of the most affluent neighborhoods in the state, Roosevelt felt a compulsion to root out unjust advantage. "The Cyclone Assemblyman" they called him for the way he bore down on Albany, buffeting bosses of both parties, demanding investigations of corrupt judges and lawmakers, and decrying "the wealthy criminal class" who put their own interests ahead of the public good.

Sometimes the fights threatened to become more than verbal, as during one committee meeting when Roosevelt forestalled a riot only by brandishing a leg he'd torn from a chair in the capitol chamber.

He was the youngest member of the assembly, but the hyperactive freshman made such an impression, on his colleagues and the public alike, that at the beginning of his second term the Republicans elected him minority leader. An avalanche of progressive bills tumbled from his office, and though some were blocked by party hacks, others carried into law, including the first civil service act passed by any state, which dared to award government jobs not through the time-honored system of favors and bribes but through competitive examinations. Over three exhausting, exhilarating terms, Roosevelt relied on his wiles, ambition, and bulldog persistence to press his statehouse crusade. And before it was over, his name was known not just in Manhattan or New York State, but across America.

In his sophomore year at Harvard, Roosevelt had been profoundly shaken by the death of his father, Theodore Sr. But on Valentine's Day 1884 came a personal tragedy sufficient to veer even a cyclone from its course. At three o'clock that morning, Roosevelt's mother, Mittie, died of typhoid in the family's Fifty-seventh Street town house. Then, at two o'clock that afternoon, in the same house, his wife, Alice Lee Roosevelt, succumbed to kidney disease—just two days after giving birth to their daughter. "There is a curse on this house," Roosevelt murmured as he hunched over Alice's bed. In his diary, he wrote a big black *X* and the words "The light has gone out of my life." He was twenty-five years old.

Roosevelt served out the remaining months of his term, but when the legislature adjourned that summer, he fled New York and all its memories. Leaving baby Alice in the care of his unmarried older sister, Bamie, he boarded a train for the bleak Badlands of the Dakota Territory, where he already owned a ranch. Donning buckskins, he went to work raising cattle, serving as a deputy sheriff and leading the rugged, restorative life of the cowboy. "There were all kinds of things I was afraid of at first," he wrote in his diary, "ranging from grizzly bears to mean horses and gunfighters; but by acting as if I was not afraid I gradually ceased to be afraid."

By 1886, he was back in New York City, accepting his party's nomination for mayor, though everyone knew no Republican had a chance of beating the Democratic candidate, Abram Hewitt, that year. But a turn as sacrificial lamb, Roosevelt realized, was the price of resuming his political career.

A month after losing the election, Theodore married Edith Kermit Carow. A close friend of his sister Corrine, Edith had practically grown up in the Roosevelt household. She and Theodore, with their shared love of nature and of books, had been childhood playmates. Then, as Edith had matured into a tall young woman with blue-gray eyes and dark, fine hair, they had become sweethearts. They'd had a falling-out while Theodore was in college, and he'd been smitten by the beautiful Alice Hathaway Lee, cousin of a Harvard classmate. When he'd announced his engagement to Alice, Edith had concealed her heartbreak behind her habitual reserve. But in September 1885, during one of Theodore's visits to New York, they had revived their romance. He proposed two months later, and in December of the following year they were married in London. Reunited with baby Alice, they moved into Sagamore Hill, the estate Roosevelt had begun planning before Alice's death, in Oyster Bay, on Long Island's affluent North Shore. Sagamore Hill was the only house that Theodore and Edith ever owned, and it was there that they raised their family, which came to include another girl, Ethel, and four boys, Ted, Kermit, Archie, and Quentin.

By 1889 Roosevelt was in Washington as a member of the US Civil Service Commission. The agency had been a backwater since its creation, but during the six years of his tenure, Roosevelt proved so ferocious (and so ostentatious) in his purging of favoritism and corruption that the commission (and the commissioner) became a staple of front pages nationwide. Sometimes President Benjamin Harrison seemed to regret his appointee's zeal, grumbling that Roosevelt "wanted to put an end to all evil in the world between sunrise and sunset." Roosevelt returned the compliment, finding the president "a cold-blooded, narrow-minded, prejudiced, obstinate, timid old psalm-singing Indianapolis politician."

John Schrank was nineteen when he first fixed his particular attentions on Theodore Roosevelt. It was in 1895, and Roosevelt had just been appointed president of the board of the New York City police commissioners. The force was so corrupt in those days that policemen called their profession "the business," and with good reason—according to a state senate investigating committee, the department generated illicit revenues of more than $10 million a year, twice its government appropriation. On assuming control of the three-man board, Roosevelt began to purge the ranks. He forced the resignation of Superintendent Thomas Byrnes, who had managed to amass a fortune of $350,000 on his municipal salary of $2,000 a year. And the new commissioner became famous for cruising the streets at night, often in full evening dress, hauling in beat cops caught napping or otherwise slacking in their duty.

The senate committee reckoned that almost $2 million of the police department's extracurricular income came from bribes paid by the city's nearly fifteen thousand saloonkeepers. For four decades, New York State had forbidden the sale of alcohol on Sunday. But the dry law didn't go down well in the City, where German and other European immigrants couldn't see the harm in passing a weekend afternoon at a beer garden or tavern. So the bar owners, including John Schrank's uncle Dominick, locked their front door on the Sabbath but kept the side entrance ajar, slipping the police an occasional five- or ten-dollar bill to look the other way. And every liquor dealer voted Democratic, at least in local elections, to ensure the continued protection of Tammany Hall, the notorious political machine that had been dispensing patronage for more than a century.

Though a near teetotaler, Theodore Roosevelt was no lover of prohibition. Still, he knew he could never end police corruption without enforcing the blue laws and eliminating the kickbacks they generated. So, beginning on June 23, 1895, Sunday mornings found police stationed outside the city's saloons, including the Flammangs' bar on East Tenth Street. And with the fear of Roosevelt in them, no patrolman dared to look the other way now.

Imbibers missed their refreshment, but the liquor merchants missed their Sunday patrons even more; after the crackdown, nearly a quarter of the city's bar owners were reported close to bankruptcy. The campaign was particularly hard on the Germans, not only because they were among the most enthusiastic beer drinkers in the city, but also because many earned their living in breweries and saloons.

In August, Schrank's countrymen mounted a mammoth protest in Yorktown, turning out thirty thousand lederhosened demonstrators and hundreds of bicycles, carriages, wagons, and floats, all parading down streets adorned with purple bunting and black crepe. ROOSEVELT'S RUSSIAN RULE read one banner; ROOSEVELT'S RAZZLE DAZZLE REFORM RACKET charged another. The organizers had dared the commissioner to attend, and Roosevelt surprised them all by bounding onto the reviewing stand, applauding the marchers, laughing at their antics, and to all appearances passing a delightful couple of hours. When one nearsighted demonstrator, hoping to get a glimpse of the enemy, called out in German, "Where is Roosevelt?" the commissioner pounded his chest and fired back, also in German, "Here I am!" The crowd laughed despite themselves. "Roosevelt, you're a man!" shouted a spectator, expressing the general view. When the commissioner left, he took two of the anti-Roosevelt banners and hung them in his office.

Roosevelt's Sunday-closing campaign made national and even international headlines, and pundits began to mention a run for the presidency. But the commissioner, dubbed King Roosevelt I, had become the most reviled politician in the city. Hostile newspapers called the crackdown "Teddy's Folly." His office received a letter bomb (which failed to detonate), and people wondered how long it would be before he was shot. Worse for the Grand Old Party, Roosevelt's unpopularity was contagious, and by early November, a little more than four months into the operation, his fellow Republicans were begging him to relent. On Election Day 1895, every G.O.P. candidate in the city went down to defeat. Among the Germans, 80 percent of voters opted for Democrats.

King Roosevelt held on for two awful, arid years. Then, on the verge of losing his appointment, he finally retreated before the massed forces of the press and both political machines. In 1897, he applied to the incoming president, William McKinley, for the position of Secretary of the Navy; though McKinley thought him too excitable for that post, he did name him assistant secretary, and Roosevelt bustled off to Washington again. New York breathed a warm, wet sigh of relief that day, John Schrank recalled.

Less than a year later, the United States was at war. In early 1895, revolutionaries led by Cuban exile José Martí had landed on the island to seize its independence from Spain. The American public threw their sympathy behind the rebels, especially after reports of brutal Spanish reprisals, and voters pressed McKinley to intervene. So did American entrepreneurs, worried over their considerable investments in Cuba, in everything from sugar and tobacco to iron and manganese. Joseph Pulitzer's *New York World* and William Randolph Hearst's *New York Journal* outdid each other (and swelled their circulations) with calls for war. Within the administration, Theodore Roosevelt was the loudest voice for intervention. Sometimes it sounded as though the assistant secretary was spoiling for battle, any battle. "I rather hope that the fight will come soon," he wrote. "The clamor of the peace faction has convinced me that this country needs a war."

In January 1898, McKinley dispatched the USS *Maine* to Cuba, a decision that has been likened to lighting a candle near an open cask of gunpowder. On the evening of February 15, the battleship exploded in Havana Harbor, killing 266 crew members. When an American board of inquiry ruled that the *Maine* had been the victim of a mine, the drumbeat for war grew more insistent. On April 20, McKinley signed a resolution demanding Spanish withdrawal from Cuba. The next day, Spain severed diplomatic relations and the US Navy launched a blockade of the island. On April 25, the US Congress declared war.

Roosevelt finally had his fight, and he meant to take an active part. Resigning from the Navy Department, he helped to organize the First US Volunteer Cavalry Regiment, nicknamed the Rough Riders. Though its thousand troopers consisted mostly of cowboys from Arizona and other western states, the regiment also attracted its share of eastern equestrians from Roosevelt's own social stratum. He was offered the rank of colonel, but having no previous combat experience, he accepted a lieutenant colonelcy under his friend and experienced Army surgeon Leonard Wood.

The Rough Riders landed in Cuba toward the end of June, and when Wood was promoted out of the regiment, Roosevelt assumed command. On the first of July came the moment that the Colonel would always call "my crowded hour" and "the great day of my life." Sporting his custom-tailored Brooks Brothers uniform and straddling his chestnut gelding Little Texas, he led his (dismounted) troopers on their charge up the grassy slopes of San Juan Heights. Fire was brutal, and fifteen of the thousand or so Rough Riders were killed, with another seventy-three wounded; the Colonel himself was grazed in the elbow. But before the end of the day, the Americans had claimed the crest, the Spanish had fled, and the Rough Riders had played a pivotal role in the decisive land victory of the war.

By August 7, the first American forces were already being withdrawn. The Spanish had been evicted from Cuba, the United States had seized the strategic islands of Puerto Rico in the Caribbean and Guam and the Philippines in the Pacific, and Theodore Roosevelt had come home a certified war hero. That same year, he was tapped by the G.O.P. bosses to run for governor of New York—not out of any belated affection for the problematic progressive, but because they figured he was the only Republican with a chance of winning.

They were right. On November 8, Roosevelt narrowly defeated Augustus Van Wyck, scion of another venerable New York family and justice of the state Supreme Court in Brooklyn. After his inauguration, the forty-year-old "boy governor" ran up against the same party hacks who had jockeyed against his anticorruption bills when he was an assemblyman back in the early 1880s. But now, as then, Roosevelt was bent on reform. Working his popularity and charisma, he befriended the press and took his program directly to the voters. And by the end of his first year in office, he'd rammed through the legislature a raft of bills attacking "the combination of business with politics and the judiciary which has done so much to enthrone privilege in the economic world." There were taxes on the state's lucrative gas, tunnel, and rapid-transit franchises; a new civil service law (to replace the one he'd sponsored as an assemblyman, which had been repealed in 1897); and measures to improve working conditions in sweatshops and factories, to bolster the educational system, and to conserve the state's wilderness areas. "All together," he admitted, "I am pretty well satisfied with what I have accomplished."

There was no doubt that the popular governor would be reelected, and he was widely expected to run for the presidency in 1904, when William McKinley would be finishing his second term. But when Vice President Garret Hobart died of heart disease in November 1899, the New York Republicans pressed for Roosevelt as the president's new running mate the following year—just to get the gadfly out of Albany.

Roosevelt would have preferred the War Department to the vice presidency, which he seemed to consider a dull dead end for somebody of his talents and ambition. But the New York delegation outmaneuvered him at the nominating convention, and in the end he let himself be drafted onto the ticket. That fall, McKinley was reelected in a landslide over the Democrat William Jennings Bryan. And by the following September, McKinley was dead and Roosevelt was president.

⌐⌐

At age forty-two, Roosevelt was the youngest man to hold the presidency. But mounting his "bully pulpit," he seized the initiative from Congress and established himself as the driving force in government. His first target was the corporate trusts. Recognizing the efficiency and competitiveness that the corporations gave American industry, he didn't seek to dismantle them but to direct their efforts toward the public good. "Great corporations exist only because they are created and safeguarded by our institutions," he reminded Congress in his first annual message; "and it is therefore our right and our duty to see that they work in harmony with these institutions." It was a question of restoring the equilibrium between capital and labor and between industry and government, of protecting workers from exploitation and preserving ordinary citizens' voice in the political process. And so the president filed lawsuits to bust only the trusts that he considered "predatory," including the widely hated Standard Oil, the American Tobacco Company, the Northern Securities railroad conglomerate, and the meatpackers Swift & Company.

He also persuaded Congress to create the Department of Commerce and Labor to regulate the corporations. With new irrigation projects, he opened three million acres to farming in fourteen western states. And in 1902, after Pennsylvania coal miners struck for higher wages and recognition of their union, threatening the nation with civil unrest and economic calamity, he took the daring, unprecedented step of meeting with both sides and persuading them to accept the judgment of an independent commission (which ultimately supported most of the workers' demands). Barely a year into his term, Roosevelt's popularity soared.

Overseas, the young president claimed an audacious new role in world affairs. Expanding the Monroe Doctrine, he asserted the United States' right, duty even, to preserve order in the hemisphere. When Colombia refused to ratify a treaty for the construction of a transoceanic canal in its province of Panama, Roosevelt dispatched warships and troops to abet a revolution there. Then he sealed a hasty pact with the breakaway nation, paying $10 million plus an annual rental of $250,000 for the right of the United States to build and administer the waterway. It was a venture of mind-boggling scope and hubris—a French effort had already ended in disaster—but Roosevelt was confident that his Yankee engineers could pull it off. When completed several years hence, at a cost of $375 million, the canal would permit American merchant vessels (and warships) to pass from the Atlantic to the Pacific in just three weeks instead of the two to three months the voyage now required.

At home, the economy was surging, and most Americans, at least outside Congress and Wall Street, welcomed Roosevelt's brash magnetism and muscular, progressive government. Yet no vice president who had become chief executive through the death of his successor had ever been elected to another term. Roosevelt relished power, and he determined to break that precedent and prove that his administration was no accident. So fierce was his determination that his friend the writer Henry Adams said, "Theodore thinks of nothing, talks of nothing, and lives for nothing but his political interests. If you remark to him that God is Great, he naively asks how that will affect his election."

He needn't have worried. In November 1904, he routed the colorless Democratic nominee, New York Appeals Court Judge Alton B. Parker, winning by the widest margin of popular and electoral votes in the nation's history. Though the *Staats-Zeitung* (along with Pulitzer's *World* and Hearst's *Journal*) had endorsed Parker, many Germans cast their ballots for the incumbent.

In his second administration, Roosevelt's influence only expanded, until it seemed to permeate every crevice of government. He signed a bill giving the federal branch the authority to regulate railroad rates. He approved a meat inspection act and a pure food and drug law. He established the Forest Service, set aside millions of acres of new national forests, created five national parks and some fifty wildlife refuges, and signed the Antiquities Act, giving the president responsibility for protecting "wonders of nature." He even oversaw an extensive renovation of the Executive Mansion, which he renamed the White House.

Roosevelt built more than fifty new warships, making the US fleet second only to that of Britain and earning for himself the title "Father of the Modern American Navy." Then he sent sixteen battleships, a dozen auxiliary vessels, and fourteen thousand sailors on a fourteen-month, fifty-thousand-mile, around-the-world cruise in an unprecedented show of American military might and technical prowess. After the Russo-Japanese War broke out in 1904 over Russia's expansion into Manchuria and Korea, Roosevelt negotiated an end to the conflict, a feat that won him the Nobel Peace Prize, the first Nobel awarded an American in any field.

Roosevelt had reshaped the presidency, and as his second term drew to a close, even his bitter opponent Senator "Pitchfork Ben" Tillman of South Carolina had to admit that he had become "the most popular president the country has ever had." The venerable Mark Twain went further, calling him "the most popular human being that has ever existed in the United States." Not just across the country, but around the globe, Theodore Roosevelt was recognized as a titan, a force of nature, the precise embodiment of his nation and his time, the preeminent personality in the world.

Roosevelt loved being president perhaps more than any man before him. If he had decided to run for a third term, there would have been no one to stand in his way. But in 1904, on the night of his great electoral triumph, he had made a strange announcement that would haunt the rest of his career. Citing "the wise custom which limits the President to two terms," he had said, "under no circumstances will I be a candidate for or accept another nomination."

Now, despite the "still, small voice" tempting him to break his word, Roosevelt stood by his rash promise of four years earlier. And so he engineered the nomination of his close friend William Howard Taft to finish the work he had started. One year older than Roosevelt, Taft had been born near Cincinnati, Ohio, the son of Alphonso Taft, who had been Secretary of War and Attorney General under Ulysses Grant. Like his father, "Will" had entered government service soon after his graduation from Yale, where he'd been a champion wrestler and had finished second in his class academically. Proving a gifted administrator, the younger Taft had been appointed, in quick succession, justice of the Cincinnati Superior Court, Solicitor General of the United States, a federal judge, and Governor-General of the Philippines, before Roosevelt had named him Secretary of War toward the end of his first administration.

Taft had the advantage of not being beholden to Wall Street, and Roosevelt hoped his friend could unite the progressive and conservative wings of the Republican Party. On hearing of Roosevelt's plan, Taft confessed to his brother, "My ambition is to become a justice of the Supreme Court." But bowing to the will of the president (and Mrs. Taft), he continued: "I presume, however, there are very few men who would refuse to accept the nomination of the Republican Party for the presidency, and I am not an exception." In November, he trounced the Democrats' perennial populist William Jennings Bryan—though his victory did seem to owe more to the Roosevelt afterglow than to any exceptional qualities of his own.

After the election, Roosevelt admitted his ambivalence on leaving the White House: "Of course, if I had conscientiously felt at liberty to run again and try once more to hold this great office, I should greatly have liked to do so and to keep my hands on the levers of this mighty machine. I do not believe that any President has ever had as thoroly [*sic*] good a time as I have had, or has ever enjoyed himself as much. Moreover I have achieved a greater proportion than I had dared to think possible of the things I most desired to achieve. . . . But I am bound to say in addition that I cannot help looking forward to much enjoyment in the future. In fact, I am almost ashamed to say that while I would have been glad to remain as President, I am wholly unable to feel the slightest regret, the slightest sorrow, at leaving the office."

Just weeks after Taft's inauguration, Roosevelt sailed for Africa, a continent that had fascinated him since boyhood (and that was conveniently far from reporters hounding him about his future plans and his opinion of his successor's performance). Over the next ten months, with his second son, Kermit, he tramped through the savannas of East Africa, living a primordial dream—and shooting more than five hundred big-game animals, which were destined for display in the Smithsonian and the American Museum of Natural History. (J. P. Morgan, meanwhile, was rooting for the other team. "Wall Street," he said, "expects every lion to do its duty.")

Early the following spring, on his way home, the ex-president made an extraordinary six-week triumphal tour of Europe, delivering speeches, reviewing troops, conferring with monarchs, and being received, in the words of one reporter, as "something more than a king" himself. "Never since Napoleon dawned on Europe has such an impression been produced there as has been made by Theodore Roosevelt," observed the French newspaper *Le Temps*. The general assumption, sometimes spoken, sometimes not, was that the dynamic fifty-one-year-old was destined to be President of the United States again one day. In June, after representing his country at the funeral of

England's King Edward VII, the ex-president/war hero/adventurer/ Nobel laureate finally boarded a ship for America. For Roosevelt, the departure came just in time. "I felt if I met another king," he said, "I should bite him!"

———

When Roosevelt's steamer, the *Kaiserin Auguste Victoria*, entered New York Harbor on June 18, 1910, it was greeted by a battleship, five destroyers, and dozens of lesser craft. When the Colonel stepped ashore at Battery Park, the ovation was so thunderous that he was moved to tears. Afterward, there was a tickertape parade up Broadway and Fifth Avenue, with military bands, Rough Riders, mounted police, and the ex-president standing in his carriage, wearing a frockcoat and waving his top hat to hundreds of thousands of cheering New Yorkers. It was said to be the largest crowd that ever gathered in the city for any occasion. As in Europe, most of the spectators assumed that, his earlier denial notwithstanding, the Colonel would soon announce his candidacy for the White House.

Then, in the coming months, Roosevelt and Taft had an ugly, public falling-out. Roosevelt regretted leaving office at the height of his popularity and power. And apparently he and the more cautious, more conservative Taft had never been as compatible as it had seemed. Soon after his inauguration, Taft had offended Roosevelt by replacing several of his predecessor's cabinet members, despite reassurances to the contrary. He'd also signed a controversial new tariff.

For twenty-five years, the tariff had been the single most divisive issue between Democrats and Republicans. Since the federal government levied no income tax, it derived more than 40 percent of its revenue from these duties, which also protected American producers from cheap foreign imports. The Republicans, taking their time-honored stance that what was good for industry would ultimately prove good for the worker, clung to the protective tariff as an article of faith, the very foundation of the economic expansion the country had enjoyed since the Civil War. But to ordinary citizens, the high tariff had outlived its usefulness.

For one thing, the tariff by itself could no longer generate enough revenue to support the new federal regulatory agencies. And with mechanization cutting production costs, and new marketing techniques increasing demand for goods and services, American businesses now seemed less in need of government protection. To many people, the duties protected industrialists too well, at the expense of workers. Depending on the type of goods, the tariff raised the retail price of imports between 5 and 75 percent. It even raised the price of domestic goods, since, with reduced foreign competition, American producers were free to increase their prices as well. It was estimated that the tariff cost the average family $115 a year, or nearly 20 percent of the typical worker's earnings. Only about $16 of that money found its way to the federal treasury, and even less trickled down to the worker in the form of higher wages; the rest of the price increases were pocketed by the corporations—giving them even more lucre to dole out to compliant politicians. Farm families, which included 60 percent of Americans, suffered the worst. Most of their crops didn't need protection from foreign imports, but thanks to the tariff, every time they bought a plow blade or a hoe, they were forced to pay a premium. And this was on top of the gouging they were already taking at the hands of banks, middlemen, and railroads.

In the election campaign of 1908, Taft had promised to review the tariff issue. So when he called Congress into special session early in 1909, it was generally expected that a reduction was in the offing. But instead the legislators produced the Payne-Aldrich Tariff Act, a tepid compromise that had little effect on the status quo. Though Taft had hoped for more of a decrease in tariff rates, he balked at imposing his will on a recalcitrant legislature. Not only did he sign the disappointing measure, he called it "the best tariff bill that the Republican Party ever passed." After that, even many of his fellow Republicans began to long for a decisive leader like Theodore Roosevelt.

After a life spent as a follower, the uncharismatic Taft appeared incapable of leading. In a letter written as Roosevelt was leaving for Africa, Taft had confessed that on being called "Mr. President," he would turn to see whether his predecessor had entered the room. "I want you to know," he'd gone on, "that I do nothing in the Executive Office without considering what you would do under the same circumstances and without having in a sense a mental talk with you over the pros and cons of the situation." He'd begun to nap during the day, and seemed to prefer the golf course to the newly constructed Oval Office. While Roosevelt was still in Africa, *Life* magazine had expressed the general disillusionment:

> Teddy, come home and blow your horn,
> The sheep's in the meadow,
> The cow's in the corn.
> The boy that you left to tend the sheep,
> Is under a haystack, fast asleep.

As Taft's administration wore on, voters also questioned his dedication to the crucial issue of trust reform. Although he prosecuted more suits under the Sherman Anti-Trust Act than Roosevelt had, he believed that government already had the tools it needed to control the corporations. To progressives, it seemed that the president had abandoned the great fight that his predecessor had called the "conflict between the men who possess more than they have earned and the men who have earned more than they possess."

The Colonel felt his progressive legacy threatened by Taft's shortcomings. He also worried for his own reputation, since he'd named the man as his successor. "What a floppy souled creature he is," Roosevelt lamented. The final break came in October 1911, when Taft filed an anti-trust suit against J. P. Morgan's U.S. Steel to block its acquisition of Tennessee Coal and Iron, a merger that Roosevelt had personally approved while president. Concluded on terms highly favorable to U.S. Steel, the deal had been a quid pro quo for Morgan's role in containing the Panic of 1907, but now Taft was claiming that Roosevelt had been duped.

In February 1912, the Colonel did what so many had so long expected, coming out of retirement to challenge Taft for the Republican nomination. "The fight is on and I am stripped to the buff!" he announced. What about his promise not to seek a third term? He'd meant three consecutive terms, he now claimed, so after a four-year hiatus, he was free to run again. He explained the decision this way: "Frequently when asked to take another cup of coffee at breakfast, I say 'No thank you, I won't take another cup.' This does not mean that I intend never to take another cup of coffee during my life; it means that

President William Howard Taft speaking in Springfield, Massachusetts, on April 25, 1912, during the fierce campaign for the Republican nomination. "Roosevelt was my closest friend," he sobbed to a reporter.

I am not accepting the offer as applying to that breakfast, and that my remark is limited to that breakfast." His detractors found the homey but convoluted analogy unconvincing.

But the old Rough Rider was as beloved as ever by the common folk. And so he decided to bypass the Republican machine and to focus on states that had adopted primary elections, a recent reform that allowed citizens, not the bosses, to choose their party's candidates. He began to barnstorm the country by train, once again taking his case to the voters. Opinion polls showed him running 66 percent ahead of Taft among Republicans, and when the votes were counted, Roosevelt won nine of the twelve states with primaries, getting more votes than the other two G.O.P. contenders, Taft and Wisconsin's fiery progressive senator Robert La Follette, combined; he even outpolled Taft in the president's home state of Ohio.

The primary elections extended the campaign season and forced the candidates to travel more than in previous contests, increasing their expenses. Even before the nominating convention, Taft and Roosevelt together laid out the unheard-of sum of more than $1 million. Since contributions from the public totaled only about $5,000, the rest had come from a few wealthy men. It was a dangerous trend, wrote muckraking journalist George Kibbe Turner in *McClure's* magazine, which amounted to "the underwriting of presidential campaigns for hundreds of thousands of dollars—exactly as a bond issue is underwritten before it is offered to the general public. . . . No matter how good individual motives may have been, it is not a practice that can be continued."

Not only was the campaign expensive, it was nasty, with Taft labeling the challenger a "dangerous egoist" and Roosevelt calling the president a "fathead" who had "brains less than a guinea pig." Sitting in his private railroad car, Taft wept as he told a reporter, "Roosevelt was my closest friend." To Mrs. Taft, he wrote, "Sometimes I think I might as well give up as far as being a candidate is concerned. There are so many people in the country who don't like me."

At the Republican convention in June, 1,078 delegates were to be seated, with 540 needed to nominate. Roosevelt arrived in Chicago with 469½ (including those won in the primaries), to Taft's 454½. But the majority of the Colonel's supporters were "shadow" delegates who claimed they had been defrauded of their seat by double-dealing in their home states, especially in the South. The Republican National Committee reviewed 254 disputed delegates and surprised no one by awarding 235 of the contested places to Taft, versus 19 for Roosevelt. The Colonel's close friends Henry Cabot Lodge and Elihu Root were among those who deserted him, though Root lamented, "I care more for one button on Theodore Roosevelt's waistcoat than for Taft's whole body."

With his hopes for the nomination slipping away, Roosevelt boarded an overnight train from New York to Chicago, where he

Theodore Roosevelt arriving in Chicago during the Republican convention in June 1912; the streets were so clogged with supporters he could barely reach his hotel.

found the station and streets so packed with supporters that his car could hardly reach his hotel. In the Auditorium, he addressed a crowd of five thousand, with another twenty thousand milling outside. "We are fighting for honesty against naked robbery," he exhorted. "Fearless of the future, unheeding of our individual fates; with unflinching hearts and undimmed eyes; we stand at Armageddon, and we battle for the lord." On the convention floor, there were fistfights and cries of "We want Teddy!" When it came time for the nominating vote, Roosevelt instructed his remaining delegates to abstain in protest. On the first ballot, there were 561 votes for Taft, 107 for the Colonel, and 41 for the even-more-radical "Fighting Bob" La Follette.

Faced with Taft's "theft" of the nomination, Roosevelt and his followers bolted from the Republicans and created a new party, the Progressives. A National Committee was elected, with members drawn from every state; distinguished supporters were enlisted, including governors such as Hiram Johnson of California, US senators such as Joseph M. Dixon of Montana, Albert J. Beveridge of Indiana, and Moses E. Clapp of Minnesota, and prominent journalists such as William Allen White of the *Emporia* (Kansas) *Gazette* and O. K. Davis of the *New York Times*. Financing was procured, and headquarters were opened in Chicago and New York. A platform was written, and a slate of candidates was assembled to contest state and local elections.

But beneath the Progressives' obvious zeal and frenzied activity, even the party faithful realized that their departure would likely throw the election to the Democrats. Watching this long-building rupture between the conservative and progressive wings of the Republican Party, many observers agreed with Chauncey Depew, ex-senator from New York, when he pronounced the general election moot. "The only question now," he said, "is which corpse," Taft or Roosevelt, "gets the most flowers."

John Schrank was a member of no political party, had no affection for the Republicans. But it was indecent what Roosevelt had done, abandoning his friends and claiming that President Taft had stolen the party's nomination. From the start, Roosevelt had taken to power with an unseemly keenness, as though forgetting the unspeakable tragedy that had brought him to office. Throughout his presidency, he'd shown a raw ambition and a frightening love of command. And now King Roosevelt was plotting his return from exile. But the two-term tradition was a sacred pillar of American democracy, a bulwark against oppression. The great Washington had refused a third term of office, and none of his successors had ever been granted such a mandate. So why did Theodore Rex feel entitled? It was undemocratic and un-American. *The New York World* had gotten it right when they called Roosevelt "the most cunning and adroit demagogue that modern civilization has produced since Napoleon III."

On this cool August morning, in the White House Hotel, Schrank picked up his newspapers and started to read. At the Progressive convention, Roosevelt had stood waiting at the podium beneath dozens of American flags, a portrait of himself, and the head of a giant bull moose. After fifty-eight minutes, when the cheers had finally ebbed, he began to fill the Coliseum with his reedy, patrician cadences. "To you men and women who have come here to this great city of this great State formally to launch a new party, a party of the people of the whole Union, the National Progressive party, I extend my hearty greeting," he began. "You are taking a bold and a greatly needed step for the service of our beloved country. The old parties are husks, with no real soul within either, divided on artificial lines, boss-ridden and privilege-controlled, each a jumble of incongruous elements, and neither daring to speak out wisely and fearlessly what should be said on the vital issues of the day."

Then Roosevelt launched into his "confession of faith," trotting out the same hackneyed promises—presidential primaries, popular election of United States senators, public disclosure of campaign contributions, a minimum wage, safety standards for workers, a reduced workweek, the end of child labor, old-age and disability insurance, women's suffrage, conservation of natural resources. And how would these so-called progressive goals be accomplished? By surrendering more power to the president, of course. "It is utterly hopeless to attempt to control the trusts merely by the antitrust law," King Roosevelt was saying. "The administrative branch of the government must exercise such control." By "the administrative branch," naturally, he meant himself.

Roosevelt, it seemed, wanted to scrap the justice system altogether. "The acts of the courts should be subject to and not above the final control of the people," he told his disciples in Chicago. "The people themselves must be the ultimate makers of their own Constitution. . . ." Judicial recall. Schrank had heard the argument before, but that didn't mitigate the shock: That the common people should decide what the Constitution meant, and vote to overturn the decisions of their courts! It would be the end of government by law and the beginning of mob rule, just as the editors of the *World* had warned.

John Schrank hunched over the newspaper, absorbing the words like a poison. "It little matters what befalls any one of us who for the time being stands in the forefront of the battle," Roosevelt went on. "I hope we shall win, and I believe that if we can wake the people to what the fight really means we shall win. But, win or lose, we shall not falter. Whatever fate may at the moment overtake any of us, the movement itself will not stop."

His speech went on for two hours, with his minions interrupting him 145 times for applause. Then, like a revivalist minister, he launched into his apocalyptic peroration. "Our cause is based on the eternal principles of righteousness; and even though we who now lead may for the time fail, in the end the cause itself shall triumph. . . . Now to you men, who, in your turn, have come together to spend and be spent in the endless crusade against wrong, to you who face the future resolute and confident, to you who strive in a spirit of brotherhood for the betterment of our nation, to you who gird yourselves for this great new fight in the never-ending warfare for the good of humankind, I say in closing,"—and then he pronounced the line they'd been waiting for, the same one he'd used during the Republican convention to such spectacular effect—"we stand at Armageddon, and we battle for the Lord."

It was Armageddon, all right, but the candidate was confusing the Messiah and the Anti-Christ. As Schrank brooded over Roosevelt's words, something came together in his brain, something ineffable that suddenly crystallized into words and sentences. He pushed aside the newspapers and took up his fountain pen.

He wrote to warn his fellow citizens of the immediate danger, but he also wrote for history. "When in the course of human events," he began, echoing the hallowed Declaration of Independence, "it becomes necessary for one people to dissolve the political bonds which have hitherto connected them with another, due respect to mankind requires that we should declare the cause of such action."

Then John Schrank poured out his own confession of faith, scribbling feverishly, barely pausing to start a new paragraph. "In the present campaign for the first time in American history we are confronted by a man to whom practically nothing is sacred and pretends to stand above tradition. This man abused our constitution, he wants it amended until it is abolished. . . . He has abused our highest Courts, he has spoken in the profanest language of our legislators, he has abused our best and most venerable citizens, calling them liars and scoundrels, he has shamefully abused our president, thereby undermining the dignity of the office, how can we expect our foreign born citizens to respect our institutions when an ex-President circumtravels the Union telling everybody that those honorable men at Chicago were thieves and crooks."

Schrank had to expose the lies, and the unquenchable ambition behind them. "The third termer," he went on, refusing to dignify the man by writing his name, "claims that it is not a third term, if not followed by two consecutive terms, then a second term would not be a second, if given to a man 8 years after his first, I wonder what to call such term, after a while he will tell us that a monarchy in this country is not a monarchy if the monarch is a native born."

There was no denying Roosevelt's popularity and persuasiveness. But no third-party nominee had ever won the presidency, and Schrank doubted that even this pretender could manage that feat. And so it wasn't the prospect of his winning that was most frightening, but the likelihood of his losing. Because when he was defeated, having already shown his lack of loyalty, his unslakable thirst for power, his tyrannical cravings, what would prevent King Roosevelt from inciting his followers simply to seize the reins of government?

"The dangers in this campaign are these, the third termer is sure that the nomination has been stolen and that the country and the job belong to him, therefore if he gets honestly defeated in November he will again yell that the crooks of both parties have stolen the election, and should he carry a solid West, he and the hungry office seekers would not hesitate to take up arms to take by force what is denied him by the people, then we face a civil war, and it was Ab. Lincoln who said that war is hell and that he who wilfully invited war deserves death. We would then be compelled to wash out the sin of violating the third term with the blood of our sons."

As the shadows shifted across his rented room, Schrank wrote on. Even another civil war was not the greatest danger, he argued. With the United States consumed by warfare at home, what would prevent America's enemies from launching their own campaign of conquest? "Does anybody think that the European powers would sit idly while we are disunited, would a certain power hesitate to help the third termer and make good the gravest mistake that power has made in

1861 by not keeping this country disunited and separated while we are just getting ready to become their greatest competitor on the seas after the completion of the Panama Canal. Our strength is not in our Army or Navy nor in our Money power, our strength is in our Union."

As a naturalized American, Schrank could discern the truth that his fellow citizens failed to see. But would they heed his warning? "In this critical time I find that men have more interest in the baseball results than to register, think and vote. But of course some people have no more sense than three guinea pigs." Would they see the ravenous wolf wrapped in the fleece of progressivism? "His movement is not progressive, they are insurgents, insurgents and revolutionary. Hardly any revolution has started without pretending that their movement was progressive. . . . Naturally the third termer would prove too in 1916 that the fourth term is only his second, to do this he would have to become the conquering hero, we would commit the same faults France did 100 years ago," with the rise of Napoleon Bonaparte.

Sheet after sheet John Schrank filled with his manifesto, pouring out the injustice and treachery and unworthiness and un-Americanism of Theodore Roosevelt. Finally, he sat back and considered the pages of crabbed black script. Then he allowed himself to recall that night almost exactly eleven years before. Every detail of the dream was fixed in his memory—the cascades of flowers, the polished coffin, the hard glint in President McKinley's eye, the monkish figure of Theodore Roosevelt cowering across the room. "This is my murderer and nobody else! Avenge my death!" the president had commanded.

John Schrank had often puzzled over the dream, wondered whether it had been a simple nightmare or something more. Was it possible that Leon Czolgosz hadn't acted alone? Could there have been a conspiracy to assassinate the president? Theodore Roosevelt had had the most to gain from McKinley's death. And now, after wielding his ill-gotten authority for two terms, the tyrant considered even that span as insufficient to his greatness. Bent only on power, he would betray his friends, destroy his party, ruin his country. Wasn't someone capable of all that wickedness also capable of murder? History was full of such treachery, and worse.

Countless times, Schrank had asked himself whom President McKinley was exhorting that night from his funeral bier. Through Roosevelt's two terms and all his antics afterward, Schrank had waited for someone to step forward and pick up the slain president's challenge. But even now, with the nation on the verge of catastrophe, no one seemed to recognize the third termer's threat. So once again, John Schrank posed the question he had pondered all that time: Could it be that President McKinley had been speaking to him? Was he, a common immigrant, to be the agent of divine vengeance, the savior of the nation? Carefully, tenderly, he folded his warning to the American people and slipped it into his breast pocket.

It little matters what befalls any one of us, Roosevelt had proclaimed. *Whatever fate may at the moment overtake us. . . .* To John Schrank, the words lay on the page like a gauntlet.

TWO

"God Has Called Me to Be His Instrument"
Saturday, September 14, to Sunday, September 15

THERE WAS A *CLANK* OF COUPLINGS AND A *CHUFF* OF STEAM, AND THE campaign special lurched to a halt. The Colonel raised himself stiffly from his seat. He pushed his black Stetson over his bristly auburn hair, collected his tan army overcoat, and passed brusquely down the aisle of his private car, the *Mayflower*. Favoring his rheumatic ankle, he stepped out into the dark and down to the tracks below.

He breathed in the sea air. The night was fair and mild, and he decided to keep the overcoat folded over his arm. In the breast pocket of his suit coat was the text of his speech. By God, he'd give it to Wilson tonight. On this western tour, he'd been lulled onto the defensive, parrying the Democrat point for point rather than making any thrusts of his own. But tonight he'd draw blood. Across the bay, in San Francisco, he'd make his most important speech since his Confession of Faith at the Progressive convention back in August. And tomorrow morning, he'd be on front pages across the nation. This afternoon, as his train had sped through the California countryside, he'd forsaken the usual whistle-stops, intent on honing his words.

The Colonel was no stranger to long railroad journeys. In 1903, as president, he'd made a two-month, fourteen-thousand-mile, twenty-five-state tour, terminating in San Francisco, where he'd broken ground for a monument to his slain predecessor, William McKinley. Earlier this year, during the brawl for the Republican nomination, he'd lived on trains for weeks at a time. Then, after kicking off his Bull Moose campaign in New England in August, he'd barnstormed for two weeks through Missouri, Iowa, Minnesota, North Dakota, Montana, Washington, Oregon, Utah, and Nevada, before arriving in California. On the return journey, he'd loop through the Southwest and the Deep South. Before he slept again in his bed at Oyster Bay, at the end of this month, he would have logged ten thousand miles.

In out-of-the-way places like tiny Cache Junction, Utah, he would perch on the *Mayflower's* rear platform, accepting accolades from city fathers and bouquets from schoolchildren, and he would limit himself to brief, off-the-cuff remarks. But in the larger cities, like Des Moines and Spokane, he would address ten or fifteen thousand citizens in an auditorium or public park. Tailoring his speeches to local concerns, he had come out against an unpopular trade treaty in the border state of North Dakota and argued for more irrigation projects in arid Nevada.

Everywhere, he would press the need to regulate the corporations, to protect the worker, and to restore the people's voice to government. Both Republicans and Democrats were "parties of privilege," he would thunder, a "crooked alliance between crooked politics and crooked business" intent on preserving their own prerogatives. But the Progressives would restore government to the citizens. That was why primaries and the direct election of US senators were so important, he'd explain, not as theoretical adjustments to the democratic process, but as a practical means of circumventing the party bosses. Often in these speeches, the Colonel would invoke the spirit of Abraham Lincoln, the first Republican president, who in another perilous time had, as Roosevelt put it, "dared to go forward for righteousness' sake." Like Lincoln, the Colonel implied, he was battling for justice and freedom—in this case, for the millions of men and women enslaved by the industrialists and politicians.

President Taft, meanwhile, had spent a quiet summer at his seaside retreat in Beverly, Massachusetts, north of Boston. He claimed

to be honoring the tradition that a sitting president not actively campaign for reelection (a custom that both McKinley and Roosevelt had
observed as incumbents). But in truth, the president had no stomach
for electioneering. "I have been told I ought to do this," he confided
to a reporter for the *New York Times*, "ought to do that, ought to say
this, ought to say the other; that I do not keep myself in the headlines,
that there is this or that trick I might turn to my advantage. I know it,
but I can't do it." Taft did have a few appearances planned for the fall,
but in the meantime he would rely on interviews, paid advertisements,
and speeches by party loyalists to carry his campaign. He'd get no help
from his vice president, James S. Sherman, who, suffering from heart
disease, was unlikely to see Election Day.

Taft's principal speech of the summer had come three months earlier, during his acceptance of the Republican nomination in Chicago.
Pointing to his administration's aggressive prosecution of the trusts,
the president had warned against "demagogues" who sought to foment
"popular unrest" with their quasi-socialist "appropriation of what
belongs to one man, to another." As for Theodore Roosevelt, he was
advocating "dangerous changes to our present constitutional form of
representative government and our independent judiciary."

In the same speech, Taft had turned to the vital question of the
tariff, an issue his opponents had been debating all summer. Roosevelt, arguing for "a tariff for labor," wanted to hold duties high,
to generate revenue and keep American industry competitive; but
he would also create a federal commission to root out abuses and
ensure that wage earners saw their fair share in their pay envelopes.
Wilson, who was calling the existing system "stiff and stupid," had
a more radical proposal, to gradually decrease the tariff until it still
generated revenue but no longer posed a burden for consumers. But
Taft was defending the status quo, warning that Wilson's plan would
cause "serious injury to a large part of our manufacturing industry"
and "would halt many of our manufacturing enterprises and throw

many wage earners out of employment, would injure much the home markets which the farmers now enjoy for their products, and produce a condition of suffering among the people that no reforming legislation could reform or mitigate."

Since Wilson had no hope of winning the Progressive West and no fear of losing the Solid South, he had also passed much of the season by the shore, at the governor's official summer residence in Sea Girt, New Jersey. Toward the end of September, he planned to mount two short tours, one in the Northeast, the other through the Midwest. Meanwhile, his opponents eyed him closely, hoping for some misstep. But in his first national contest, Wilson was proving poised and supremely confident, a gifted orator and a tough, smart campaigner. If the bookmakers were right, he would also be the next President of the United States.

Woodrow Wilson had gotten a later start in politics than Theodore Roosevelt, but once begun, his rise had been even swifter. Whereas Roosevelt was born to wealth, Thomas Woodrow Wilson had entered life—in 1856, two years ahead of the Bull Moose—as the son of a Presbyterian minister. At the time, the family was living in Staunton, Virginia, in the bucolic Shenandoah Valley. But as Joseph Wilson sought to advance his career in the church, they moved among a succession of other Southern cities—Augusta, Georgia; Columbia, South Carolina; and Wilmington, North Carolina. Just as Roosevelt recalled watching Abraham Lincoln's funeral procession pass his grandfather's New York town house in 1865, Wilson's earliest memory was the announcement of Abraham Lincoln's election in 1860, which even the young "Tommy" understood would bring civil war. But when the fighting did come, the family never found itself in the path of battle.

As the Wilsons' third child and first son, Tommy was his parents' favorite and a self-described mama's boy. Like "Teedie" Roosevelt, he suffered from a childhood disability, though in Wilson's case the problem was intellectual. He managed to learn his letters only at age nine and didn't read fluently until he was twelve. Like Roosevelt, he overcame his handicap through intense effort. To compensate for his difficulty writing, he learned shorthand at age sixteen, but on finishing high school, he still complained about the slowness of his reading.

The boy grew into a lanky young man, with a long nose, angular jaw, and piercing gray-blue eyes. He matriculated at North Carolina's Davidson College, but after a year transferred to another Presbyterian school, the College of New Jersey, better known as Princeton. Since the school's curriculum was notoriously unchallenging in those days, he spent much of his time reading independently, especially in history and politics; he also joined a debating society and became managing editor of the school newspaper. His first choice of career was government, but after graduating from Princeton, he bowed to family pressure and matriculated at the law school of the University of Virginia. Still, his "brightest dream," he confided to a friend, was "the great work of disseminating political truth and purifying the politics of our own country. . . . When I get out of this treadmill of the law I intend to devote every scrap of leisure time to the study of that great and delightful subject."

After a year and a half of law school, Woodrow, as he'd started calling himself, left the university and began independent studies for the bar. Intending to open a practice with a friend in Atlanta, he sat for the exam in Georgia, where he posted the highest score that year. But he found the law stultifying, unremunerative, and "antagonistic to the best interests of the academic life," and after just a year he began to prepare for an academic career. He would still have preferred to enter politics, but no doubt thinking of Theodore Roosevelt and his ilk, he wrote, "No man can safely enter political life nowadays who has not an independent fortune . . . . Therefore the most I can hope to become is a speaker and writer of the highest authority on political subjects."

Instead of an actor on the governmental stage, he would content himself with being a spectator and critic.

In 1886 he was awarded a doctorate in history and political science from the Johns Hopkins University. The year before, he had published *Congressional Government*, the first, most original, and most influential of the half-dozen books he would write during his teaching career. Besides more treatises on government, the works would include popular biographies and collections of essays, as well as articles for magazines such as *Scribner's* and *The Atlantic Monthly*.

Also in 1885, he had married Ellen Louise Axon, daughter of a prominent Presbyterian minister. Wilson had first noticed his bride in 1883, during a church service in Rome, Georgia, where he was tending to legal business. He'd been instantly attracted by her intelligent expression and mischievous brown eyes, and on his next trip to the city, a month later, he'd invited her for a carriage ride and a stroll. During his third visit, the two sat together at a picnic; by the time he'd departed, he had determined to marry her. Over their twenty-nine-year marriage, the couple would have three daughters, Margaret, Jesse, and Eleanor.

Wilson hoped to return to his alma mater as a professor, but with no opening there, he taught for the next several years at other prestigious Eastern schools—Bryn Mawr, Johns Hopkins, and Wesleyan— where he was popular with the students and respected by the faculty. In 1890, he received the long-awaited appointment as professor of political economy and public law at Princeton; soon he was recognized not only as a standout among the faculty but also as the preeminent political scientist in the country. He was also a leading advocate of academic reform, and after the college's president was forced out in 1902, Wilson was the trustees' unanimous choice to take the position.

On hearing of Wilson's appointment, then President Theodore Roosevelt hailed him "a perfect trump" whose selection "overjoyed" him. The pair had first met in 1896, when they had both addressed a municipal-reform meeting in Baltimore. In the meantime they had kept in touch, with Wilson asking for counsel on a faculty appointment and Roosevelt soliciting political advice. In 1901, while still vice president, Roosevelt had invited Wilson to Sagamore Hill, along with professors from Harvard and Yale, to discuss strategies for recruiting promising young men to government service.

As president of Princeton, Wilson made good on his promise of reform, distancing the school from its Presbyterian roots, expanding the faculty, revamping the curriculum, and molding it into a major university. With his busy speaking schedule and frequent magazine articles, he became an effective representative of his institution and the most famous college president in the nation. Building on that rising reputation, he began to dabble in his first love, politics—as a conservative Democrat, attacking reformers in both parties, including President Roosevelt. (After Roosevelt announced his Square Deal, Wilson complained, "What we need is not a square deal, but no deal at all," just "an old-fashioned equality and harmony of conditions.") In 1907, New Jersey Democrats paid Wilson the compliment of nominating him for US senator, with the understanding that, in those days before the popular election of senators, the Republican-controlled legislature would choose a member of their own party. In 1908 he was mentioned as a possible contender for the presidency, though that year the Democrats once again nominated William Jennings Bryan.

By then Wilson had moved away from his earlier conservatism and was steering more with the progressive current of the times. All over America, on farms and in cities, ordinary people were determined to claim a greater share of the profits of industry, and to wrest control of government back from the corporations and corrupt party bosses. Wilson admitted that in his case the shift was partly opportunistic. And despite his progressive tendencies, the Democrats were excited by the prospect of a newcomer on the scene; in 1910 they nominated him for governor.

In his closing address of that campaign, Wilson showed how far he had veered from his onetime conservatism: "We have begun a fight that it may be will take many a generation to complete—the fight against special privilege, but you know that men are not put into this world to go the path of ease; they are put into this world to go the path of pain and struggle. . . . We have given our lives to the enterprise, and that is richer and the moral is greater." Reading these words in the newspaper, ex-president Roosevelt, returned from his African safari, might have mistaken them for one of his own speeches.

On Election Day, Wilson received the second-widest margin of votes of any governor in New Jersey history. His win, he said, was not a triumph of just the Democrats but "a victory of the 'progressives' of both parties, who are determined to live no longer under either of the political organizations that have controlled the two parties of the State." As at Princeton, Wilson followed through on his promises, though this time it meant turning his back on the party machine that had secured his election. In his first year, he guided through the Democratic assembly and Republican senate a sweeping program attacking corruption, regulating utilities, mandating food safety, improving working conditions, protecting women and children in the workplace, enhancing education, instituting primary elections, and authorizing initiative, recall, and referendum on the municipal level. As for how he found the transition from academia to government, he allowed, "After dealing with college politicians, I find that the men with whom I am dealing . . . now seem like amateurs." Like Roosevelt's earlier reforms in New York, Wilson's changes were popular in his own state and admired beyond its borders, and after just a year in office he was already considered a contender for the Democratic presidential nomination in 1912.

Despite his popularity, Wilson harbored two secrets that, if they had ever become public, would have thwarted his run for governor, never mind for national office. The first was that in 1906, while president of Princeton, he had suffered a stroke; although he appeared to have made a full recovery, his health was fragile and he was partially blind in his left eye. The second secret was that, also while still at Princeton (and married), he'd had a years-long infatuation with a divorcee named Mary Allen Hulbert Peck, whom he'd met on vacation in Bermuda. Though there was no proof that his passion had been consummated, he had visited Mrs. Peck's New York City apartment alone, and he had written her scores of intimate letters. During the presidential race, some of these were offered to the Taft and Roosevelt campaigns, but both declined to purchase them. There was no point, Roosevelt joked, because "no evidence could ever make the American people believe that a man like Woodrow Wilson, cast so perfectly as the apothecary's clerk, could ever play Romeo."

As the campaign for the Democratic nomination opened in 1912, Wilson's slender experience and his feud with party operatives made him a dark horse. Seen as overly friendly to the cities and to big business, he failed to excite the party's important agrarian wing. But he also held undeniable appeal. For one thing, despite his differences with the New Jersey bosses, his short tenure in Trenton hadn't given him time to make many enemies or to collect much political baggage. And though he was fifty-five years old (and his avian features tended toward the plain), he was still seen as a fresh face in national politics, with fresh ideas.

Even so, if the Bull Moose hadn't come charging out of Oyster Bay, Wilson may never have ventured from Trenton. Whatever the Democrats thought of the governor in private, the astute among them grasped that the party must change if it weren't to be swept away by the rising progressive tide. They recognized that the Republican split offered their best chance of retaking the White House in sixteen years, and they understood that it was the charismatic Roosevelt, not the weary Taft, who stood in their way. Roosevelt was painting himself the candidate of the future, battling two corrupt parties mired in the past. If the Democrats nominated a conservative like Taft, they would only give credence to Roosevelt's claim. Worse, the Democrat and Taft would split the moderate and conservative vote, clearing the way for Roosevelt, who would be the race's only viable progressive. But in Wilson, the Democrats could offer an alluring alternative to the Bull Moose—a progressive with mainstream appeal. Over the past few years, as Wilson had shifted to the left, the line separating his and Roosevelt's positions on the issues had blurred; but their mounting rivalry meant that the two would never share the collegiality they'd enjoyed back when the only presidency Wilson aspired to was that of Princeton University.

At the start of the primary season, it looked as though the Democratic Party might rally behind Oscar W. Underwood of Alabama, the diligent House majority leader, or James Beauchamp "Champ" Clark of Missouri, the mildly progressive Speaker of the House. In Democratic primaries throughout the spring, Wilson didn't approach Roosevelt's success in the Republican races, taking only five of thirteen contests. "It begins to look," he lamented to a friend, "as if I must merely sit on the sidelines and talk, as a mere critic of the game I understand so intimately—throw all my training away and do nothing."

By the time the nominating convention opened in Baltimore on June 25, the sixty-two-year-old Clark had emerged as frontrunner, with between four hundred and five hundred delegates, while Wilson was in second place with about two hundred fifty. On the first ballot, Clark received 440½ votes to Wilson's 324, with 322½ spread among the other candidates. But whereas the Republicans' bylaws required a simple majority of delegates to nominate, the Democrats' called for two-thirds of the votes—an antiquated rule that Wilson had criticized. A fierce floor fight ensued, with battles over seating of delegates and rules for voting, and ferocious behind-the-scenes deal making. On the tenth ballot, Tammany Hall threw its support behind Clark and cast New York's ninety votes for the Speaker, giving him a majority but still not the required two-thirds.

The Tammany endorsement inspired party patriarch William Jennings Bryan to come out for Wilson, perhaps hoping to force a stalemate and position himself as a compromise candidate. Instead, Bryan's move swung the convention, and on July 2, after a bruising forty-six ballots, the man from Trenton became the Democratic nominee, marking one of the great upsets in American electoral politics. The nomination was "a sort of political miracle," Wilson admitted. But in accepting it he said, "I feel the tremendous responsibility it involves even more than I feel the honor."

Woodrow Wilson on July 2, 1912, immediately after learning he had won the Democratic nomination; his convention victory was "a sort of political miracle," he said.

Theodore Roosevelt's strategy that summer was to play to his own strength, his enormous personal popularity. Wherever he stopped on his cross-country pilgrimage, he attracted such multitudes— at depots, outside hotels, along city streets—that newspaper wags were comparing him to John the Baptist. Sometimes the well-wishers threatened to get out of hand. On September 13, in Reno, Nevada, a huge crowd welcomed Roosevelt at the train station. In the tumult, he was separated from his escorts and forced to shoulder his way through the throng. But "he went at it like a football player," reported the Ogden (Utah) *Evening Standard*, "and, after a few minutes of scrimmaging, reached his automobile before the rest of his party."

In Blackfoot, Idaho, he was conducted through the streets by whooping cowboys and red-bandana-toting Indians. Again, the reception was so raucous that the Colonel's entourage was unable to get near him. Later, at the county fairground, he spoke to eight thousand people, including five hundred schoolchildren who gave a squeaky rendition of "America." As the Colonel assured the crowd that he had no dictatorial intentions in seeking a third term, he was interrupted by an attractive woman in the audience.

"I guess you don't know who I am," she called out.

"Who are you?" he asked.

"I'm Nell Raphael, sister of Otto Raphael, of New York."

"Well, by George!" he answered, to the crowd's delight. "The sister of one of the best men I ever appointed to the New York police force. What are you doing away out here?"

She was a teacher, she said, chaperoning the children who had sung for him.

The Colonel explained that when he was police commissioner, some fifteen years before, he'd heard about a man who'd rushed into a burning house to rescue a young stranger. "I said, 'By George, he is a game fellow, and I would like to hunt him up.' If you recall," he told the sister, "he was at the Bowery branch of the YMCA. He is not as good-looking as his sister," the Colonel said, warming to his story, "but I found he was an honest lad, and I put him on the force. And he made an A-one officer. He did not feel kindly toward me during the Spanish War because he wanted to join my regiment and I could not take him. He was an A-one policeman, as I have said, but he did not know one end of a horse from the other. I think he had a general knowledge that horses did not have horns." The crowd roared with laughter.

At Pocatello, Idaho, the Colonel spoke from a platform erected in front of the public school, while dozens of children squirmed at his feet. "Now, all you kids keep perfectly quiet," he warned. But even as he assured their parents of his supremacy over Taft and Wilson, he was unable to dominate the youngsters. "I've taken a whole lot of you on board—" he scolded, "sit down there, you boy, sit down—but you've got to be—little girl, don't make so much noise—you've got to be quiet. I like kids—now, children, children, please be quiet." At which point a small boy threw himself on the floor and hugged the candidate's ankles. "I'll have to appeal to the marshal for protection," the Colonel said, lifting the youngster out of the way. "Any boy who stands up from now on goes right off the ground." And so he'd finally managed to quiet the children, though he was obliged to halt his remarks and shush them from time to time.

With his popular touch, the Colonel was perhaps the most skilled campaigner the country had ever seen. Still, he understood that just because multitudes came out to see him in mountain rain and desert sun, that did not guarantee they would vote for him. "Pure Barnum and Bailey," he'd told a reporter during the primary campaign. "Pure Barnum and Bailey. It's my past that brings them, not my future." Next month he would turn fifty-four. Ever since Cuba, he'd been prone to recurring fevers. Though he concealed it, he (like Wilson) had been blinded in his left eye, by a boxing injury sustained while he was president. His weight had crept up to two hundred pounds, and his blood pressure was chronically high, helping to explain his ruddy features. On the stump, his overtaxed voice had grown so frayed that he was limiting his remarks wherever possible in order to conserve it.

The Colonel hadn't campaigned for office since 1900, when he'd run as McKinley's vice president, and the truth was that he was exhausted. Reporters had noticed and had begun to say so in their papers. His aides saw that he was becoming stale, repeating himself instead of scoring new points, and they'd scheduled a few days' rest at the end of this journey to revive him before his October swing through the Midwest and Mid-Atlantic. But there were thousands of miles to cover first, and hundreds of speeches, starting with tonight's major address in San Francisco, which his advisers hoped would reinvigorate, if not the candidate, then at least the campaign.

An inveterate optimist, Roosevelt still recognized the odds against him. If he'd managed the Republican nomination, his tremendous popularity would have posed a serious threat to Wilson. But by bolting from his own party and founding the Progressives, he'd opened the door for the Democrat—even as he closed it on Taft. Unable to forgive this betrayal, and appreciating that their candidate was unelectable, the Republicans had vowed to work first of all to defeat, not Wilson, but the traitor Roosevelt. As Vice President Sherman argued, "It was essential, both for the life of our party and the continuance of our Government that the Bull Moose and his ilk should be sidetracked." Taft put it less vindictively, admitting privately that Roosevelt's bolt meant "a long hard fight with probable defeat. But," he went on, "I can stand defeat if we retain the regular Republican party as a nucleus for future conservative action."

The Colonel knew that some Republicans would follow him out of the G.O.P., yet likely not enough to secure the election. If he were to win, he would have to take votes from the Democrats—a task they had complicated by nominating a progressive themselves. As early as July, there had been signs that Democratic voters were not abandoning Wilson. Then in September, the Vermont state elections had given the Bull Moosers added reason to worry. The Colonel had campaigned there in late August, before heading west, and though the state had voted Republican as always, the Democrats had picked up ground. It was a bad omen for November, and as the summer began to wane, so apparently did the Colonel's chances of returning to the White House. Still, Progressive candidates would appear on state and local ballots across the country, and the crucial thing, the Colonel pointed out, was to elect as many as possible, to establish the new party and guarantee the future of the movement. Only then would it "be able to give the right trend to our democracy, a trend which will take it away from mere greedy shortsighted materialism."

It was a few minutes past eight p.m. when the Colonel's train sighed to a stop in Oakland. Enveloped in aides, Roosevelt crunched down the gravel beside the tracks and passed the hissing locomotive. He climbed into an automobile, which rumbled onto the Oakland Pier. A ferry was standing in the slip, black smoke billowing from its stacks. One hundred and fifty people were waiting on the ferry's rear apron, hoping to catch a glimpse of the most famous person in the world.

A dozen well-dressed men stood apart. Among them the Bull Moose recognized the bald, bespectacled features of George Crothers, trustee of Stanford University and chairman of the state's independent Republicans. His chin thrust forward, the Colonel charged Crothers and clasped his hand. "My wife and family send greetings to you and San Francisco," Roosevelt told him.

There was an awkward pause while Crothers searched for a response. Finally, he waved a hand toward the dark water all around them. "See, Colonel," he said, "we are to have a bridge across the bay, and it is to cost millions."

The bridge in question would link Oakland with San Francisco, which lay on a bulbous peninsula to the west. The project had been under discussion for forty years but had grown more urgent over the past decade, as Oakland's population had more than doubled to one hundred fifty thousand plus, thanks in part to refugees from the great earthquake and fire that had ravaged its neighbor in 1906, killing some three thousand people and leaving more than two hundred thousand homeless. Though San Francisco, still claiming more than four hundred thousand souls, remained the preeminent metropolis of the West, the city was eager to be linked to the mainland by rail and road, lest it lose more ground to its rival across the bay, or even to Los Angeles to the south. But the bridge would have to span three miles of open water, and so far the solution had eluded engineers and financiers alike. In the meantime, passengers arriving by train from the east had to disembark on this pier, which jutted more than two miles out into the bay, since any closer to Oakland the estuary was too shallow to accommodate ships.

As the crowd peered through the phalanx of policemen and detectives surrounding him, the Colonel and his reception committee occupied several more minutes with small talk. Among the pleasantries, his greeters failed to mention an incident that same day involving a Berkeley resident named Carl Olson. Styling himself an inventor, Olson had been approaching officials of the various presidential campaigns, peddling gilt-covered hat pins featuring an image of their candidate. But as the Colonel's special train sped west from Reno, Olson had dashed among Oakland's telegraph offices, warning that Roosevelt's life was in danger if he dared to enter California; when he'd gone to a police station with the same message, he'd been arrested.

There seemed to be something about this bitter, superheated campaign that could incite seemingly rational citizens to desert their senses. But, having seen three presidents shot down and having succeeded to the presidency because of an assassination, the Colonel had always accepted the possibility that someone might try to kill him. After McKinley's murder, the Secret Service had assumed responsibility for protecting the chief executive, but as president, Roosevelt had chafed at their constraints and had more than once conspired to escape them. And preferring to rely on his own resources, he had often carried a loaded revolver (which once caused a stir when it peeked out of his trousers pocket during services at Christ Church in Oyster Bay).

He'd already had a narrow escape. One night in September 1903, he'd been working late in his library at Sagamore Hill, when he'd heard a scuffle in the driveway. Going out to investigate, he found Secret Service agents wrestling with a young man who'd ridden up in a carriage. The man was wielding a pistol, and when he saw Roosevelt, he yelled, "There he is!" Some of the guards pushed the chief executive into the house, while others subdued the youth. As he was being led away, the man confessed, "I came to kill the president" for not doing enough on behalf of the workingman.

No longer president but only a candidate, the Colonel was now ineligible for Secret Service protection. Although he counted a few bodyguards among his entourage, it was understood that they and the police assigned to him in every city could offer only nominal protection from the enormous crowds that swarmed him. And so the authorities had no choice but to take seriously crackpots like Carl Olson from Berkeley, California.

Finally, the great paddle wheels began to churn, and the ferry slid into the black waters of San Francisco Bay. The Colonel climbed the steps to the comfortably furnished cabin deck. With him, besides the press and members of the local Progressive Committee, were Lt. Governor J. A. Wallace, who had met him yesterday at the border; George Emlen Roosevelt, the Colonel's cousin, three years out of Harvard, who was traveling with the campaign as a secretary; Cecil Lyon, Rough Rider, former chairman of the Republican Party in Texas, Progressive National Committee member, personal friend of the Colonel, and sometime bodyguard; Scurry Terrell, M.D., a throat specialist from Dallas, charged with coddling the Bull Moose's failing voice; and two young stenographers, John W. McGrath and Elbert E. Martin. After half an hour, the tall, square clock tower of the San Francisco Ferry Building hove into view above the fog. Throttling back, the ship bumped into a narrow slip, where another knot of men were waiting.

Among them was Francis J. Heney, who would introduce the Colonel tonight. Fifty-three years old, Heney still cut a dapper figure with his impeccable suit and his trim gray hair oiled flat and parted in the middle. In 1906, as a crusading prosecutor, Heney had brought bribery charges against San Francisco's notoriously corrupt mayor Eugene Schmitz and political boss Abe Ruef. During jury selection, after Heney exposed a potential juror, Morris Haas, as an ex-convict, Haas drew a revolver in open court and shot Heney in the jaw. Supposing his assailant to be one of Ruef's henchmen, the assistant D.A. vowed, even as he lay sprawled on the courtroom floor, "I'll get him yet!"

Not only did he survive the wound, but after another prosecutor, Hiram Johnson, took up the case, Heney recovered in time to make a dramatic return to the courtroom and hear Ruef pronounced guilty. Mayor Schmitz was also convicted, but when Ruef refused to testify against him, the verdict was thrown out on appeal. Morris Haas was found shot to death in his cell; a pistol lay beside him on the cot, but it was never determined how it had gotten there or whether he had died by his own hand. As for Johnson, his prosecution of the case earned him statewide acclaim, and in 1910 he was elected governor. Less than two years later, the Colonel tapped him as his Bull Moose running mate, giving the ticket coast-to-coast representation—and ensuring that California would vote Progressive.

In the ferry terminal, Francis Heney extended his hand to the Colonel and gave a sonorous hello. The Colonel reciprocated with a flash of his perfect teeth, then accompanied the others through the building's high, handsome arcade. Outside, nine automobiles were waiting. The Colonel, his hosts, aides, and the press filled seven; the other two were reserved for the police guard.

The Colonel's motorcades customarily meandered at parade speed, with the candidate standing and waving to supporters along the route. But tonight he had been delayed when the Southern Pacific train to which the *Mayflower* was to be hitched had fallen behind schedule. The campaign had ordered a special train instead, but still they'd arrived nearly two hours late. So now the order was given to waste no time, and the Colonel remained planted in the auto's leather seat.

The motorcade had barely started south on Market Street when an urchin leapt on the Colonel's car to get a closer look at his hero. As the driver accelerated, the boy struggled to hold on, his legs dangling dangerously close to the rear axle. Finally, the car slowed at Fourth Street, and spectators were relieved to see the boy jump off.

Racing down Market, avoiding the trolley tracks in the center of the road, the driver coaxed the automobile to fifty miles an hour. Even at that speed, it was obvious that San Francisco, once the quintessential boomtown, was booming again. Founded by the Spanish in the late 1700s, the settlement known as Yerba Buena had at first consisted of a mission and a presidio. Then, in 1848, at the end of the Mexican War, it had passed to the United States, along with the rest of California and a great chunk of the American Southwest. That January, gold had been discovered at Sutter's Mill, about a hundred miles to the northeast, and in a single astonishing year, the city (renamed San Francisco) had seen its population surge from one thousand to twenty-five thousand grasping souls. Now, only six years after the earthquake and fire, new buildings lined Market Street; in another few years, it would be impossible to tell that more than three-quarters of the city had been in ruins.

At Battery Street, a throng pressed together under the Mechanics Monument, a colossal bronze sculpture of five naked men clambering over a giant punch press; presumably the sculptor's intent was heroic, but on first glance it wasn't clear who had the upper hand, the workers or the machine. A few blocks farther down, the motorcade passed skyscrapers sheltering hotels, banks, and newspaper offices, and then sped by the US mint, the post office, and city hall. Turning west, the cars climbed to a comfortable residential area that had been spared by the earthquake, and then saved from the fire when the wind had abruptly shifted and blown back the flames. Just past nine o'clock, the motorcade came to rest in front of the Coliseum, on Baker Street between Oak and Fell, at the eastern tip of Golden Gate Park. Across the street, the Colonel could see a tall granite plinth surmounted by a bronze statue of a woman grasping a palm frond in one hand and a sword in the other; it was the memorial to President McKinley for which Roosevelt had broken ground nine years earlier.

The Colonel was accustomed to overflow crowds in the streets around his campaign venues, but tonight the front of the Coliseum was strangely deserted; when he was delayed, those without tickets apparently had gone home. But light and noise were seeping from every crevice of the ungainly, barrel-shaped building, which looked like an airplane hangar dropped in the center of the city. A crowd of eleven thousand—half of them standing in the aisles and along the walls—had been waiting since the Coliseum opened its doors at six forty-five. They had amused themselves by singing patriotic songs and listening to a droll speech by W. S. Scott, Bull Moose candidate for state assembly. Now, as they caught sight of the Colonel, the audience erupted, tossing hats into the smoky air and giving a cheer that drowned out the brass band.

With Lieutenant Governor Wallace on one side and Francis Heney on the other, the Colonel mounted the speaker's platform to tremendous applause. Acknowledging the ovation, he ran across the stage, leapt onto the dais, and gave the crowd a crisp military salute. The cheering continued for nearly a quarter hour, while the candidate peered out from the platform at a sea of waving red bandanas.

When Heney was finally able to begin his introduction, he kept it short: "I have the great pleasure and the great honor of introducing to you tonight the man who made it possible for San Francisco to celebrate in 1915 the opening of the Panama Canal, which will make us the metropolis of the Pacific Ocean. You came here to hear him, and I will introduce him now—Theodore Roosevelt."

The Colonel asked for three cheers for Heney and expressed his pleasure to be back in San Francisco and California. Then, brushing aside the Republican Party, which, he said, "has abandoned the people and has abandoned every principle of honesty and of popular rule and surrendered itself to servile subjection" of the bosses, he closed in on his main target of the evening, the Democratic contender, Woodrow Wilson.

As his jumping-off point he took a recent speech Wilson had made at the New York Press Club. Though the talk had been given five days earlier, on September 9, the text had just come to Roosevelt's attention, when a copy of the *New York Tribune* had caught up to his train. "Liberty has never come from the government," Wilson had told his audience. "Liberty has always come from the subjects of the government. The history of liberty is a history of the limitation of governmental power, not the increase of it." The statement had been part of a larger argument, but Roosevelt offered it as evidence that Wilson's conversion to progressivism had been incomplete, that he still harbored his earlier conservative views.

Though Wilson and Roosevelt were both progressives, they prayed at different altars of that faith. They agreed on the need for tariff revision (though they differed on the specifics). They agreed on democratic reforms such as direct primaries and the popular election of US senators. And they agreed on laws to guard the safety and improve the wages of factory workers. But their essential difference was on how to control the corporations.

Wanting to preserve the economic growth and international competitiveness that big business could provide, Roosevelt sought to maintain the trusts but to prevent them from exploiting employees and exerting undue influence over public officials. The only way to accomplish this balancing act, he argued, was through the regulatory power of a robust federal government. Both industry and labor, moreover, needed to put aside their selfish concerns and work together for the common good. Roosevelt called his philosophy "The New Nationalism," a term borrowed from *The Promise of American Life* by influential progressive thinker Herbert Croly.

Wilson had honed his ideas in conversation with prominent progressive attorney Louis Brandeis. Finding Roosevelt's approach too limited and paternalistic, Wilson argued that government should not content itself with regulating the trusts but must stimulate competition and encourage new businesses to enter the marketplace. Whereas Roosevelt believed that individuals must act altruistically for the public welfare, Wilson believed that the national well-being was best served when citizens were free to act in their own self-interest. And so he sought to renew society from below, by providing the conditions for talented and energetic people to prosper. To underscore this liberation of creativity and competition, he called his plan "The New Freedom."

Roosevelt's and Wilson's programs were rooted in fundamentally different assumptions about human nature and the proper role of government, and as the campaign unfolded, the nation witnessed a substantive philosophical debate the likes of which hadn't been seen since the days of Thomas Jefferson and Alexander Hamilton. But that didn't mean the candidates had left posturing and electioneering behind. Addressing the crowd this evening in the Coliseum, the Colonel launched his most personal attack yet on the Democrat, dismissing Wilson's ideas as "a bit of outworn academic doctrine which was kept in the schoolroom and the professorial study for a generation after it had been abandoned by all who had experience of actual life."

Which progressive programs would Wilson eliminate in the interest of minimizing the federal government? Roosevelt wanted to know. Would he repeal the Interstate Commerce Act, which regulated the railroads and other industries doing business across state lines? Did he object to the forty-hour workweek? To workmen's compensation and workplace safety? He "must be against every single progressive measure," the Colonel concluded, "for every progressive measure means an extension instead of a limitation of government control."

"The trouble with Mr. Wilson," he went on, was "that the history of which he is thinking is the history of absolute monarchies and oriental despotisms. He is thinking of government as embodied in an absolute king or an oligarchy or aristocracy. He is not thinking of our government which is a government by the people themselves. The only way in which our people can increase their power over the big corporation that does wrong, the only way in which it can protect the working man in his conditions of work and life, the only way in which people can protect children working in industry or secure women an eight-hour day in industry or secure compensation for men killed or crippled in industry, is by extending instead of limiting the powers of government.... Our proposal is to increase the power of the people themselves and make the people in reality the governing class.... We propose to use the whole power of the Government to protect all those who, under Mr. Wilson's laissez-faire system, are trodden down in the ferocious, scrambling rush of an unregulated and purely individualistic industrialism."

As Roosevelt slammed his opponent, the crowd interrupted often with cheers, and afterward thousands swarmed the platform to shake the Colonel's hand. Finally, at midnight, he retired, as a reporter described him, "wearied, hoarse, and rest-seeking." The Colonel had drawn blood. But would it be enough to change the course of the campaign? And could he press the attack beyond California, in the less-welcoming political climes of the South and Southwest?

The night that Theodore Roosevelt made his speech in San Francisco's Coliseum, John Schrank awoke in his tiny room in Manhattan's White House Hotel. It was nearly one thirty in the morning—the eleventh anniversary, to the hour, of the dream in which William McKinley had sat up in his coffin and commanded, "Avenge my death!"

Schrank had pondered the dream often in the intervening years, but since August 6, when Roosevelt had made his "Confession of Faith" to the Progressive convention, he had thought of little else. As he'd sat alone in his room or made his long ambles through Manhattan and Brooklyn, he'd brooded on the third termer and the catastrophe awaiting his adoptive country. The dream had been searing, and he still recalled every detail. But he'd asked himself time and again: How could he shoot a man down on the basis of a dream? "All dreams," he reminded himself, "don't come true."

Earlier that evening, Schrank had sat at his wooden worktable, wrestling with a new poem. His mind had swirled with images of manly duty and its terrible price, but he hadn't found the words to fit. Setting down his pen, he'd given up and gone to bed. But now, as he lay in the darkness, the ideas arranged themselves into sentences and stanzas. He pushed the bedclothes aside, padded to his writing table, and lit a lamp. Hunched in the halo of light, he began to write:

Be a Man
Be a man from early to late
When you rise in the morning
Till you go to bed
Be a man.

Is your country in danger
And you are called to defend
Where the battle is hottest
And death be the end
Face it and be a man.

When you fail in business
And your honor is at stake
When you bury your dearest
And your heart would break
Face it and be a man.

But when night draws near
And you hear a knock
And a voice should whisper
Your time is up; Refuse to answer
As long as you can
Then face it and be a man.

As he bent over the table in the midnight stillness, John Schrank was startled by a soft, sad voice behind him: "Let no murderer occupy the presidential chair for a third term. Avenge my death!"

He felt a gentle hand on his left shoulder. Turning, he saw the wraithlike face of William McKinley.

The martyred president vanished. But the visitation left Schrank with a certainty he had never known before. Tonight he wasn't asleep, and this summons was no dream.

They would say he was mad, of course. But hadn't they called Joan of Arc mad after the Holy Virgin appeared to her in a vision? When Moses glimpsed Yahweh in a burning thorn bush, then again in a pillar of cloud, didn't his own followers call him mad? And if God had appeared before in times of great crisis, why should He not appear again today, in the likeness of the slain president?

Schrank didn't care what others thought. He had no bother about law. He had been called to self-sacrifice, and where self-sacrifice began, the power of law reached its limit. He had an inviolable right to act. And even if this summons resulted in his death, what was his life compared to the salvation of his country? Tonight he had seen his duty, and he would face it like a man.

Putting the poem aside, he scribbled another document:

September 15th, 1912.
To the people of the United States
September 15, 1901—1:30 a.m. in a dream I saw president McKinley sit up in his coffin, pointing at a man in a monk's attire in whom I recognized Theo. Roosevelt. The dead president said This is my murderer, avenge my death.
To prevent is better than to defend.
Never let a third term party emblem appear on an official ballot.
I am willing to die for my country, god has called me to be his instrument.
So help me god.

Then he added, in German, the opening line of "A Mighty Fortress Is Our God," the hymn that had sounded as the *General Slocum* pulled away from the Third Street Pier with Elsie Ziegler aboard:

Eine fester burg ist unser gott

And beneath that the cryptic afterthought:

Innocent Guilty.

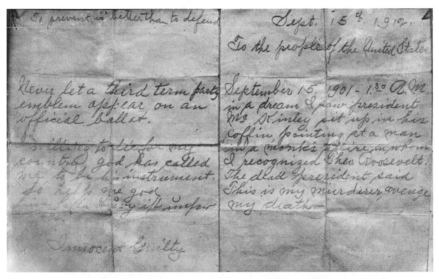

John Schrank's letter to the people of the United States, written on September 15, 1912. "I am willing to die for my country," he swore, "god has called me to be his instrument."

THREE

"We Want No King"
Saturday, September 21, to Sunday, September 22

PEERING OUT THE WINDOW OF THE WHITE HOUSE HOTEL, JOHN Schrank saw that the morning had broken sunny and crisp. He buttoned his vest over his generous middle, slipped into his suit coat, and tapped his bowler onto his head. In his pocket, he nestled his bankroll of $350. He had borrowed the money on a ninety-day note from Herman Larunger, brother of Edward, his former landlord at the Homestead Hotel. Though Schrank still owned the tenement in Yorkville (and had hired Edward Larunger to collect the rents), he found himself barely able to keep up with the mortgage and hadn't managed to put anything aside. After getting the money, Schrank had sent Herman Larunger a note: "I have just received news that a rich uncle of mine died in New Orleans. I am going there at once. Will send you a postal from Charleston, S.C."

Making his way down the steep front stairs of the White House Hotel, Schrank saw that Canal Street was already crowded with Saturday shoppers. Long-skirted ladies paused under shop awnings, corralling string-tied bundles in one hand and sloe-eyed children in the other. Men in long mustaches and blue serge suits chatted on the corner, while newsboys in knickerbockers and tweed caps darted through traffic. Their headlines trumpeted the perils of city life: POLICE GET "THE MIDNIGHT BURGLAR," reported the *Tribune*; DOCTOR KILLED, WOMAN HURT IN AUTO CRASH, related the *Sun*.

Schrank crossed Elizabeth Street and headed west, passing brick tenements with zigzag fire escapes, and cast-iron storefronts with wide, arched windows. He ticked off the blocks: Mott, Mulberry, Baxter. Beyond Baxter, he was skirting the northern boundary of Five Points, a neighborhood synonymous with crime and misery for the better part of a century. The name derived from the prominent intersection of Baxter, Park, and Worth Streets, but the district owed its origin to a pool known as Collect Pond. For hundreds of years before the arrival of Europeans, the fifty-acre, spring-fed pond had been an important source of drinking water. But by the early 1700s, it had been polluted by tanneries and other industries along its banks. The pond was drained by a forty-foot-wide canal, which angled westward across Manhattan to the North River, as the Hudson was known. In 1811, the pond was filled, and the channel, now covered, became Canal Street.

But the underground spring continued to flow, and the wooden buildings constructed over Collect Pond started to subside. Residents with the means sought higher, healthier ground, and those who remained, free blacks and poor immigrants, saw their neighborhood degenerate into a slum, rife with gangs, robbery, gambling, prostitution, brawls, and murder. Calls to clean up Five Points began as early as 1830, and by the 1860s the missionary societies had gone to work. By the turn of the twentieth century, the neighborhood had been razed, and one of its most dangerous precincts, Mulberry Bend, had been transformed into a public park. But even now Five Points was home to the infamous New York Halls of Justice and House of Detention, better known as the Tombs, a reminder of the district's notorious past.

Beyond Elm Street, John Schrank turned left onto Broadway, the island's preeminent artery ever since its days as an Indian trail. Behind him, to the north, lay the Great White Way, world famous for its dazzling electric billboards and theater marquees. Before him, to the south, rose some of the great buildings of the world, shrines to American industry and, some would say, greed. At the corner of Broadway and Leonard was the stately New York Life Insurance Building, surmounted by its stalwart stone clock tower. Farther on, between Cedar and Pine, had once stood another monument to the actuaries, the Equitable Life Building. When it opened in 1870, the seven-story structure had been the world's first office building equipped with a passenger elevator. Then, just this past January, the Equitable had been destroyed by fire. The new Equitable Building, rising on the same site, would be the largest structure in the world, rising nearly forty stories and encompassing almost two million square feet. Still on the drawing board, the leviathan-to-be was already controversial for its overpowering scale and the permanent shadow it would cast over everything around it.

On the corner of Liberty Street and Broadway, the delicate, needlelike tower of the Singer Building soared forty-one stories above the sidewalk. When it was completed in 1908, it had been the tallest structure in the world—until the following year, when the title was snatched by the Metropolitan Life Building at Madison and Twenty-third Street. But farther down Broadway, between Park Place and Barclay, even now was rising the massive Woolworth Building. When that Gothic Goliath was completed next year, it would rise an incredible fifty-eight stories and be dubbed the Cathedral of Commerce.

Striding past theaters, hotels, banks, and stores, John Schrank finally stopped before a window whose hand-lettered sign promised GUNS. Without even glancing at the name of the business, he entered.

Over the past six weeks, as he'd been honing his scheme, Schrank had been careful to confide in no one. When he'd asked his landlord, Gustav Jost, to hold his mail, he'd told him he was planning a trip to the Pacific Northwest to visit an uncle. The month-and-a-half of silent waiting had been excruciating. But there had been no alternative, because after the Progressive convention in early August, the third termer had retreated to his Long Island estate. Schrank had determined not to act in New York, because if he did, the world would think he'd been hired by Wall Street. Then, no sooner had Roosevelt launched his campaign in New England, he'd bolted out west. But now, finally, he was on the return, drawing closer to striking distance with every passing day.

Schrank knew nothing about guns, though he'd shot a Colt .38 into the air a few times to celebrate the Fourth of July. In fact, he already owned such a pistol, but it was in storage with the rest of his things in Yorkville, and he dared not go to the warehouse to retrieve it.

Now he told the man behind the counter that he wanted to buy a .38, and the clerk lifted a revolver from the glass case. Schrank took the gun into his hands and felt its cold, silent weight. He ran his fingers over the nickel-plated barrel and down the hard-rubber grip. The price was fourteen dollars, the clerk said. That seemed high to Schrank. But the gun was brand new, and it looked like a serious weapon for a serious purpose. He'd take it, Schrank told him, and a box of bullets. The clerk placed a carton of .38-caliber Smith & Wesson Longs on the counter. That would be an extra fifty-five cents, he said.

Before handing over the gun, the salesman asked to see Schrank's pistol permit, as required under the Sullivan Act, the controversial law that had gone into effect thirteen months before. In 1910, Manhattan had seen a record 108 homicides by shooting. So the following year, after a sensational murder-suicide near Gramercy Park, state senator and notorious Tammany operative Timothy Sullivan had sponsored a bill requiring a license to carry a concealed weapon. Some complained that the law would only succeed in disarming lawful citizens, while others suspected that Sullivan was just trying to rein in the thugs on his own payroll. Either way, the measure made it a felony to carry an unlicensed handgun in the state.

John Schrank wasn't about to apply to the police for a pistol permit. When he told the clerk he had no license, the man said he would simply remove a small screw from the body of the pistol, rendering the trigger inoperable. But what good was a pistol that wouldn't fire?

Schrank explained that he was leaving New York on a steamship that same afternoon, and fished the ticket from his pocket. In that case, the clerk said, the gentleman could take the gun as is.

The clerk knew the Sullivan Act contained no allowance for disabling weapons or for leaving the state within a certain period after purchase. But whereas the law made it a felony to carry an unlicensed pistol, it was only a misdemeanor to sell one. So dealers found it worth the risk to deal in illegal guns—and had sold an estimated five thousand of them in the twelve months after the Sullivan Act's passage. In that period, Manhattan's gun-murder rate had dropped by a grand total of two from the record set the year before.

John Schrank took his bankroll from his pocket and counted out fifteen dollars, while the clerk placed the revolver in its wooden box.

That evening, thirteen hundred miles west of New York City, Theodore Roosevelt thrust his barrel chest over the dais of the Topeka Auditorium, glowered through his spectacles, and came the closest he ever had to calling Woodrow Wilson a liar. The Democrat had made the offending remarks the day before, in Detroit, over the crucial issue of the trusts. Wilson had deliberately distorted the Progressives' ideas, Roosevelt was charging, with "misstatements of the facts," "deliberate misrepresentations," assertions "not in accordance with the facts," and several other synonyms for *falsehoods*. In reality, he went on, Wilson's plan for controlling the corporations—which was "in effect only Mr. Taft's plan with a slight variation of sound and fury in the preamble—would leave the supremacy of the trusts unchallenged," whereas "our [Progressive] plan for an extension of Governmental power will establish the Government in absolute and complete supremacy over the trusts."

It was the same aggressive note the Colonel had sounded in San Francisco, one week and twenty-five hundred miles ago. The day after his speech in the Coliseum, he had slept late and, following his custom, had scheduled no campaign events on the Sabbath. Leaving the city at ten o'clock that night, he'd made brief remarks the next day in several California towns, including Santa Barbara and Ventura, before arriving in Los Angeles at two forty-five in the afternoon.

There had been new threats against the Colonel's life, which authorities were attributing to the radical trade union the Industrial Workers of the World, known as the Wobblies. So, at the Los Angeles depot his train was met by three carloads of plainclothesmen carrying pistols and sawed-off shotguns. But the show of force didn't dispirit the candidate, who stood in his open car waving his black Stetson, or deter the spectators, who flooded the streets in what newspapers called the most raucous reception in the city's history. The three-mile parade route was festooned with flags, banners, and Chinese lanterns, and in places the crowd spilled into the road, forcing the motorcade to a halt until mounted police could clear the way. That afternoon the Colonel made a speech to a standing-room audience in the Temple Auditorium, then that evening he gave another at the Shrine. At ten p.m., he departed on the *Mayflower*, bound for Arizona, New Mexico, Colorado, and points east.

He had planned to stop next in Phoenix, but the Arizona Progressive Committee insisted that he add an appearance in Tucson and dispatched a special train to fetch him. When he finally did reach Phoenix, he was greeted by two companies of state militia, a brass band, and Governor George W. P. Hunt, who had taken office the previous Valentine's Day, when Arizona had become the forty-eighth state admitted to the Union (just behind New Mexico, admitted on January 6).

After a pause in Albuquerque, where he spoke from a bandstand near the depot, the Colonel barnstormed through Colorado, stopping at dusty towns such as La Junta, Rocky Ford, and Trinidad and substantial cities such as Pueblo, Colorado Springs, and Denver. Then he churned across the Nebraska prairies like a spring tornado, making twelve speeches in a single day, in places such as Lincoln, Holdrege, and Hastings; at the last of these he assured his listeners, "Mr. Taft is a dead cock in the pit."

In Oxford, Nebraska, he was awakened at seven thirty a.m. by the unmelodious notes of a local boys' band. Throwing on some clothes, he said a few words from the *Mayflower's* platform and then retreated inside for something to eat. Though he rarely missed any meal, the Colonel seemed to have a special affinity for breakfast, where in a single sitting he'd been known to consume two whole grapefruits, four soft-boiled eggs, four lamb chops, and a pair of wheat cakes.

Roosevelt was still taking his sustenance when he was visited by George W. Norris, Nebraska Bull Moose leader, congressman, and candidate for the US Senate. But when Norris tried to enter the *Mayflower,* he was stopped by a porter, who told him, "You can't come in here."

"I guess I can," he answered. "I am Congressman Norris, and I'm an invited guest."

"But my orders are that the Colonel is not to be disturbed until after breakfast, and that goes," the porter insisted.

"Well, but I was invited," Norris sputtered, and flashed a letter from the Progressive National Committee.

A conductor was called, and though he read the letter he sided with the porter. Furious, the congressman stormed into an ordinary Pullman, until one of the Colonel's aides, hearing of the contretemps, came and rescued the candidate from his constituents.

That evening, the Colonel spoke in Omaha, where he lambasted the political bosses of both parties. He'd had no choice but to bolt from the Republicans, he told the attentive but undemonstrative audience, because the hierarchy was crooked, and "the only way you can reform that kind of man is with a club."

While he slept, his train sped across Kansas, arriving September 21 in Topeka, where, in the packed Auditorium, he was now calling Woodrow

Wilson all but a liar. In the middle of his speech, a voice rose from the audience: "How about Perkins?"

The reference was to Roosevelt's friend, adviser, and contributor George W. Perkins. Now fifty, the charming, soft-spoken, beautifully tailored Perkins had risen from office boy at New York Life to the company's presidency. After J. P. Morgan had taken him on as a partner, Perkins had been instrumental in the founding of the great trusts U.S. Steel and International Harvester. Then two years ago, he'd retired, though he still served on the boards of eighteen corporations. Perkins had been influential in Republican politics, and, like Roosevelt, he believed that the answer to the trusts lay not in eradication but in regulation. As the Progressives' largest donor, he'd been appointed chairman of the party's executive committee, over the objection of some of the Colonel's closest advisers, who worried that Perkins's ties to America's largest corporations undermined the party's calls for reform.

Roosevelt had been fending off similar insinuations for years, since reports had surfaced that his 1904 campaign had accepted huge contributions from the same trusts he proposed to regulate. In December 1911, as he was mulling his run for a third term, the rumors had intensified, and this past May the US Senate had named a special subcommittee, chaired by Moses E. Clapp of Minnesota, to investigate corporate contributions to Roosevelt's and Taft's campaigns. In August, William Randolph Hearst's monthly magazine had reported that in 1904 Republican Senator Boies Penrose of Pennsylvania had taken a check for $25,000 from Standard Oil, with Roosevelt's knowledge. Penrose was now claiming the money had been intended for the president's election campaign. He also charged on the Senate floor that the Roosevelt campaign committee had solicited a contribution from railroad financier Edward H. Harriman, whose Northern Securities Company had been sued under the Sherman Anti-Trust Act in 1902 and ordered dissolved by the Supreme Court two years later.

Penrose was hardly known as a paragon of legislative virtue. Born to a patrician Philadelphia family, he had graduated from Harvard Law School in 1881 and had entered politics as a reformer. But eventually he had joined the Republican machine and had been elected to the Senate in 1897, becoming the undisputed political boss of Pennsylvania and a major factor in the national party. He had once explained his philosophy of government this way: "I believe in the division of labor. You [industry] send us to Congress; we pass laws under which you make money . . . and out of your profits, you further contribute to our campaign funds to send us back again to pass more laws to enable you to make more money." But in leveling his condemnation of Roosevelt, Penrose was joined by a senator who was known for his probity, frustrated Republican candidate Robert La Follette. Together, the pair demanded that the Senate investigate Penrose's allegations.

Appearing before the Clapp Committee, John D. Archbold, president of Standard Oil, testified that Roosevelt's campaign manager, the late Cornelius Bliss, had solicited a $100,000 contribution from him, with Roosevelt's approval. Since there were no legal limits on corporate donations to political candidates at the time, it was unlikely that the committee would uncover any criminal activity. The intent was not to prosecute Roosevelt but to embarrass him, to show that his dealings with the corporations had not been as pure as he'd pretended. In the Senate, La Follette encouraged this inference, claiming that whereas only 140 trusts were operating in the United States at the beginning of the Roosevelt administration, there had been 10,000 at its close.

In his defense, Roosevelt produced a letter he had written Bliss, instructing that any donation from Standard Oil be returned. But apparently the funds had already been spent and were never sent back, as Roosevelt almost certainly knew when he dictated the letter. Now the Colonel was demanding to appear before the Clapp Committee to clear his name, but since Congress was about to adjourn for the summer, his testimony would have to wait until late September or early October.

And now, during this address in Topeka, a voter was raising the troublesome matter of George Perkins. The Colonel answered that Perkins had once admitted to him that he didn't worry for his children's financial future. But, he'd added, he knew that the United States wouldn't be a good place for his children unless it was a good place for everybody's children, and it was out of this enlightened self-interest that Perkins supported the Progressives' reforms.

"Didn't you know then that Perkins had not severed his connection with the Harvester Company?" the man in the audience pressed. Harvester was one of the corporations on whose boards Perkins still served.

The auditorium went still. Turning to face the questioner, the Colonel snapped, "Listen and learn if you are an honest man. I knew perfectly well. He asked me whether he should sever his connection, and I told him, 'No.' I told him any man who would object to that would be a man whose shriveled soul wasn't worth taking into account."

The crowd broke into cheers, and when the din subsided, the Colonel added that he welcomed the assistance of any man, rich or poor, as long as the supporter expected nothing but the "reward that will come through the triumph of the principles in which they believe." Still, Roosevelt knew that until he could testify, the issue would throw a shadow over the campaign, just as his political enemies intended.

During this third week of September, Woodrow Wilson was finishing a campaign swing that had taken him to Indiana, Iowa, South Dakota, Minnesota, Ohio, and Michigan. And, like Roosevelt, he was on the attack. Whereas the Democrats wanted to expand freedom, Wilson charged, the Republicans wanted "not to take you out of the hands of the men who have corrupted the Government of the United States, but to see to it that you remain in their hands and that that government guarantees to you that they will be humane to you."

Privately, Wilson admired the Colonel and even admitted to the fusty academic image that Roosevelt was trying to paint of him. "The Bull Moose," he wrote a friend, "appeals to their imagination; I do not.

He is a real, vivid person, whom they have seen and shouted themselves hoarse over and voted for, millions strong; I am a vague, conjectural personality, more made up of opinions and academic prepossessions than of human traits and red corpuscles."

But Wilson exuded an uncommon inner strength. "I never met a man who gave such an impression of quietness inside," found journalist John Reed. Deep within the man was "a principle, a religion, a something, upon which his whole life rests. Roosevelt never had it, nor Taft. Wilson's power emanates from it. Roosevelt's sprang from an abounding vitality."

Despite his immense popularity, the Colonel still harbored doubts over his electability. The day he spoke in Topeka, a story appeared in the *New York Times* under the headline ROOSEVELT HAS LOST HOPE, reporting that he had written to friends in London saying he had no chance of success on November 5. When the *Times* reporter traveling with the campaign asked Roosevelt for a comment on the article, the candidate tried to make a joke of it. "If they'll specify the person I wrote to and the place where he lives," he said, "I'll search my memory and try to recall it. I don't see why London was picked as the place from which to send this revelation. Why not Polynesia or Tibet?"

To some, the humor was strained. And even the Colonel couldn't say how many votes he'd added with this interminable barnstorming. Ahead lay a long, difficult journey through the solidly Democratic South. But tomorrow, at least, he would have a day of rest and a Sunday visit with an old friend.

While Theodore Roosevelt was taking Woodrow Wilson to task in Topeka, the nominee of the Socialist Party, Eugene Victor Debs, was campaigning sixty miles to the east, in Kansas City. Like the Colonel, Debs had been stumping the country in September, with stops from New York to California and from Minnesota to Texas.

Eugene Victor Debs, candidate of the American Socialist Party. "Let us make the numerals 1912 appear in flaming red in the calendar of the century," he told his followers.

But while Roosevelt, Taft, and Wilson dominated the front pages, reporters—and his fellow candidates—scarcely took note of Debs. Taft had refused an invitation to debate the Socialist, and when the Colonel mentioned him at all, it was to argue that the Progressives' reforms were necessary to ensure peace between labor and capital and to prevent a Socialist revolution. Debs, meanwhile, saved his most biting criticism for Roosevelt, whom he called a charlatan who had stolen his ideas and watered them down for popular consumption. No one could accuse the Socialists of diluting their own beliefs: Their platform, among other points, called for the collective ownership of banks, industry, communication, and transportation; the abolition of the US Senate; and the elimination of the presidential veto.

Debs, aged fifty-six, was making his fourth run at the White House. Though not a brilliant politician, he was sincere in his sympathy for the workingman and utterly dedicated to his cause. Lanky and bald, with a prominent nose and intense blue eyes, he was a mesmerizing speaker who drew large, fervent crowds. His vote tallies had risen from less than a hundred thousand in 1900 to around four hundred thousand in both 1904 and 1908. And during that time, his party had made undeniable progress. The year 1910 had seen the election of the first Socialist congressman, Victor Berger of Wisconsin, along with fourteen legislators in that famously left-leaning state; across the country, some thousand Socialists now held local and state offices. With a rudimentary party organization and a tiny budget of $66,000, Debs didn't delude himself that he had a chance of being elected president. But by drawing even more votes this year, he hoped to show the inexorable Socialist rise. "Let us make this our year!" he exhorted. "Let us make the numerals 1912 appear in flaming red in the calendar of the century."

Debs had been born in Terre Haute, Indiana, the son of impoverished Alsatian immigrants who founded a successful grocery store. At age fourteen, against his parents' wishes, he left school and went to work for the Vandalia Railroad as a paint scraper. Within a year, he was promoted to locomotive fireman, before losing that job in the international depression known as the Panic of 1873, brought on largely by the speculative, unregulated expansion of the railroads.

Through a connection of his father, Debs found a job as an accounting clerk for a large wholesale grocery. Though he never worked for the railroad again, he remained intensely involved in the industry. In 1875 he joined the Brotherhood of Locomotive Firemen, at the time more a fraternal organization than a labor union. Rising to influence in the local chapter, he was elected two years later as the Brotherhood's grand marshal. He became active in Democratic politics and was elected Terre Haute's city clerk, then a state assemblyman. But frustrated with the sluggishness and uncertainty of the legislative process, in 1888 he refused the Democratic nomination for the Terre Haute city council. Turning toward union organizing, he helped to found chapters of carpenters, coopers, and printers, as well as a Central Labor Union, all the while continuing his work with the Brotherhood of Locomotive Firemen, where he'd been named treasurer-secretary.

At the time, the Brotherhood didn't involve itself in labor disputes, so Debs played no role in the nation's first major rail walkout, the Great Railroad Strike of 1877. Beginning in West Virginia in mid-July, after the Baltimore & Ohio and other financially pressed railroads cut workers' wages, the strike spread across the country and, during six violent weeks, exacted more than a hundred lives and millions of dollars in property damage before being put down by militiamen and federal troops. The bloodshed and destruction shocked the nation, and by hardening the already bitter divisions between employees and management, set the stage for future rail strikes. In these later disputes, both the Brotherhood and its treasurer-secretary Eugene Debs showed themselves increasingly aggressive advocates for workers. Beginning in February 1888, Debs led his first strike, of engineers and firemen who walked off the Chicago, Burlington & Quincy Railroad over work rules and compensation. When the company hired strikebreakers, the Brotherhood suffered an unalloyed defeat.

In 1893, Debs cofounded the American Railway Union, the railroads' first truly industry-wide labor organization. That same year, yet another depression was sparked by the collapse of the overextended Reading Railroad. The following spring, when the Great Northern reduced employees' wages for the third time in eight months, Debs led the strike and by submitting their case to arbitration, won virtually all the workers' demands. It was the first time that a union had ever been victorious in a dispute with an American railroad. American Railway's membership soared to a hundred and fifty thousand, and Debs was hailed as a national labor leader.

That same summer, railroad unions faced an even greater challenge, from the Pullman Palace Car Company. George Pullman, inventor of the sleeping car, had founded the business in 1867 and had later built a workers' community called Pullman City south of Chicago. Clean, comfortable, and attractive, Pullman City was vaunted as a model community, where workers lived in company-owned houses, prayed in company-owned churches, and shopped in company-owned stores, living by company-set rules and paying company-set prices. Then in response to the Panic of 1893, Pullman decreased employees' wages between a third and a half, without offsetting reductions in the cost of food or rent. Workers organized a local of the American Railway Union, and on May 11, three thousand workers lay down their tools; the remaining union members were locked out.

Though he worried that the union wasn't ready for another major confrontation, Debs announced that beginning June 25 his workers would not move any train carrying a Pullman car. The action paralyzed railroad travel, especially in the western states, and after workers rioted in Chicago on July 3, management won a federal injunction against the strike on the basis that it interfered with the US mail, disrupted interstate commerce, and violated the Sherman Anti-Trust Act (which had been intended to regulate the corporations, not labor unions). Some twelve thousand federal troops were sent to Chicago to reinforce the police, and in the resulting violence, dozens of workers were killed and scores were wounded. But Debs's call for a general strike went unheeded, and when the rival American Federation of Labor, under Samuel Gompers, refused its support, the American Railway Union was broken.

Debs and other leaders were arrested, convicted of contempt of court for defying the injunction, and sentenced to six months in prison. In a second trial, on the more serious charge of conspiracy, they were represented by two Chicago lawyers, Clarence Darrow and S. S. Gregory. When the proceedings began to go against the prosecution, the government suspended the trial and never resumed it. But the American Railway Union never recovered from the disaster; after it disbanded, some of its members, including Debs, went on to form the Social Democratic Party of America. Meanwhile, Debs's leadership in the strike and his incarceration only burnished his reputation. On leaving prison, he turned once more to politics, and on January 1, 1897, announced his conversion: "I am for Socialism because I am for humanity. . . . Money constitutes no proper basis of civilization. The time has come to regenerate society—we are on the eve of universal change." Like Theodore Roosevelt, he claimed Abraham Lincoln, the Great Emancipator, as his personal hero.

By 1900, Debs was recognized as the leading American socialist. That year he was the Social Democratic Party's candidate for president, and in 1901 was one of the founders of the Socialist Party of America, a merger of the Social Democrats and a faction of the Socialist Labor Party. In 1904 he ran on the Socialist ticket. And now, eight years later, he found himself pitted against an incumbent president, a former president, and a college-president-turned-governor in this bruising four-way contest of ideas.

On Sunday, September 22, Theodore Roosevelt slept until eight o'clock and then enjoyed breakfast in the *Mayflower*, parked on a siding in Emporia, Kansas. A vehicle was waiting outside the depot, but today it wouldn't convey him to an auditorium or a parade. Today, the only hand waiting to be shaken belonged to his old friend William Allen White, editor of the *Emporia Gazette*.

Born here in Emporia, his mother a schoolteacher and his father a doctor, White had been working on newspapers since age eleven, when he got an after-school job as a printer's devil, rolling ink and picking stray type off the floor. Later, while a student at the College of Emporia and then the University of Kansas, he wrote part-time for several papers, and when he was offered the editorship of the El Dorado (Kansas) *Republican*, he left school before earning a degree. He went on to report for the *Kansas City Journal* and *Star* but soon realized he was unsuited to working for someone else. So in 1896, at the age of twenty-seven, he borrowed $3,000, bought the struggling *Gazette*, and returned to his hometown. With no funds to bring his young family with him, he arrived in Emporia with $1.25 in his pocket.

White made a success of the *Gazette* and became a respected author in his own right, publishing a syndicated column, articles for magazines such as the *Saturday Evening Post* and *McClure's*, and several books of fiction and nonfiction. His 1896 essay "What's the Matter with Kansas?", supporting William McKinley over William Jennings Bryan in that year's presidential election, brought him to the attention of the Republican hierarchy, and he was eventually named to the party's National Committee.

White had met Roosevelt when the president-to-be was still assistant secretary of the Navy. Introduced by a mutual acquaintance, Kansas Congressman (later Senator and Vice President) Charles Curtis, the pair had gotten together for lunch at a Washington hotel. It was a meeting that would change White's life. "I was afire with the splendor of the personality I had met," he recalled. "I had never known such a man as he, and never shall again. He overcame me. And in the hour or two we spent that day at lunch, and in a walk down F Street, he poured into my heart such visions, such ideals, such hopes, such a new attitude toward life and patriotism and the meaning of things, as I had never dreamed men had. . . . So strong was this young Roosevelt, hard-muscled, hard-voiced, even when the voice cracked in falsetto, with hard, wriggling jaw muscles, and snapping teeth, even when he cackled in raucous glee, so completely did the personality of this man overcome me that I made no protest and accepted his dictums as my creed. . . . After that I was his man."

White found Roosevelt's rift with Taft "heartbreaking," but he supported the Bull Moose in his battle for the Republican nomination and was instrumental in delivering Kansas to the Colonel. When Roosevelt bolted to form the Progressives, White bolted with him, serving as a key delegate at the party's August convention. Though he took exception to some of Roosevelt's notions (such as judicial recall) and found George Perkins a "sinister figure" who "represented money and the power of money," White was the Colonel's unwavering friend, confidant, and adviser.

At the time of Roosevelt's visit, Emporia was a community of ten thousand souls, two colleges, an opera house, more than thirty churches, and not one cigarette stand or saloon. Though the town boasted a score of automobiles, White, to his neighbors' chagrin, elected to meet their illustrious guest at the station in his antiquated fringe-topped surrey drawn by his venerable black horse, Tom. It was said that Tom was so old that everyone had either lost track of his age or declined to mention it out of respect.

Mrs. White dared not abandon the dinner preparations, but Mr. White brought along to the station the district attorney, the town banker, and the resident poet. While the delegation clip-clopped under arching elms and past spacious lawns and porches, White and Roosevelt shared the front seat, taking turns driving Tom, while the other passengers sat behind. Riding with the local dignitaries was the Colonel's young cousin George Emlen Roosevelt.

The streets were quiet, since White had asked his neighbors to grant the Colonel a day of rest; visiting reporters had been ushered off to the country club, where they nibbled chilled watermelon and spent an uncustomarily dry Sunday. The plan was to escort the visitor to the Congregational sanctuary, which was packed for the occasion. But the Colonel asked to be taken to the Lutheran church, where his appearance startled the forty assembled worshipers. The minister paled as the ex-president walked up the aisle, and during his sermon he made only passing reference to their guest. When it came time to sing, the Colonel stood with the congregation and thundered four verses of

"How Firm a Foundation, Ye Saints of the Lord" without as much as a glance at the hymnal. Roosevelt had a "rough bass," White found, "about a half-tone off-key, and no ear for music, melody, or harmony. But he bellowed through the hymn without 'da-daing' on a line, so I was proud of him."

After the service, they drove to the White home at 927 Exchange Street, a large, comfortable house called "Red Rocks" for its Colorado sandstone. White's wife, Sallie, came out with their children, Mary, eight, and William, Jr., twelve. Then everyone (except little Mary, who preferred to eat in the kitchen) sat at the dining room table and passed platters of fried chicken and mashed potatoes with gravy.

Afterward, the Colonel lay down for an hour. Then the old friends sat in the front room "considering the cosmos," along with more earth-bound matters. Roosevelt confided he had a fair chance of winning the election, and that he believed he could count on Kansas in the Progressive column. He chuckled as he reported that in Denver, where he'd just been, Progressive National Committee member and longtime judge Ben Lindsey was being called "the bull mouse" for his diminutive stature. Then, regretfully, the Colonel excused himself and left for the Bartlett Hotel, where he had an appointment with a businessman from Chicago.

Harry O. Sooy was an employee of the Victor Talking Machine Company. Though he'd arrived on the train at one-thirty that morning, he'd gotten up early to make sure that everything would be ready. When the Colonel entered, Sooy thought he looked tired despite the day of rest. As the entourage blustered into the hotel room, Roosevelt was complaining about having to walk up a flight of stairs because the elevator was out of order. He threw his hat on the dresser. Then he sat at a table facing a large metal cone, which would capture his voice and transmit it to a needle that would cut grooves in a thick wax disk. Back at headquarters, the company would manufacture twelve-inch, 78-rpm records, which would sell for $1.25 apiece. For the campaign, the recordings meant that the candidate's voice could reach places that he would never go. It wasn't Roosevelt's first time making such recordings; in August, he had produced four for the Edison Company. Taft and Wilson made similar disks.

Without the benefit of notes, Roosevelt began to speak into the metal cone. For three minutes and thirty-seven seconds, he discoursed on "The Liberty of the People," reprising his criticism in San Francisco, that Wilson's idea of freedom was "an academic statement of history in the past," which didn't recognize that governmental power now resided in the electorate. "The liberty of which Mr. Wilson speaks today," he went on, "means merely the liberty of some great trust magnate to do that which he is not entitled to do. It means merely the liberty of some factory owner to work haggard women over hours for under pay and himself to pocket the proceeds. It means the liberty of the factory owner who crowds his operatives into some crazy death-trap on a top floor, where if fire starts the slaughter is immense. It means the liberty of the big factory owner who is conscienceless and unscrupulous, to work his men and women under conditions which eat into their lives like an acid. It means the liberty of even less conscientious factory owners to make their money out of the toil, the labor, of little children. Men of this stamp are the men whose liberty would be preserved by Mr. Wilson. Men of this stamp are the men whose liberty would be preserved by the limitation of governmental power. We propose, on the contrary, to extend governmental power in order to secure the liberty of the wageworkers, of the men and women who toil in industry, to save the liberty of the oppressed from the oppressor. Mr. Wilson stands for the liberty of the oppressor to oppress; we stand for the limitation of his liberty thus to oppress those who are weaker than himself."

His piece spoken, the Colonel stood up and collected his hat. It fell to Mr. Sooy to inform him that the company was expecting at least four such recordings.

Roosevelt threw his hat back on the dresser. "I don't know what to talk about," he muttered.

Cousin George suggested a few words about John D. Archbold, Boies Penrose, and the Senate campaign-finance investigation.

"A good suggestion, a good suggestion," the Colonel agreed. And he proceeded to rail for another three and a half minutes against "the big bosses of the political field, the beneficiaries of privilege in the field of industry, the men who represent that sinister alliance between crooked politics and crooked business, which has done more than anything else for the corruption of American life," as exemplified by Senator Penrose of Pennsylvania and Mr. Archbold of the Standard Oil Company.

Pursuing this theme, he recorded another track on "The 'Abyssinian Treatment' of Standard Oil," pointing out that any campaign contribution from the corporation to his 1904 election had clearly bought no influence, since, as Archbold himself had testified before the Senate committee, "Darkest Abyssinia can show nothing to compare with the treatment administered to the Standard Oil Corporation during the administration of President Roosevelt."

In the fourth track, the Colonel explained "Why the Trusts and Bosses Oppose the Progressive Party": "They dread you, the people. You and those like you who make up the people of the United States. They know that their time has come once the people obtain real power." He then made yet a fifth recording, "The Farmer and the Business Man," in which he promised to promote the interests of the common people over the trusts, in order "to promote prosperity and then to see that prosperity is passed around."

Finally, Sooy asked whether he would like to make a nonpolitical track, to preserve his voice for posterity.

"No," Roosevelt snapped. "I don't care a damn about the preservation of my voice. No, I would not think of such a thing." And with that, he and his entourage bustled out.

Back at Red Rocks, the Colonel posed for pictures with the White family on the lawn and the deep, plant-filled porch. Then he bid goodbye to Sallie and the children, and he and White returned to the station in the fringed surrey. The rest of the afternoon he spent in the *Mayflower*, parked on its siding, dictating correspondence. That night, when his train left Emporia, several hundred people collected at the depot to see him off. He told the crowd that he'd enjoyed his visit, thanked them for their hospitality, and bid them farewell and good luck. Though the comments were simple pleasantries, they were received reverentially, without applause. As the *Mayflower* pulled out of sight, tears were seen to stream down the cheeks of grown men.

In New York City, John Schrank strode west across Canal Street. Block after block he toted his suitcase, passing cast-iron storefronts and brick tenements and even a few prim town houses from early in the previous century. Finally, after more than a mile, he stepped onto Pier 36 on the North River, at the foot of Spring Street. All about him was the bittersweet bustle of departure—uniformed porters manhandling trunks; smug businessmen with stiff collars and neat leather grips; somber couples sauntering arm in arm, as if to forestall the inevitable. Just downriver among the phalanx of docks lay the slip operated by the Savannah Line, which shuttled among Georgia, Alabama, New York, and Boston. Upriver were the three piers reserved for the great White Star Line, where the *Titanic* would have landed after its maiden voyage this past April, if it hadn't rendezvoused with an iceberg in the North Atlantic.

Schrank peered up at the vessel alongside Pier 36, a screw steamer christened the *Comanche*. At 350 feet, the *Comanche* was long and low. It looked fast, with its raked black hull. Above the white superstructure, a single stack was spewing smoke from the coal fires smoldering deep below decks. On the short rear mast fluttered a pennant with a bright-red *C* set in a white field and bordered top and bottom by a narrow, royal-blue band. The *C* stood for "Clyde," the line that operated the *Comanche* between New York and Jacksonville, Florida, along with her sister ships the *Apache, Mohawk, Huron, Lenape*, and *Arapahoe*. According to company literature, the *Comanche* boasted every feature to ensure the safety and comfort of its three hundred passengers—watertight compartments, a radio, steam heat and baths, electric lights and bells, a large dining saloon, a social hall, smoking rooms, and a spacious promenade deck. Cruising speed was advertised at fifteen knots.

Clutching his suitcase, John Schrank climbed the *Comanche's* narrow gangplank. From the railing of the first deck, he could look down on the knots of well-wishers standing on the dock waving to other passengers. Before long he heard the bass blast of the ship's horn and felt the urgent throbbing of the enormous engine beneath his feet. Cautiously, like a matron rising from a sofa, the *Comanche* eased from its berth and turned downriver toward the harbor. In forty hours, the ship was scheduled to make its first landfall, at Charleston, South Carolina. After a half-day's layover, it would be another ten hours' cruise to Jacksonville.

Onshore, enveloped in gray sky and gray water, rose the gray buildings of Manhattan. John Schrank had never seen New York from this perspective, and he couldn't say when he would see it again. Though the city had been his home for more than two decades, he wasn't leaving with much more than he'd brought as a gawky thirteen-year-old—some three hundred borrowed dollars, an extra suit of clothes, a change of underwear, a razor, a couple of books, his naturalization papers, and the deed to his boardinghouse, all packed into his new, three-dollar suitcase.

Much of the case was taken up with his own writings, some carefully copied in notebooks, others scratched on the backs of envelopes and paid utility bills. One was a letter addressed "Dear Lady" but never sent, begging her forgiveness for making love in such an abrupt manner. Some of the pages held his philosophizing: "I never had a friend in my life; my uncle was more than a friend, and God was my guardian." "Our face is the image of the sins of our fathers." And: "Your future success depends as much upon the bad you omit doing as the good you do." Of course, there was poetry:

> When the hand leads the head life will be hell;
> But let the head lead the hand and all goes well.

> When the sun has set and we recall the day,
> We know well what happened and what should have;
> But that makes us no wiser than the birds that sing
> As to what the following day will bring.

Most of the texts were political: "Wealth is accumulated poverty." "People who cannot rule themselves are not worthy of a king." "Roosevelt is trying to commit race suicide on the American nation." "Two terms is enough for the best President: Washington." "Roosevelt's ambition murdered me: McKinley." "Let us not follow the Socialism of the old world. We are the new world, and it is a living world; let the old world follow us."

Scribbled on the back of a water and light bill was a slightly longer inspiration: "Theodore Roosevelt is in conspiracy with European monarchs to overthrow our Republic. Theodore Roosevelt's unscrupulous ambition has been the murder of President McKinley, to satiate his thirst for power. Down with Theodore Roosevelt, we want no King; we want no murderer. The United States is no Carthage. We will not yield to Rome."

And another: "One of Ohio's most noble sons, one of the best Presidents the Union has ever had, was compelled to make room for this unscrupulous, ambitious adventurer. I am also a son of Ohio, and I am proud of it, but should I also drop like my noble countryman, I shall do so while fighting to maintain our republican institutions.

"When victory is nearest, it looks most like defeat. You will never enjoy life if you have never been down and out. He calls it bull moose; just let the bull loose. When we get through with the kid it will look like ————. Those who venture most have to brave the storm."

Also in the suitcase, along with the notebooks and sheaves of precious papers, lay a carton of bullets and, snug in its wooden box, the gleaming Colt .38.

FOUR

"A Perfect Stranger"
Monday, September 23, to Saturday, September 28

IT WAS LATE AFTERNOON WHEN THE SS *COMANCHE* CLEARED THE jetties and began the seven-mile run up Charleston Harbor. The long, sack-shaped inlet was the reason the English had built their city here in 1670. And in 1829, it was to protect the port that the federal government had piled tons of granite boulders at its mouth and constructed a low, five-sided fort named in honor of native Revolutionary War hero General Thomas Sumter. Three decades later, the fortress had vaulted from local landmark to national icon, when soldiers of the Confederate States had trained their cannons on its five-foot-thick, brick-and-masonry walls. At the end of the thirty-four-hour bombardment, the rebels had claimed the smoldering rubble as a prize of war. But today the reconstructed fort was once again garrisoned by US troops; as the *Comanche* steamed past, the muzzles of their howitzers could be seen jutting through the square gun ports.

Charleston was built on the tip of a peninsula, which hung down into the harbor like a bunch of grapes. The Ashley River flowed to the west of the city, but the *Comanche* eased off to starboard and headed up the wide, shallow estuary of the Cooper. It was on the town's east side that most of the docks were situated, receiving passenger ships from New York, Baltimore, Georgetown, Florida, and Europe, and freighters from the West Indies and Central America.

As the *Comanche* neared the low, flat city, church steeples seemed to rise out of the sea. Then came into view the handsome esplanade and lush lawns of the Battery, studded with live oaks and magnolias. Situated around the park were some of Charleston's finest houses, boasting pillars, porticos, and elegant, multistory verandas.

The ship glided past a dozen wharves, then backed its engines and churned into one of the four slips reserved for vessels of the Clyde Line. Hawsers as thick as a man's wrist were thrown overboard and secured to huge metal cleats. Passengers surged forward. Some would disembark at Charleston, while others intended only to stretch their legs and see a bit of the city during the layover. But John Schrank's purpose was far from casual: After two days without a paper, he was desperate for news of the third termer.

He was carried along with the crowd, down the gangplank to the pier, where a boy was hawking papers. Schrank gave him a nickel and scanned the headlines. Today the Progressive campaign had released their candidate's itinerary for the rest of the month. Schrank pulled up short: Roosevelt was scheduled to reach New Orleans on the morning of September 27—just three and a half days away.

He calculated time and distance. From Jacksonville, the *Comanche*'s last port of call before returning to New York, he'd been planning to find a ship bound for New Orleans. But the *Comanche* wouldn't land in Florida until tomorrow morning. And he needed to reach New Orleans by the evening of the 26th to be on hand for Roosevelt's arrival the following day. There wasn't enough time to book passage and make the long voyage around the Florida peninsula. Worse, after his speech in New Orleans, Roosevelt would speed northward in his private car, while Schrank would have to creep along on regular service. If the third termer escaped in New Orleans, he could be back in Oyster Bay before Schrank caught up to him again.

Schrank could rush to New Orleans by train, but it would be a journey of more than seven hundred miles from Charleston and more than five hundred from Jacksonville. Then he saw in the paper that after New Orleans, Roosevelt was scheduled to swing through Alabama and Georgia, stopping for a major speech in Atlanta on the evening of the 28th. Atlanta was less than three hundred miles away. If Schrank started tomorrow, he would have four days to make the journey. He could take his time, checking newspapers along the way and watching for any change of schedule. Maybe he could even intercept the third termer before he reached Atlanta.

Schrank turned back toward the deserted steamer, went to his cabin, and retrieved the locked grip. Exiting the terminal, he found himself on a street called Concord, near the corner of Broad. The afternoon was cool and overcast. There were still puddles on the sidewalk from rain earlier in the day. To the north was the United States Customs House, with its wide marble steps and grand Corinthian columns. Schrank headed west on Broad, passing long, low sheds loaded with ship's stores, coal, cotton, fertilizer, rice, and lumber. Then, after a few blocks, the warehouses gave way to two- and three-story, brick-and-stone buildings housing banks and offices.

At the corner of Broad and Meeting, he came to one of the city's major intersections, judging from the prominent buildings rising on all four corners. To the south was St. Michael's Church, with its classical pediment and five-tiered wedding-cake tower, one of the spires visible from the deck of the *Comanche*. Across the street was the Italianate post office, looking more like an opera house than a department of the federal government. And on the other two corners were the pale, restrained facades of the county courthouse and city hall.

Schrank knew no one in the city, and no one knew him; he was, he realized, *a perfect stranger.* Turning north on Meeting Street, he passed the modern, deluxe St. John's Hotel, at five stories among the tallest buildings in view. Compared to New York, Charleston appeared a squat, mean city. There were few pedestrians on the sidewalks, and among the little traffic clattering over the red bricks and cobblestones were more mule drays than motorized trucks. Whereas New York was a booming, striving metropolis of the future, Charleston seemed a down-at-heel relic of the past.

In another few blocks, he passed Market Street, lined on both sides with old-fashioned shops. Then, on the corner of Society Street, he spied what he was looking for: a three-story, wood-frame building whose sign announced the Moseley National House. The hotel seemed modest but respectable.

Standing behind the desk was the proprietor, E. H. Moseley. As the stranger entered, Mr. Moseley took the man's measure with his professional eye: Short, stout, nearly forty, reasonably well dressed. The suitcase was new, most likely purchased for this journey. When the man asked for a room, he was surprisingly well spoken, with just the hint of a foreign accent. He seemed polite, meek even. Utterly innocuous, Moseley decided, nothing to threaten the tranquility of his establishment. Yes, he told the stranger, he had a room. Could he have it for a week? the man wanted to know. Mr. Moseley offered the register, and the stranger took the fountain pen and signed as John Schrank of New York City. Taking a roll of bills from his pocket, he laid eight dollars on the counter for the week. That wasn't necessary, Mr. Moseley said. But John Schrank insisted. He was planning a side trip to Columbia and perhaps as far as New Orleans, he explained, and he wanted to leave his suitcase in the room until he returned in two or three days' time.

❧

On Monday morning, as the SS *Comanche* was steaming toward Charleston, Theodore Roosevelt awoke feeling recharged from his day's rest in Emporia, Kansas. He had breakfast in the *Mayflower*, then reviewed his schedule, which called for barnstorming along the Kansas-Missouri border. Through the car's window, he could see that the weather would be perfect for campaigning.

This was mining country, and the train raced past hills, forests, rivers, and rock outcrops blasted to create the right-of-way. In the morning, he paused at Arcadia, Liberal, Lamar, and other towns, where the Bull Moose calls were so boisterous that his frayed vocal chords could scarcely compete. In the afternoon, the *Mayflower* stopped at Pittsburg, Kansas. A large crowd had gathered in the main square, and boys and grown men had shinnied up trees and telephone poles for a better look. The day had turned warm, and a woman called, "Don't you want an umbrella, Colonel? The sun is mighty hot." But a parasol wouldn't do for the hero of San Juan Heights. "Oh, no," he hollered back, "you'll have to use a club to kill me." Not long after, a woman fainted. Rushing from the platform, the Colonel elbowed the crowd aside, unfastening the lady's high collar and calling for a glass of water.

But despite the cheers, the Colonel couldn't shake the feeling that, as he approached the Solid South, he was facing a long, slow march into enemy territory. That morning in Lamar, as he'd stood on the *Mayflower*'s platform, he'd spied a banner challenging WE WANT TAFT; LET WELL ENOUGH ALONE. The Colonel hadn't been able to let it pass. "Any man who supports the receiver of stolen goods," he'd told the crowd, "stands on a level with the receiver of stolen goods. He is a dishonest man, and is unfit to associate with honest men." As the train had pulled from the station, he'd shouted, to underscore the point, "Goodbye, honest men!"

Later that day, in Springfield, Missouri, he spied another Taft banner on the street, and a cluster of men wearing Republican buttons. "I have noticed several Taft badges in your town," he told the seventy-five hundred men and women packed into the city's auditorium. "And they are the appropriate color of yellow. There never was a yellower performance than that of the Republican managers at the Chicago convention, and the badges are just the right color. The man who puts one on shows that he has a yellow streak somewhere."

Notably absent from the hundreds of hands that the Colonel had shaken today was that of Missouri's Republican governor, Herbert S. Hadley. The young, debonair Hadley had been one of seven progressive governors who'd signed the original petition urging Roosevelt to contest Taft's renomination. He had been a steadfast ally during the convention, and the Colonel (as well as Taft) had even considered him as a running mate. But when Roosevelt had bolted to form the Progressives, Hadley (and three of the other petition signers) hadn't joined him. And today, the governor had failed to welcome his visitor. Yet the Colonel was still hopeful that his onetime supporter would come around. "I wish to express my appreciation of the way Missouri stood by me in the primaries and the way a man I have always admired, Governor Hadley, stood by me," he told the crowd in Springfield. "I not only hope but believe that Governor Hadley will decide to stand with us." If Hadley didn't oblige, Roosevelt knew he had no chance of carrying the state.

In the coming week, before heading home to Oyster Bay, the Colonel would cross Missouri, Arkansas, Louisiana, Mississippi, Alabama, Georgia, Tennessee, and North Carolina. It was a journey his closest advisers had counseled against, preferring that he invest his time in states where the crowds would be friendlier, and more likely to vote Progressive.

Roosevelt understood the risks of his strategy. Like everything in the South, presidential politics was entangled in race, and he knew he was straddling a perilous line. Blacks were ambivalent toward the Colonel because he had shown himself ambivalent toward them. While in office, he had scandalized white Southerners by dining with Booker T. Washington in the White House and by hiring more blacks to federal civil service jobs than had any of his predecessors. But based on scanty, biased evidence, he'd ordered the dishonorable discharge of 167 black soldiers for allegedly rioting in Brownsville, Texas, in 1906. And though he'd used his bully pulpit to condemn lynchings, which still claimed more than sixty lives per year, he hadn't wielded the big stick of the federal government to curb the outrage or to enforce black voting rights.

Now candidate Roosevelt was holding to this dual course. In the North, he welcomed blacks into the Progressives, but in the South, he bowed to traditionalists and opened the membership rolls to whites only. It was a devil's bargain, and he knew it. He could only hope that it would be temporary, that by appealing to "the best white men in the South, the men of justice and of vision as well as of strength and leadership, and by frankly putting the movement in their hands from the outset, we shall create a situation by which the colored men of the South will ultimately get justice." But the compromise didn't endear him to the country's 10 million blacks, two-thirds of whom lived in the South and 2.5 million of whom were men of voting age.

Nor were Southern whites won over. Since before the Civil War, the region had flocked to the Democrats, the party of states' rights and white supremacy. Though Roosevelt now called himself a Progressive, to white Southerners he still embodied the party of Lincoln, whom the Colonel often cited as his inspiration. Concluding that there were few votes to gain in the region, Roosevelt's advisers had pleaded with him not to waste limited resources on this weeklong tour. But the Colonel was determined to crack the Solid South, which hadn't supported a Republican for president since 1876. Even if he didn't carry a single state there, he rationalized, a respectable showing would leave the Progressives a foothold to build on in future elections.

Neither did Woodrow Wilson have much to offer black voters. True, he had invited Booker T. Washington to his installation as president of Princeton, but once in office he'd blocked the matriculation of a black student. During the present campaign, Wilson had made a few conciliatory gestures toward blacks, such as condemning lynching, but he'd been quick to point out the chief executive's powerlessness in ending race violence. A Southerner born and bred, he supported segregation. President Taft was hardly an advocate for blacks either, since he'd named few persons of color to government posts. And so, as the country prepared to mark the fiftieth anniversary of the Emancipation Proclamation, black voters struggled to find a candidate in any major party who represented their interests.

The Colonel ended his Monday in Joplin, Missouri, where he was driven down Main Street while standing in an open car singing "There'll Be a Hot Time in the Old Town Tonight," the Rough Riders' favorite tune. Addressing a crowd of twenty thousand in the Miners Park baseball field, he compared his situation to that of native son and Speaker of the House Champ Clark, whom Woodrow Wilson had outmaneuvered at the marathon Democratic convention. At the mention of Clark's name, the audience gave a terrific cheer lasting for more than three minutes. "Mr. Clark carried the primaries in Missouri by a majority of two hundred thousand," Roosevelt reminded them. "The bosses did not want him nominated. They wanted another candidate, and they got him by overriding the vote of the people in not only this but in every state whose primaries Mr. Clark carried. It was as willful a disregard of the desire of the voters as was evidenced in the Republican convention at Chicago. The nomination at Baltimore belonged to Mr. Clark, but the bosses handed it over to Mr. Wilson." The crowd cheered again.

Before the speech, as the Colonel was shouldering his way to the speaker's platform, he'd been set upon by souvenir seekers. Now, from the dais, he opened his gray suit coat to display the damage. The lining on one side had been ripped out by a woman, he reported, and that on the other side by a man. He'd brought no other clothes. "I'm only praying that the suit may last until I get to New York," he told them. "Then I am willing to throw it away." The audience roared again, with laughter and applause. But as his own men watched their hoarse, plainly exhausted candidate, they could only hope that, by the time the *Mayflower* creaked into Oyster Bay, there would be something left of the Colonel himself.

The next day there was a newspaper story about a man in San Jose, California, named George W. Johnson. The week before, after intense brooding over politics, Johnson had taken a hen to live inside his house. He'd also claimed to have written out the will of God, which he would permit Theodore Roosevelt to present to the American people after his election. Now, according to the article, Johnson was resting at a state mental hospital, another victim of the fevered presidential campaign.

On Wednesday, September 25, John Schrank sat in Charleston, poring over a stack of newspapers for word of the third termer's progress. As expected, Roosevelt was headed for New Orleans.

At his hotel, Schrank reminded Mr. Moseley that he would return for his grip in two or three days. He mailed a casual postcard to Gustav Jost, landlord of the White House Hotel in New York. Then he set out for the depot. The rain of the past two days had finally broken, and the morning was cool and blue. Though two trolley lines ran to the station, Schrank chose to walk the half-mile.

As he left the Moseley House and turned north on Meeting Street, it felt strange to be without his new suitcase. Though Mr. Moseley seemed honest enough, Schrank wished he could have gotten a receipt for the bag. But since the establishment was a boardinghouse, not a hotel, there was no provision for checking luggage. Schrank had locked the grip and left it in his room. Still, he worried over it and all his papers—his naturalization documents, the deed to his tenement in Yorkville, his essays and poetry. Since he would need to move quickly and unencumbered, he brought with him only what he could wear or carry in his pockets—his brown suit, his bowler, the rosary around his neck, his bundle of bank notes, the Letter to the People of the United States that he'd written after being visited by President McKinley, the Colt .38, and eleven bullets, six chambered in the gun, another five rattling loose in his pocket. Everything else he would buy along the way or do without. To fit the revolver in his vest, he'd sliced open the bottom of its left-hand pocket; now, with every step, he could feel the cold steel barrel press against his leg.

In a few blocks, Schrank passed the handsome lawn of Marion Square and the turreted façade of the Citadel, the Military College of South Carolina, whose cadets had been among those firing on Fort Sumter in April 1861. Then he turned east on Columbus Street and walked through the center of a public park called Hampstead Mall. Before him, rising out of a web of trolley wires, were the brick, Spanish-baroque towers of Union Station (named, like all Union stations, North and South, for the disparate rail lines they united, not to celebrate the enemies of the Confederacy). Schrank crossed the stone-paved plaza in front of the depot, passed a rank of horse-drawn hacks, and entered under the building's red-tiled eaves.

He bought a ticket and hurried through the waiting room to the cavernous train shed. Locating the cars with the red-and-black logo-type of the Atlantic Coast Line, he climbed aboard. There was a piercing whistle, and the train lurched into the brilliant sunshine. Hugging the Cooper River, it passed the city limits, the Magnolia Cemetery, and the country club. Augusta lay 150 miles away, just over the state line in Georgia, about halfway to Atlanta.

As the locomotive gained momentum, John Schrank's car began to sway. He had never been on an intercity train before. Nor, before yesterday, had he ventured south of the Mason-Dixon Line. It was strange, gazing out the window at the lush, peaceful landscape, to think of the blood that had been shed here five decades before. And it was more terrifying still to think of the carnage that would be exacted again, if the third termer succeeded in plunging the nation into another civil war. Why did no one else see the threat? Why had he alone been called to be God's instrument?

Making a wide western turn, the train crossed the Ashley River. It gained the Atlantic Coast Line trunk and added speed. Untiring, unswerving, it raced toward its destination.

It was afternoon when Schrank's train rattled into Augusta. Leaving the depot, he walked south on Ninth Street. In a few blocks, he came to the Planters Hotel, at 945 Broad on the corner of Macartan Street, hard by the river. The hotel was a big, boxlike affair of three stories, with iron balconies projecting from one side. It was said that Jefferson Davis, Robert E. Lee, Ulysses Grant, and Philip Sheridan had all been guests at one time or another. On the first floor, besides the office and dining room, there was a laundry, a saloon where Schrank could enjoy his customary ration of beer, and a barbershop where he could have a shave—which he'd need, since he'd left his razor with his other nonessentials in Charleston. At the Moseley House, he'd given his real name to avoid any question when he returned to claim his suitcase, but now he signed the register as Walter Ross of New York City. If the clerk noticed that Mr. Ross carried no luggage, he didn't comment on the fact.

The next day, as Schrank studied the daily papers, he saw that the third termer had reached Little Rock early the previous morning. In heavy rain, he'd been greeted at the depot by the city's leading citizens and then paraded through the streets by a horde of Progressive officials, a pair of brass bands, two companies of the Fourth US Infantry, and a motorcade of seventy-five automobiles. Despite the weather, the crowds had been large. Roosevelt was in Little Rock to address a meeting of the Deep Gulf Waterways Association, which was petitioning the federal government to dredge the Mississippi to promote river traffic and prevent more floods like the record-breaking deluge this past spring, which had exacted $100 million in damage. Here in Augusta, in the street in front of the Planters Hotel, the Savannah River had risen to the height of a man's knees.

The Little Rock convention hall was packed with six thousand delegates from Illinois, Missouri, Arkansas, Tennessee, Mississippi, and Louisiana. Among the worthies onstage were two Arkansas Democrats, US Senator James P. Clarke and long-serving Congressman

Joseph Taylor Robinson, who had voted for many of then President Roosevelt's progressive reforms. But one of their colleagues, populist Arkansas Senator Jeff Davis, who had once branded Roosevelt a "dictator and demagogue," refused to join them and listened impassively from a back row.

The crowd cheered the third termer for several minutes after he mounted the dais. Then John M. Parker, a New Orleans cotton broker and Progressive National Committeeman, introduced the candidate as the "author of the Panama Canal, future author of the Mississippi Waterway, and the greatest living American." For once, Roosevelt set aside his stump speech and laid out an ambitious (some said preposterous) scheme for deepening the Mississippi, using equipment and personnel transferred from Panama after the canal's completion two years hence. It was exactly what the audience wanted to hear, and they applauded noisily.

Late in the day, he left for Memphis, where his train huffed into the depot in a light rain. A throng filled the street in front of his hotel, and five hundred people jammed the lobby. Pleading exhaustion, the Colonel went straight to his room. But the crowd began chanting for him. A member of the local Progressive committee came onto a balcony and told them, "Colonel Roosevelt is very tired and hoarse." The people shouted, "Go back and sit down! We want Teddy!" After five more minutes, the candidate appeared on the balcony and thanked them for the warm reception. Then he said, "If there are any of the crowd I went bear hunting with here, I want them to come right up and talk about b'ars."

He knew his audience would remember his hunting expedition in the Mississippi Delta back in November 1902. Though he'd come at the invitation of Mississippi Governor Andrew Longino, the president was widely despised by white Southerners for his comparatively liberal views on race (James Vardaman, Longino's opponent for governor, had notoriously called Roosevelt that "coon-flavored miscegenist in the White House"), and so armed guards formed a perimeter around the hunting grounds to deter assassins.

For five days, as the party bivouacked amid the swamps and canebrakes, Roosevelt didn't manage even a shot at a bear, to the consternation of visitor and hosts alike. Then late one afternoon, after the president had returned to camp, the hounds flushed out a young specimen. The hunters stunned it with a rifle butt, tied it to a tree, and summoned the president so he could have the honor of shooting it. But Roosevelt refused such an unsporting deed and ordered the creature put out of its misery. The incident was reported in the press, and *Washington Post* artist Clifford Berryman immortalized it in a front-page cartoon. Captioned "Drawing the Line in Mississippi," it depicted a disgusted Roosevelt being presented with the black bear cub lassoed around its neck by a white man—apparently a reference to Roosevelt's condemnation of lynchings.

Coincidentally, the German toymaker Steiff had begun marketing stuffed bears for children around the time of Roosevelt's hunting trip, and now Brooklyn storekeepers Rose and Morris Michtom promoted their own button-eyed model, which they called the "Teddy Bear." (Later, around the time of William Taft's inauguration, another company tried to market a stuffed animal called "Billy Possum," but the toy failed to catch on.)

In Memphis, there were a few of Roosevelt's bear-hunting companions in the crowd outside his hotel, and despite the third termer's fatigue, he and they sat up late into the night reminiscing. This afternoon, Roosevelt was due in Montgomery, where he'd be feted at a luncheon at the Marion Hotel before addressing the convention of the Interstate Levee Association, again to tout his plan to dredge the Mississippi River. After that, he would leave for New Orleans, passing through Mississippi in the night.

Schrank made his decision. Tonight he would rest here in Augusta. Tomorrow he would check the morning papers. Then, assuming

Roosevelt was still bound for Atlanta, he would make the short journey there. And when Roosevelt arrived in two days' time, Schrank would be waiting.

The Colonel was passing through the high, curved portal of New Orleans's Union Station when he heard the noise. It began as a low growl and then ascended in volume and pitch until it reverberated off the station's glazed red brick. His train had pulled in at 10:10 a.m., fifty minutes behind schedule, but the throng had waited, filling the park in front of the depot. And when they saw his battered black Stetson, they erupted.

The police held back the crowd as the Colonel, his traveling party, the reception committee, and the press corps left the station. Overseeing security were Chief Inspector James W. Reynolds and Chief of Detectives George Long of the New Orleans Police Department, whose handpicked men would guard the ex-president during his stay.

The Colonel's grizzled mustache lifted in a smile as he acknowledged the ovation, but those lucky enough to have a place in front could see that his eyes were etched with exhaustion. As he walked, chatting with one of his companions, he lifted his hand and absentmindedly brushed something from his face or collar.

Thirty automobiles were waiting in front of the station. The Colonel climbed into one of the open cars and took his place on the back seat. Gears ground, exhaust spewed, and the motorcade rumbled down St. Charles Avenue to wide, bustling Canal, the city's principal commercial street. Despite its commanding location near the mouth of the Mississippi, New Orleans had been slow to develop after its purchase by the United States in 1804, due not least to the yellow fever that was endemic to the area. Blockaded by the Union, the city had seen its commerce all but halted during the Civil War, and it wasn't until 1880 that the economy had rebounded to antebellum levels. Today New Orleans boasted the largest sugar refinery in the world, and the port shipped nearly a third of US cotton, as well as molasses, rice, tobacco, corn, wheat, oats, and pork. Yet its sewers had been open troughs until 1900, and even now the city seemed, if not worn by care, at least by time.

Turning onto Decatur, the motorcade entered the quaint, usually peaceful French Quarter, an enclave of clay tile, wrought iron, and louvered shutters. The cars passed the sober gray edifices of Jackson Square, then along the river, the thick stucco columns of the old French Market. They veered north and snaked all the way to the lush, watery landscape of City Park, near Lake Pontchartrain, before looping south and regaining the city center via Audubon Park. Everywhere, cheering crowds massed under cool and cloudy skies.

But even as he waved his hat to the crowd, the Colonel's thoughts skipped ahead to the speech he would make this afternoon. If only there were a way to capture this outpouring of good feeling and channel it into support for his ideas, and into votes on Election Day. If only he could convince Southerners to shake the cold, dead grasp of the past. That was the alchemy he needed to perform, not only in New Orleans but throughout the South. He was certain that untold thousands of Southerners sympathized with his progressive vision for the country. Those were the men he had to reach, with as direct and personal an appeal as he could mount. And he would make his case this afternoon, here in New Orleans.

The motorcade finally jerked to a stop in front of the lavish, fourteen-story Gruenwald Hotel, just off Canal Street, between Baronne and O'Keefe. The two finest suites, B and C, had been reserved for the Colonel, along with four others for the rest of his party. He wouldn't be staying the night, but the rooms would offer a place to rest before and after his address. On arriving, the Colonel stripped off his clothes and availed himself of a cool bath.

At twelve thirty, he attended a luncheon in his honor at the venerable French Quarter restaurant Antoine's. Given the choice of a public event or a private one, he had opted for the private. So the white-covered tables had been set for just fifty, and he'd been assured he needn't make a speech. After the guests took their places, a toast was offered to the candidate and the cause. Then, as course after elaborate course came steaming from the kitchen, calls arose for a few words from Cecil Lyon, the former Rough Rider from neighboring Texas.

Finally, before the coffee and cognac were served, the slender, silver-haired, elegantly mustached Lyon stood and shared some amusing anecdotes from the campaign. Then he introduced the guest of honor, who gave a few words of thanks and reminded the assembled gentlemen of the need to place country ahead of self. When the luncheon adjourned, the Colonel went back to the Gruenwald to rest before his late-afternoon speech. Not that there was much rest to be had, with the constant stream of visitors and the torrent of correspondence to be dictated to his two young stenographers, Elbert E. Martin and John W. McGrath.

Even before the Colonel reached the Gruenwald, the crowd had begun to gather at the recently remodeled Winter Garden Theater, down the street on Baronne between Girod and Lafayette. When the doors opened at two thirty, there was a Sooner-like dash for the four thousand seats. To entertain the audience during the wait, a band and glee club performed popular tunes, including "Casey Jones," Mississippi," and a new ditty whose lyrics went, "Who are we? Bull Moose. What's the use? What's the use? Nothing to it but Bull Moose."

When the Colonel appeared through the Girod Street entrance, there was a roar, and the musicians broke into the familiar "There'll Be a Hot Time in the Old Town Tonight." He stood onstage, bowing and waving to the crowd, and when the applause finally slacked, he took his chair, flanked by a collection of Progressives, Republicans, and even a few Democrats.

The band and glee club launched into "They Are Calling from the Mountains, 'We Want Teddy,'" which the West Virginia delegation had made famous at the Republican National Convention in June. Then John M. Parker rose to introduce the Colonel, whom he lauded as "the most loyal friend the Mississippi Valley has ever had," for his work on flood control, yellow fever eradication, and the Panama Canal, which promised to benefit the Crescent City more than any other American port. "Shoot it to 'em, Parker!" someone in the audience called.

The musicians performed "Roosevelt, O Roosevelt," to the tune of "Maryland, My Maryland," and finally the Colonel rose to speak. From his first words, he sounded the personal appeal that was the heart of his message here in the South. "Mr. Chairman and friends, men and women of Louisiana, men and women of this great city . . . there is no speech that I have made during this campaign that I am as anxious to make as the one I am making now; because, friends, I am not willing to admit that you and I are on opposite sides, and I came down here to make my plea for the right to stand shoulder to shoulder with those who look face to face with the great problems from the standpoint I do."

In the matter of the Panama Canal, he reminded the audience, "I think I represented the South better than its own senators," many of whom had opposed the vast project. Then he raised two points calculated to appeal to even the most conservative Louisianans, control of the Mississippi River and the duty on imported sugar, which the Republicans, despite their generally pro-tariff stance, were threatening to eliminate. "If Louisiana believes in no protection" for sugar, he said, "all right, go against us, but if you believe with us, I want you to feel that you have a right to go with us."

His journey through the South, he went on, reminded him of a trip he'd once made to Texas, where he was given a souvenir of his visit. "There were ten thousand people present when the loving cup was presented, and the man who presented it said: 'This is from Texas, where you have more admirers and fewer voters than in any other state.'

"Now I'll tell you an anecdote of Louisiana," he added. "A member of a certain club in New Orleans said to me: 'There was no more rejoicing anywhere than in our club when you were elected.' I replied that there were no symptoms of such a feeling in the vote cast in Louisiana, and he said, 'Well, of course, we all voted against you, but we were anxious to see you win.'" That was precisely the kind of blind tradition that he was determined to crack here in the Solid South.

By this point, the Colonel realized that his speech had gone a little long. "You are such a nice audience that you are a little responsible," he kidded. But instead of concluding, he broached a new theme, the need to level the playing field between employers and workers and between the wealthy and everyone else. Not that he ever preached class hatred, he reminded the audience, except as it applied to "crooks." But even then, he didn't hate the crooks, only their crookedness.

At this, Cecil Lyon approached the Colonel and told him that Dr. Terrell insisted he sit down and conserve his ragged voice, so the candidate launched into his peroration, on the need to protect the common man and woman from the oligarchs. If they believed that the Progressive Party could improve their lives, they must, "in the name of their own independence and manhood," come and join with him "in making the republic one where the people rule and secure the industrial and social good of all." And if they were in accord with his program, they must forget sectional politics and vote for him as readily as would a citizen in New York or Chicago or San Francisco.

Applause thundered through the Winter Garden as the Colonel was escorted out the Lafayette Street exit and back to the Gruenwald Hotel, where he spent the rest of the afternoon dictating letters, meeting with local dignitaries, and chatting with old friends. After a quiet dinner in his suite, he left for the station, where the *Mayflower* pulled out at 8:00 p.m., attached to the Louisville & Nashville's New York Limited. The Colonel reckoned that his ten-hour stump through the city had gone well. But he still couldn't say how much of the cheering had been for him and how much for his ideas. It was, after all, pure Barnum and Bailey.

—⁓—

On the morning of September 27, as the *Mayflower* was racing toward New Orleans, John Schrank awoke in Atlanta. The previous afternoon, he had come from Augusta and, passing through Terminal Station's elegant, high-ceilinged waiting room, had exited on West Mitchell Street. Adjacent to the depot, he had spied a sign for Child's Hotel, a three-story buff-brick building trimmed with terra cotta and surmounted by a carved stone cornice. Picking his way across the trolley tracks, he'd bypassed the ground-floor storefronts and climbed the stairs to Reception, where he'd signed the guest book as Walter Ross.

Now, as he riffled through a stack of newspapers, he saw that the third termer's schedule hadn't changed. Today Roosevelt was expected in New Orleans, and tomorrow he would barnstorm through Alabama and Georgia, reaching Atlanta late in the afternoon. There was nothing to do but wait.

Yet for John Schrank, waiting was the cruelest measure. Hours had never rested easily in his hands, and it had been the long, black expanse of empty time that had propelled him on all those solitary rambles through Lower Manhattan and Brooklyn, as he'd composed his verses and brooded over politics. Then he'd wasted eleven long years waiting for someone to step forward and end King Roosevelt's tyranny, before he'd finally realized that McKinley's summons had been intended for him alone. Once he'd accepted his destiny, the waiting had grown truly hellish. Having committed to act, he longed to act.

There was also the matter of his valise, which he hoped was still sitting in his room in Charleston. He'd told Mr. Moseley that he'd be back to collect it in two or three days, but that span was quickly lapsing. He'd taken the room for only a week. If he didn't return by then, what would become of the suitcase? Would they force the lock and rummage through his papers? Would they sell the brand-new grip and chuck his writings in the trash?

The more Schrank brooded, the more determined he grew to do something. There were nearly five hundred miles between New Orleans and Atlanta. Though the newspapers reported the time the third termer was due, they didn't specify his itinerary. But north of the Gulf Coast, only one city of any consequence beckoned en route. Coal and steel and railroads had molded Birmingham, Alabama, into the industrial behemoth of the South. Then, just a couple of years ago, the city had incorporated several surrounding towns, swelling its population to more than a hundred and fifty thousand. It was inconceivable that Roosevelt would bypass all those potential voters. And Birmingham was only a hundred and fifty miles from Atlanta. Schrank consulted his train schedule and then he decided. He wouldn't waste his time for the next thirty-six hours, waiting for the third termer to come to him. When Roosevelt reached Birmingham, John Schrank would already be there.

Rain pinged on the *Mayflower's* roof on the morning of September 28, and when the reception committee from Montgomery, Alabama, arrived to escort the Colonel to breakfast, they found him still asleep in his berth. As he'd rested, the train had passed through Mississippi and then arced north through Alabama to the state capital, where he was scheduled to make a speech this morning.

Following a rushed meal, the Colonel was escorted to the New Exchange Hotel, located downtown at Court Square, on the corner of Commerce and Montgomery Streets. Though this incarnation of the hotel had opened only six years before, the name was celebrated in Southern history. Constructed in 1848 on this same site, the original Exchange Hotel had been the seat of the Confederate government immediately after secession, before the capital was moved to

Richmond. It was from the balcony of the Exchange Hotel that Jefferson Davis had first addressed his countrymen after his election as their president. But by 1904 the building was so dilapidated that it was beyond even misty-eyed Southerners to salvage it. It was demolished, to rise again on the same site, two years later, as the New Exchange Hotel.

The Colonel was escorted to the second-floor balcony to address the crowd. Despite the rain, a throng had collected in the square below, just as they had once done to hear President Davis. Roosevelt was determined to disarm them with a personal appeal like the one yesterday in New Orleans. "If you are against me," he told his listeners, "I have nothing to say. The man I am trying to reach is the man who is for me but votes against me because his father and grandfather voted that way. The way for you to honor your forefathers is to face the issues of the day fearlessly. . . . I ask you for your support only to the extent that you think it responds to your interests."

As he spoke, Roosevelt absentmindedly rested his hand on an insulated electric cable strung across the balcony. "Look out, Colonel," someone called from the street, "that wire is carrying thirty-five hundred volts!"

Without a pause, the candidate removed his fingers from the wet cable and went on. "I want to ask you of the South to leave your place at the end of the procession, and to take up the position held in the olden days. The only way you can do this is to deal with living issues, and not the ghosts of dead issues." Then the Colonel noticed that one of his companions on the balcony had also gripped the cable. "Get away from that wire, please," Roosevelt ordered. "I don't want to lose any Bull Moose by electrocution." The crowd hooted with laughter.

After Montgomery, the *Mayflower* slogged in the rain through Alabama, pausing for just five minutes at the smaller stations along the way. In Chehaw, the Colonel encouraged some farmers to approach the car's rear platform. "I want to shake hands," he told them, "even if you are not Bull Moosers."

"I'm a Bull Mooser," a brakeman offered, and the Colonel gave him a robust handshake.

Standing beside the tracks, he saw a few students from nearby Tuskegee Institute. Then he spied the most famous black man in America, the school's founder, Booker T. Washington, whose invitation to dine at the Roosevelt White House had enraged white Southerners.

"By George, there's Dr. Washington!" the Colonel exclaimed.

Washington seized the opportunity to remind him, "We are going to have a trustees' meeting on the tenth. Will you be there?"

"My heavens, I can't be there on the tenth. I've got some troubles of my own and am having a middling strenuous time," the Colonel reminded him. But he might be able to make a meeting after the campaign, he offered as the train steamed away.

In Alabama, Roosevelt would stop this morning at Auburn and Opelika. Then, crossing into Georgia, he was scheduled to speak at Columbus at noon, Reynolds at 1:30, Fort Valley at 2:20, Macon at 3:00, Forsyth at 4:40, Barnesville at 5:10, Griffin at 5:40, Hampton at 6:10, and Atlanta at 7:20. Before the day was through, he would make a major address in that city's Auditorium, to an audience for whom names such as John B. Hood and William Tecumseh Sherman, Jefferson Davis and Abraham Lincoln had yet to recede into history.

━ ◦ ━

As Roosevelt's reception committee was rousing him from bed in Montgomery, John Schrank found himself in Birmingham's Plaza Hotel, a modest establishment despite its grand name. Following yesterday's change in plans, Schrank had taken the train from Atlanta. Now scanning the newspaper, he found Roosevelt's schedule. But Birmingham wasn't even mentioned. According to the report, the third termer's train would stop late that afternoon at Macon and then continue north to Atlanta.

Roosevelt had outwitted him: Instead of passing through the most populous city in the state, he'd chosen to creep along through a handful of dusty tank towns. Almost as though he knew that Schrank was lying in wait.

Schrank loaded his few possessions in his pockets—cash, newspapers, scraps of writing, pistol and bullets. Then he hurried across the street to Terminal Station. He had no idea of the schedule to Atlanta. He only knew that he had to get there before the third termer.

FIVE

"I'm Not a Fancy Fencing Match"
Saturday, September 28

Another evening, another arrival. Another depot, another auditorium, another speech. The streets of Atlanta were already dark as the *Mayflower* snaked through the city and vanished into the vast, fanlike portal of Union Depot. With its red walls and mismatched, mansard-roofed towers, the station appeared more seaside pavilion than railroad terminal. But for four decades the building had risen in the city center, on the site occupied by the original Union Station until 1864, when William Tecumseh Sherman had come to town.

If not for the railroads, there would be no Atlanta. Called Terminus at first, it was founded in 1837 as the southern extremity of the Western & Atlantic. Other lines followed, and the town, renamed Marthasville and then Atlanta, burgeoned into a manufacturing, supply, and transportation hub—which explained General Sherman's unwholesome interest in the place. During the depths of Reconstruction, as an avowal of faith in Atlanta's future, the city had built the second Union Depot. In the new century, Atlanta's population surged to more than a hundred and fifty thousand, and the city boomed with banks, insurance companies, sawmills, cotton mills, foundries, machine shops, and patent medicine companies such as Coca-Cola. Union Depot, never handsome, hadn't grown lovelier with age, and eventually it would have to be pulled down and replaced with a larger, more modern and commodious facility.

The Colonel would make his speech several blocks from the station, at the Atlanta Auditorium and Armory. He knew the building, having spoken there (along with William Howard Taft and Woodrow Wilson) a year ago this past March, during the annual convention of the Southern Commercial Congress. Four stories tall and nearly a block square, the Auditorium and Armory served as headquarters of the US Army 197th Field Artillery Battalion as well as a venue for concerts and lectures. The hybrid structure, it was said, was "ideal for nothing" but could "accommodate anything."

Tonight it would accommodate more than ten thousand Atlantans, and the Colonel wasn't sure what to expect. His mother, née Martha Bulloch, had been born in Roswell, twenty miles north of the city, which made him, if not a native son, something of a native grandson. But Woodrow Wilson also had ties to the city, having once practiced law here—though bored by both Atlanta and the law, he'd decamped after a little more than a year to study history and political science at Johns Hopkins. So which of the candidates would the crowd embrace as its own? Tonight Roosevelt would make them choose, because he planned to take dead aim at the Democrat.

When the motorcade reached the Auditorium, an overflow crowd was swarming over the stone roadway and the trolley tracks in front. A row of American flags saluted from the roof. Surrounded by aides, police, and an official reception committee two hundred strong, the guest of honor stepped from his automobile, passed under a tall brick arch, and disappeared inside.

John Schrank watched him go. This morning, after realizing that the third termer had outwitted him and bypassed Birmingham, Schrank had boarded a Seaboard Air Line train and made the bitter, 150-mile journey back to Atlanta. It had been close, but he'd managed to arrive at the city's other main depot, the luxurious Terminal Station, half an hour before Roosevelt's train was due. With no luggage to check, Schrank hurried directly to the Auditorium. By then the venue was packed beyond capacity, and he had no choice but to stand in the street, mingling with the converted and the simply curious. Then a wave of excitement rippled through the crowd, and Schrank sensed Roosevelt's approach. He caught only a glimpse as the third termer entered the building, but even that was electrifying.

The Auditorium's high arched windows oozed yellow light, and the strains of "Onward Christian Soldiers" wafted into the street. A moment after Roosevelt disappeared inside, the building burst into cheers. A band played. Then the audience quieted and a voice droned for several minutes. Another ovation, then an expectant silence. Hugging the darkness and the crowd, John Schrank slipped toward the building's entrance.

———

Inside the hangarlike Auditorium, the three-story windows formed dead, black arches. The Colonel trotted up to the semicircular platform erected in front of the huge pipe organ and stood waving to the crowd while the band played "America" and "Dixie." The hall—the oval floor, the tiers of seats rising to the ceiling's metal trusses— was filled with a writhing mass. Thousands of red bandanas fluttered, and banners were hoisted above the crowd: THE RECEIVER OF STOLEN GOODS IS AS BAD AS THE THIEF; NO EAST. NO WEST. NO SOUTH. NO NORTH; GEORGIA WELCOMES ROOSEVELT TO THE HOME OF HIS MOTHER. But, he noted, the applause lasted less than two minutes.

The Colonel took a seat while he was introduced by his old friend, Robert Stuart MacArthur, president of the Baptist World Alliance. Then standing again, neck thrust forward and eyes sparkling, he began: "You, my fellow citizens, my fellow Americans, of my mother's state, which I claim as much my own as New York itself, I would not on any account have missed coming here to appear before you and tell the reasons for the faith that is in me. . . .

"My mission in the South is two-fold. First and most important I fight for the principle that it is your duty to vote for your own convictions. If you are in sympathy with the Progressive platform, then I hold that it is your duty to yourself, duty to your states, and your duty to the nation, not merely to support the platform, but to give your share of the leadership of the new party which has brought forth that platform.

"If you feel that we are right, then I challenge the right to your assistance and I want you to come with us now, that is, unless you are so much an 'original package' by inheritance for one political party, generation to generation, that you cannot speak your own mind and vote your convictions.

"The nation has a reservoir of national strength in the manhood and womanhood of the South. We want it drawn up in this struggle for fair play in the political, social and economic world. We need all the wisdom that this country can give, and it is not fair for the South to be robbed of its fair share of the leadership. You cannot accomplish anything in either of the old parties—they have such an inherited way of looking at things! Do not follow—lead! Stand in the forefront of the battle!"

The Colonel spoke for twenty-five minutes before mentioning his principal opponent. He was about to take the Democrat to task for again misrepresenting the Progressives' ideas on how to control the trusts, in a speech Wilson had made in Boston the night before. "Mr. Wilson has declared—" the Colonel began, giving some members of the audience their cue. "Wilson! Wilson! Wilson!" they chanted. He raised his hand for silence. When the hecklers finally quieted, after a minute and a half, he challenged them, "I was about to say that Mr. Wilson has declared the Democratic platform is not a program. Now cheer that." Then it was the turn of the Bull Moosers to roar.

A man called from the audience, "Why did you repudiate the Republican Party after you had sought the nomination at its hands?"

The faithful answered with catcalls and hisses, while Wilson supporters took the opportunity to applaud their man for another five minutes. The police tensed, expecting a riot.

When the demonstrations finally died, the Colonel tried to resume his attack on Wilson. But after he was interrupted a third time, he startled the audience by leaping onto a table that had been placed on the stage. "Now, I'm not a fancy fencing match," he glowered at the crowd. "I'm going to talk, and you can decide after hearing me if you want to believe in me. But you're going to hear me." After that, there were no more interruptions.

⌁

Mr. M. T. Floyd, of 15 Marion Avenue, Atlanta, was an ardent Bull Mooser, and he'd arrived early enough at the Auditorium to find standing room at the foot of the stage. He cheered with the others when the Colonel entered and was introduced. But as Roosevelt began his speech, Mr. Floyd was distracted by a man next to him. The stranger was of average height, he noticed, slightly rotund, with a smooth-shaven, moon-shaped face. The man seemed agitated, and Mr. Floyd was alarmed to see him try to climb onto the platform. Mr. Floyd warned him, and the man drew back. But then he tried again, and again. Finally, Mr. Floyd punched the man in the face, knocking him to the floor, all but unconscious. Stationed nearby, Chief of Police James L. Beavers saw what had happened and ordered the man carried outside. On stage, the Colonel betrayed no notice of the disturbance.

⌁

John Schrank waited in the dark street. He couldn't make out Roosevelt's voice, but he heard the crowd erupt in catcalls and cheers. From where he stood, one might have thought the Auditorium was hosting a Jack Johnson bout, not an address by an ex-president of the United States.

Schrank had snaked his way though the crowd, moving ever closer to the building's main entrance. But the nearer he drew, the more tightly packed the throng. Finally, he was unable to shoulder his way any closer. But he thought he might just be close enough.

At last, there came an ovation more sustained than the others. Schrank guessed that Roosevelt had finished. Inside his left vest pocket, he felt for the Colt .38's nubbled grip.

Around him, the crowd stirred expectantly. Like them, Schrank fixed his gaze on the Auditorium doors. They waited. He waited. The doors opened. But instead of the Bull Moose, members of the audience poured into the already packed street. What had become of the third termer? There had been some kind of altercation, people were saying. Roosevelt had been heckled. So instead of using the main exit, the men charged with his safety had quietly escorted him out a side door. The crowd began to drift away. John Schrank let himself be pushed along with them, back toward Child's Hotel.

SIX

"It Was a New Thing to Me"
Sunday, September 29, to Tuesday, October 1

THE COLONEL BEGAN THE DAY IN THE GEORGIAN TERRACE, THE elegant, ten-story hotel that had opened the year before on Peachtree Street, Atlanta's principal thoroughfare. He had an early breakfast, then, along with cousin George Emlen Roosevelt, two Progressive committeemen, and a pair of reporters, clambered into a waiting automobile.

The morning was misty, raw, and dreary. There had been rain in the night, and puddles still dotted the streets. The roads were unusually deserted, even for a Sunday; it seemed Atlanta's pastors would be preaching to half-empty pews today. In the car, the Colonel pulled his army overcoat tight around him.

Despite the weather, he was in good spirits. As it was the Sabbath, he wouldn't be making any campaign appearances today. Instead, the car turned north on Peachtree, away from the city center, and soon was cruising through open country and rolling, wooded hills. The Colonel and his entourage passed through the community of Buckhead, where wealthy Atlantans had built their country estates, barely glimpsed behind stone walls and screens of trees. Veering onto Roswell Road, they continued through Sandy Springs, with its proud old Methodist church. Then, at the end of twenty miles, they came to Roswell, a town with twelve hundred souls and a single street running its length. The car slowed, and curious residents came onto their front porches, waving shyly.

Not far from the main square, the car crested a hill and stopped before an antebellum house with a high pediment and wide white columns. The Colonel's mother, Martha Bulloch, called Mittie, had grown up here. In 1838, aged three, Mittie had come to live in Roswell with her mother, Martha Elliott Bulloch; five siblings and half-siblings; six slaves; and her father, James Stephens Bulloch. In Savannah, James had been president of the local Bank of the United States and deputy collector of the city's port; in Roswell, he would be a planter and a partner in the cotton mill. It wasn't clear what had driven the family to forsake the refinements of Savannah for the near wilderness that was Roswell in those days; some whispered it was to dodge financial difficulties, others to escape the scandal of James having married his deceased wife's stepmother.

The Bullochs constructed this fine house, and it was here, in 1849, that young Mittie met seventeen-year-old Theodore Roosevelt Sr., who had come to Roswell for the wedding of a friend. Four years later, on December 22, 1853, after Mittie had turned eighteen, she and Theodore were wed in the house's dining room, which was hung with mistletoe, holly, and pine boughs for the occasion. The couple went to live in New York City, in a town house on East Twentieth Street that was a wedding gift from Theodore's father, Cornelius Van Schaack Roosevelt. Then, three years later, after Mittie's father died suddenly at the age of fifty-six while teaching Sunday school at Roswell's Presbyterian church, Mrs. Bulloch and her daughter, Anna, moved to New York to live with Mittie and Theodore. During the war, Bulloch Hall was commandeered to billet Sherman's troops and the cotton mill was burned. In New York, far away from the fighting, Mrs. Bulloch worried over her two brothers—James, a Confederate agent in England, who oversaw the construction of the famed commerce raider the CSS *Alabama*; and Irvine, an officer on the ship. Both men survived the war, but by the time Mrs. Bulloch died, in 1864, it was clear that the Southern cause was lost. Her daughter, Mittie, though she would raise a president of the United States, would remain an outspoken Confederate sympathizer for the rest of her life.

Growing up first in the town house and later in a much grander home on West Fifty-seventh Street, young Theodore was entranced by tales of life at Bulloch Hall. In October 1905, on a tour of the South, he had visited his mother's childhood home. By then the property had passed to a Mr. and Mrs. Jehu Bartow Wing, who showed the president through the house and introduced him to "Mom Gracie," one of Mittie's former servants who still worked there. Afterward, he addressed the townspeople from a bandstand in the main square, telling them, "It has been my very great good fortune to have the right to claim my blood is half southern and half northern, and I would deny the right of any man here to feel a greater pride in the deeds of every southerner than I feel."

Today, on this return visit to Roswell, the Colonel stepped across Bulloch Hall's broad veranda and passed under the Masonic symbols carved above the door. He entered the gracious front hall, which opened onto a corridor running the length of the house. He roamed the two light-filled parlors, the grand dining room where his parents were married, the master bedroom and nursery on the first floor, and the four additional bedrooms upstairs. Occasionally he would linger, pointing out to his companions a spot that "Mother used to love." Behind the house, he peered down the vine-covered well.

After two hours he was escorted to Roswell's white-columned Presbyterian church, where his grandfather had been stricken. There was no service today, since the minister came only every other week, but the Colonel sat for a time in one of the front pews. As he left, he shook hands with the curiosity seekers gathered outside. Then he climbed into the automobile and began the drive back to Atlanta. When he arrived, it wasn't yet noon.

On this dismal Sunday morning, John Schrank found himself at Child's Hotel, on West Mitchell Street, across from Atlanta's Terminal Station. He was still dumbfounded by the night before, when the third termer had escaped by skulking out a back door. It was eerie how Roosevelt had managed to evade him twice, first in Birmingham and now here.

Turning to the morning papers, Schrank saw that today the Bull Moose was planning a pilgrimage to his mother's ancestral home, north of the city. Afterward, he was due back in Atlanta for a luncheon at the Georgian Terrace, to be hosted by Dr. Robert Stuart MacArthur, the Baptist preacher who had introduced him in the Auditorium last night. Then, sometime in the afternoon, he would retreat to his private railroad car and leave for Knoxville.

Schrank could feel precious time ebbing away, like sticky blood oozing from a wound. Tomorrow, in Washington, the Senate committee investigating the third termer's campaign finances would reconvene, with testimony from Ormsby McHarg, a Roosevelt campaign official. Roosevelt himself was scheduled to testify this coming Friday, October 4. To keep the appointment and allow for a brief stop at Oyster Bay, he would campaign through Tennessee tomorrow and North Carolina on Tuesday. Then he wouldn't pause again until he reached New York.

Schrank considered. He had no automobile at his disposal, no means of following the Bull Moose to Roswell this morning. And he certainly wouldn't be able to talk his way past the plainclothesmen at the fancy luncheon this afternoon. No, his best chance would come not in constricted areas and intimate gatherings, but in open spaces and great crowds.

He saw from the newspapers that Roosevelt's schedule had changed again. Yielding to pressure from the Tennessee Progressive Committee, he had added a stop in Chattanooga, a hundred miles northwest of Atlanta, just across the state border. He would stay there tonight and give a short address in the Auditorium tomorrow morning. Schrank could already see the reception at the station, the parade through the city streets, the tumult. And he would be among the crowd, standing, waiting again, the only island of calm in a fawning sea of humanity. Finally, he would come face-to-face with the third termer. And this time he would position himself somewhere Roosevelt could not avoid him. It would be his last opportunity before the candidate fled back up the eastern seaboard. He must not fail. Slipping the Colt .38 into his vest pocket, he made his way down the hotel stairway and onto the rain-splotched, Sunday-quiet street.

Anticipation swelled through the crowd in Dalton, Georgia. The city of five thousand lay ninety miles northwest of Atlanta, in the foothills of the Blue Ridge Mountains. Despite the unseasonable cold, several hundred people had gathered at the brick depot this evening to meet the Colonel's train. There was a whistle and a tail of black smoke, and a locomotive came into sight. Before the train had even hissed to a stop, the crowd was shoving the trainmen and streaming aboard, frantic for a glimpse of the Colonel. But on reaching the end of the train, the throng discovered that his private car was not attached. The *Mayflower*, the conductor told them, was hitched to a special train directly behind.

Minutes later, when the Bull Moose special pulled in, the crowd gave a cheer and jostled for space near the *Mayflower*'s rear platform. "Come out, Teddy!" they called. "O, you Bull Moose!" The metal door opened and the Colonel appeared. He waved his hand, and the rambunctious throng was quiet. An official presented him with a bouquet of honeysuckle, roses, and hollyhocks, which the candidate clenched in his meaty fist while he spoke. "We are on the verge of a great political upheaval," he told them. "It is the time to rid the country of corruption, corrupt politicians, and place ourselves upon record as being a government of the people."

"Amen!" someone yelled.

"That's right, brother," the Colonel went on, "we must have the support of the genuine people of this country and not the politicians and corrupt interests."

He spoke for ten minutes before the train departed. As he reentered his private car, he was heard to say, "I like it—these flowers. A simple tribute from a humble citizen."

The Colonel's next stop would be Chattanooga, and a delegation from that city boarded the *Mayflower* at Dalton. A reporter for the *Chattanooga Daily Times* was among them, along with Captain W. H. Hackett of the Chattanooga Police Department, who had come to confer with the Colonel's men about security. Several representatives of the Progressive Party had also arrived, to discuss the campaign in eastern Tennessee and their odds of beating Wilson there. It was to these men that the Colonel turned with outstretched arms.

"Delighted, captain!" he called to a gray-haired, mustached man with a military bearing. Commodore Albert L. Key had been one of Roosevelt's naval aides while he was president. "It is hard for me to say 'Mr. Key,'" the Colonel told him, "and by Jove, I'm not going to do it. How are you, anyway? You were a splendid officer, and I know you are an excellent citizen, and one any state should be proud of." As the Colonel pumped the Commodore's hand, both men turned away to hide the tears welling in their eyes. "Key, I am glad to see you," Roosevelt said. "I knew you would be for me. I wish the country had more men like you."

Then he saw someone else he recognized, a young man with a clean-shaven face and wild dark curls—S. B. Vaughn, postmaster of Augusta, Georgia, and another Bull Mooser. "Delighted!" the Colonel said. "Why Major Vaughn, what in the thunder are you doing in Tennessee? I left you in Georgia. How are you? I knew you would be for me."

He was introduced to banker John E. Edington. "We need good men," the Colonel said. "I am glad to know you are a candidate for railroad commissioner, and I hope you will be elected."

Talk then turned to Tennessee's Republican governor, Ben W. Hooper, who had been elected in 1910, after the state's Democrats split over prohibition and intramural politicking. During the past two years, Hooper had signed laws to regulate child labor and to protect workingwomen, to guarantee the purity of drugs and the food supply, and to improve education and medical care. But despite his progressive record, Hooper was straddling the fence in the presidential race. On September 20, in a speech in Jackson, Tennessee, Roosevelt had ridiculed the governor, calling him "Mr. Facing-Both-Ways," after a character in John Bunyan's *The Pilgrim's Progress* who had long served as a symbol of prevarication and political hypocrisy.

"I cannot see how any honest man can support this man Hooper," the Colonel now fumed. "He is not worthy of the support of the honest men of Tennessee. He should be defeated."

Commodore Key took the opportunity to present their visitor with an original cartoon. "This was drawn by a Confederate veteran especially for you," Key said. "It signifies conditions in Tennessee."

The Colonel pulled off his spectacles and examined the drawing. Entitled "Mr. Facing-Both-Ways," it showed a Janus-like Governor Hooper speaking out of both his mouths. "I like Woodrow Wilson," said one side. "I am supporting Taft," claimed the other.

"Bully!" Roosevelt exclaimed. "That is right. Key, I want to meet Colonel Dickinson," who had drawn the cartoon. "He has the right sort of stuff in him. It gives me the greatest pleasure to see the old Confederate veterans taking the stand they have."

Later, the Colonel ushered the reporter for the *Chattanooga Daily Times* into his stateroom for a private chat. "They tried to break up my speaking in Atlanta," he told him. "But I got them going. It was so unexpected for anyone in Georgia, especially, to jump on the Democratic candidate, I took them by surprise. They tried to break up the meeting, but they couldn't make it." Then, looking back over his tour of the South, he grew more contemplative. "I have done one thing," he said. "I have broken the ground. Nobody will ever have to break it again. I have made the furrow."

— ◦ —

The Western & Atlanta Railroad, linking Atlanta and Chattanooga, had been called "the crookedest road under the sun," and John Schrank could see why. Though the two cities lay only 102 miles apart as the crow flies, the tracks ran for 138 miles and traced the equivalent of twenty-eight complete circles as they skirted the region's many mountains. Only in one place had the engineers conquered topography and dug a tunnel of any length, a bore of more than a quarter mile through Chetoogeta Mountain.

Just as the landscape had been contorted by geologic turmoil, it had been devastated by war, as the Union and Confederate armies had battled for control of the all-important railroads. It was over these same tracks that a storied incident had occurred in 1862. On April 12, twenty Yankee troopers and two Southern supporters hijacked a train near Big Shanty, Georgia, outside Atlanta, and raced north toward Chattanooga, tearing up tracks, burning bridges, and cutting telegraph wires as they went. The idea was to prevent the Southern army from reinforcing Chattanooga, which the Union was keen to capture. For eighty miles, Confederates gave chase on foot and handcar and in a commandeered locomotive, until finally, just north of Ringgold, Georgia, the hijacked engine ran out of fuel and the perpetrators were seized. Eight were hanged as spies and the other fourteen imprisoned, though eight managed to escape to Union lines, hundreds of miles away, and the rest were exchanged the following year. Seventeen of the raiders received the United States' highest military award, the recently created Medal of Honor. But from a tactical view the raid was a failure, and the Western & Atlantic continued to serve the Confederacy until William Tecumseh Sherman finally captured it in the spring of 1864.

On leaving Atlanta, Schrank worried that Roosevelt's special train would reach Chattanooga before he did. But as he passed through Adairsville and Calhoun, he saw clusters of townsfolk huddled beside the depots, and he rested more easily: They were still waiting for the third termer. At Dalton, thirty miles southeast of Chattanooga, a wild crowd tore through the coaches, searching for their idol. On their faces shone a fierce fanaticism, the forerunner, Schrank saw, of despotism.

At last, the train approached East Chattanooga, skirting the Tennessee River, then made an abrupt turn and burrowed toward the city center. Situated on a tight bend of the Tennessee, Chattanooga was said to take its name from the Creek *Chado-na-ugsa,* sometimes translated as "Rock That Comes to a Point," a reference to Lookout Mountain, which rose over the city. Chattanooga had been founded in the early 1800s as a simple trading post known as Ross's Landing. Then, like so many Southern towns, it had surged after the railroad arrived, in this case connecting the Tennessee Valley with Savannah, which at the time was competing with Charleston to become the region's principal port. The first train passed through Chattanooga in 1849, and by the start of the Civil War, the city had grown into a strategic center, contested in three great battles, at Chickamauga Creek, Lookout Mountain, and Missionary Ridge. Now, fifty years later, with a population of thirty thousand, the city was still a major rail hub, served by nearly a dozen different lines. Industry had followed the train, and foundries, flour mills, tanneries, furniture factories, and spinning mills lined the streets, along with warehouses, saloons, and hotels. If the view from the tracks could be trusted, Chattanooga was a gritty, booming place.

It was nine thirty at night when John Schrank's train finally pulled into Union Station. Climbing down from the carriage and following the other passengers out of the depot, he saw that West Ninth Street had been closed to traffic and policemen were holding back a crowd of perhaps two thousand, who spilled for a block on either side of the station. But the police had no trouble controlling the throng. Everyone seemed to be laughing and chatting. Fathers boosted children on their shoulders. Occasionally a Bull Moose campaign song broke out.

Schrank threaded his way into the road and turned to face the depot, a stately brick façade with three square towers, tall windows, and steep mansard roofs surmounted by elegant finials. A rank of automobiles was standing before the terminal, awaiting the candidate and his party. Schrank claimed a place directly in front of the cars. Just half a dozen people stood between him and the police cordon. When Roosevelt arrived, he would pass barely ten feet away.

Schrank heard the special train pull in. So did the rest of the crowd, and they began to stir. Then there was a terrific shout, and the third termer, flanked by his staff and reception committee, exited the passenger sheds, following the same route John Schrank had taken just half an hour before. Amid the calls and applause, the waves and gesticulations, John Schrank stood motionless, every sense focused on the Bull Moose. Roosevelt was carrying his hat, and he lifted it to acknowledge the crowd. He climbed into the first auto and, standing, waved again.

The driver put the car into gear. It lurched directly toward John Schrank, precisely as he had planned. Roosevelt was still standing, still waving. A perfect target. Above the cheers, Schrank could hear the clatter of the car's engine. His hand was in his vest pocket. Trembling, he felt for the hard-rubber grip of the Colt .38. He tightened his grasp.

The auto drew closer. Thirty feet. Twenty. With the police keeping the roadway clear, the car was gaining speed. It was ten feet from John Schrank. He could see the fatigue lining Roosevelt's face. And then the car was gone.

The committee showed their guest to the Hotel Patten, just a few blocks from the station, on the corner of Market and East Eleventh Streets. Opened in 1908, the Patten was the city's first skyscraper hotel, with 251 rooms, a stylish lobby, dining room, ball room, orchestra hall, men's cafe, bar, billiard room, bowling alley, barbershop, and manicure parlors. On its opening, the *Chattanooga Times* had called the hotel "the most elegant public house in all of its appointments to be found in any city in the South" and "one of the important events in the history of Chattanooga," marking "the transition of the big town to the modern city."

This evening, the lobby was jammed with Bull Moosers, clamoring for a statement from their leader. But the candidate shoved his way to the elevators, leaving Cecil Lyon to explain that the Colonel needed some rest and in any event didn't make speeches on Sunday. As the crowd drifted off, a man approached Lyon and asked to see the ex-president in private, explaining that his twelve-year-old daughter, Julia, had written a song in the Colonel's honor, called "Hell's Broke Loose in Tennessee." Lyon told him that the title was inappropriate and sent him away. Upstairs, alone at last, the Colonel stretched out in the James Polk Suite and read a magazine.

—◡—

John Schrank trudged down Market Street, away from the noise and the crowds. Between Alabama and East Main, he came to the recessed brick doorway and garish sign of the Redmon Hotel. The building was located across from Chattanooga's other depot, the modern, luxurious Terminal Station, with its enormous brick arch marking the entrance. On either side of the hotel were wholesale liquor dealers; behind it ran a railroad siding. Once again, Schrank registered as Walter Ross of New York City, and once again the clerk showed no curiosity about his lack of luggage.

That night, Schrank had time to brood over what had happened at the depot. He could still see King Roosevelt's smug expression as the third termer stood in the car, not a dozen feet away. He could still feel the impatient weight of the pistol in his own hand. In New York, he'd heard the divine summons; he'd traveled all this way by steamship and train, deep into the black heart of the Confederacy; he'd calculated; he'd waited. But when the great moment had come, he had hesitated.

He was at a loss. It had never occurred to him that such a thing might happen. He was so sure of the morality of his crusade, so certain he had been called to rescue the Republic from civil war and foreign invasion. Why hadn't he been able to shift from conviction to action? Finally he told himself, *It was a new thing to me. I didn't just exactly have courage enough to do it.* And the car was accelerating. Before he could react, it was already past. But the next time, he swore, he wouldn't miss his opportunity. The next time he would be prepared. The next time, there would be no next time.

—◦—

The morning was still cloudy and cool, but Chattanooga was decorated as no one could remember. Along Market Street from Fourth to Ninth, every building was festooned. Old Glory fluttered from poles at city hall, the federal building, and the Hamilton National Bank skyscraper. On D. B. Loveman's store, flags waved from every window. At Miller's, two great banners unfurled from the second story, while across the way, the Live and Let Live Drug Company, the Rosebud Saloon, the Askine & Marine Company, and the Walton Furniture Company were all draped in red, white, and blue.

The railroads were putting on extra cars and offering special fares to bring in out-of-towners, and twenty-five thousand people were expected to welcome Colonel Roosevelt. The courts had delayed their sessions until ten thirty, and the McCallie School for boys had postponed the start of classes. In the *Chattanooga Times*, Close Brothers furniture store ran a large advertisement:

Roosevelt at Auditorium
Monday Morning

We shall insist of a visit from Ex-President Roosevelt to our Main and Market Street Stores to show him how very progressive we have been in selling the people House-Furnishings for less money than any other concern engaged in same like in this city. We are progressives when it comes to low prices in House-Furnishing Goods.

At eight thirty, the Colonel's car left the Hotel Patten, escorted by the Third Regiment band and a platoon of policemen. Seated beside Roosevelt was his former aide Commodore Key, who would introduce him at the Auditorium. Behind, two more cars carried Progressive officials from Chattanooga and around the state. Mounted policemen and plainclothesmen kept guard, under the direction of Chief of Police Fred Hill.

The Colonel never saw the fine decorations arrayed in his honor on Market Street, because instead of following the direct, announced route to the Auditorium, his driver turned up Broad, then doubled back to the venue. Leaning forward in his seat, the Colonel ordered the man to pick up speed, until even the mounted police couldn't keep up. Though he waved his hat to the crowd, Roosevelt seemed distracted, and he fixed his eyes toward the front.

The motorcade stopped at the Auditorium, an ungainly brick building with square towers; high, stone arches; and large, round windows on the second floor. The doors had opened at eight o'clock, and under the gaze of thirty officers, the ticketholders had streamed inside. The hall was as awkward inside as out, with a wide balcony and rows of metal poles to support the sloping roof. The stage was so small that the band had been moved upstairs to make more room for dignitaries on the platform. At nine o'clock, Commodore Key rose to introduce the Colonel.

———

John Schrank saw none of it. Everything he knew of that day he read in the newspapers—Roosevelt's short speech in the Auditorium; the brief appearance afterward on the steps of city hall; the departure of his special train at ten forty-five. All that morning, even as the streets just a few blocks from his hotel had filled with spectators, Schrank hadn't joined them. Still brooding over his failure the night before, he had decided that Chattanooga must not be the ordained location. A better opportunity was sure to come elsewhere, he told himself.

Over the next few days, Schrank followed the third termer's travels in the press. After leaving Chattanooga on Monday, Roosevelt made short stops in eastern Tennessee, including Cleveland, Athens, Sweetwater, and Lenoir City. Speaking in Knoxville's Auditorium, he was interrupted by hecklers shouting "Hurrah for Wilson!" and "Hooper! Hooper!" (the Tennessee governor whom he had called Mr. Facing-Both-Ways).

On the morning of October 1, the *Mayflower* arrived in Asheville, North Carolina. The Colonel's pocket watch said 5:50 a.m., and he elected to sleep in, figuring he had plenty of time to address the waiting crowd before the train left at 7:10. But he hadn't taken into account the change from Central Standard Time to Eastern. Presently there was a knock on his door, and a porter advised him that the train was about to leave. So the Colonel threw on his trousers, slippers, and overcoat, but no hat, and stepped into the chill morning air just in time to wave goodbye. Then, when he tried to reenter the *Mayflower,* he discovered that the train crew, under orders not to disturb him, had set the door's spring bolt the night before. He was locked out. The rest of the campaign staff was still asleep, and though he punched the door's buzzer repeatedly, no one heard it. It wasn't until twenty minutes later, at the next station, that a trainman rescued the shivering candidate.

The schedule called for only a few appearances that day, but when Roosevelt learned that people were waiting at nearly every station, he ordered additional stops. At Hickory, North Carolina, as he spoke from the *Mayflower*'s platform, some fifty students from Lenoir College gave the school's cheer, adding "Wilson! Wilson!" at the end. A melee broke out between Bull Moose and Democratic supporters, and the Colonel's train departed before he could finish his remarks.

He made more than a dozen whistle-stops through North Carolina, before Dr. Terrell, responsible for conserving Roosevelt's voice, finally overruled him. After that, the Bull Moose was reduced to waving as the *Mayflower* rattled through the intervening stations. In Raleigh, he addressed six thousand people in the Auditorium, including a section of the gallery reserved for the city's black citizens. Hoarse and visibly weary, he spoke for an hour on his social and industrial programs. Then, barely above a whisper, he ended his long campaign tour the way it had begun, telling the crowd, "We stand at Armageddon and we battle for the lord."

Shortly after midnight, the *Mayflower* left Raleigh, bound for New York City. Over the past month, the candidate had traveled nearly ten thousand miles through twenty-seven states, delivered more than four hundred speeches, and addressed a million people, from farmers to factory workers and from small business owners to prominent capitalists. He'd been lionized and vilified, applauded and heckled, and he'd had the clothes torn from his body. Before the end of the week, after a brief rest in Oyster Bay, he would face a hostile Senate committee investigating his campaign finances. When asked what he would tell the senators, the Colonel only said, "I want to reserve my fire until I see the whites of their eyes."

PART TWO

SEVEN

"A Decent, Respectable Reception"
Friday, October 4, to Saturday, October 12

FROM THE STREET, THE NEW SENATE OFFICE BUILDING APPEARED sober and restrained, as befit its occupants' public image. Dedicated three years earlier, just north of the Capitol, the three-story Beaux-Arts construction traced a sprawling irregular U, with a garden planted in the center. The main entrance lay on Constitution Avenue, on the building's shortest leg, up a daunting set of steps and through a surprisingly discreet doorway.

But inside, the edifice gave up all pretense of modesty. The entrance opened onto a rotunda of white marble and limestone, graced with Doric columns and covered by a coffered dome. Whereas the House of Representatives had chosen an understated, even plebian style for its new offices, the Senators had appointed theirs in accord with their more august station, including bronze banisters, mahogany-trimmed doors, and crystal chandeliers. Neither had they spared any comfort, such as forced-air ventilation, steam heat, and a Turkish bath. To convey them to the Capitol, there was an underground train.

On this warm, fair morning, a crowd was standing on the building's front stairs when the Colonel's car pulled up. He stepped onto the sidewalk, wearing a steel-gray suit and a blue necktie, with a gold watch chain draped across his vest; though he wore his black Stetson, he had left his overcoat at the hotel. With him were Ernest Abbott, of the progressive magazine *The Outlook*, where the Colonel was a contributing editor, and William Loeb, the Colonel's ex-secretary in the White House and the New York governor's office, who had also been called to testify. Following behind was a dark-haired young man, John W. McGrath, one of the stenographers hired to travel with the campaign. Born in Newfoundland, McGrath had played hockey for the Montreal Wanderers; today he was contending with a large valise filled with documents.

Roosevelt's party had left New York on the midnight train and had arrived at Union Station at 7:15 this morning, just as the sun caught the tip of the Washington Monument. At the depot they'd been met by Frank P. Hogan, an ex-journalist who had been on safari with the Colonel and who was now chairman of the Progressive Party for the District of Columbia. A crowd of a hundred private citizens had turned out to greet the Bull Moose. Some approached and shook his hand, which the Colonel seemed happy to oblige. Reporters were also there; one asked about Governor Herbert Hadley of Missouri, who had just come out in favor of President Taft. "No comment," the Colonel snapped.

The group passed through the station's great hall, which gleamed with marble, gold leaf, and a legion of Roman statues, then entered the main waiting room with its hundred-foot-high vaulted ceiling. Near the exit, the Colonel noticed a knot of schoolchildren who had gotten up early to welcome him. He paused and gave each a pat on the head. "There, bless you," one mother said, hugging her youngster, "you've shaken hands with Teddy."

Though the ex-president had passed through Washington in recent years, he hadn't spent the night here since leaving office in March 1909. Many old friends had offered him accommodation for this visit, but he preferred to stay on neutral ground. So from the station, he and his companions drove to the Willard, the grand hotel on Pennsylvania Avenue two blocks east of the White House, which had been the stopping place of the privileged and powerful since before the Civil War. Completed in 1904, the present building was Washington's first skyscraper, at twelve stories. The Colonel entered under the front awning, hurried through the ornate, columned lobby, and took the elevator to his suite, where he and his advisers conferred over breakfast.

At 9:55, his car stopped before the Senate Office Building and the Colonel's entourage swept through the narrow entrance and under the grand rotunda. The corridors were lined with supporters, who'd been waiting since the doors had opened two hours before; as he passed, their cheers reverberated off the polished stone walls. He entered the committee chamber, a generous room with an oversized gold mirror, elegant carpeting, and a great mahogany table. A hundred reporters and spectators were perched in chairs along the walls, and they applauded as well. As the Colonel stood to be sworn in, more cheers could be heard echoing down the corridor.

Roosevelt settled himself in the witness chair, which was set on a low platform beside the central table. William Loeb took a seat directly behind and slightly to one side, ready to confer with his former boss if needed. The witness adjusted his glasses, smiled at the committee, and waved to some friends in the room. Then he shifted to the edge of his chair, lifted his chin, and announced that he was ready.

Across the table waited four committee members who were no allies of the Colonel or his party—Republicans Wesley L. Jones of Washington State and George T. Oliver of Pennsylvania and Democrats Atlee Pomerene of Ohio and Thomas H. Paynter of Kentucky. The only kindly face was that of the chairman, Moses E. Clapp of Minnesota, a Republican who had thrown his support to the Progressives. Clapp had been appointed to the panel because he was head of the Senate's Interstate Commerce Committee, which had heard earlier testimony on Roosevelt's campaign finances. Given the patently political nature of this investigation, Clapp had accepted the chairmanship with reluctance.

Beginning deliberations in June, the committee had already heard from Republican officials who had worked for Roosevelt's election in

1904 and from industrialists who had contributed to that campaign. Former New York governor Benjamin B. Odell Jr. had testified that he'd solicited a donation of a quarter million dollars from railroad financier E. H. Harriman, and that Harriman had raised the money in a matter of hours—$50,000 from his own funds and the rest from his wealthy friends, including J. P. Morgan, railroad magnates Jay Gould and William K. Vanderbilt, Sr., and banker Hamilton Twombly. Republican Senator Boies Penrose of Pennsylvania had told the committee that the $125,000 Roosevelt's campaign had received from John Archbold of Standard Oil had never been returned, despite Roosevelt's written order to do so, and that Roosevelt had been aware of that lapse. According to Archbold, Roosevelt's campaign treasurer, Cornelius N. Bliss, had solicited the donation, with the knowledge of the president.

Even if the claims were true, there was nothing illegal about the contributions, since corporate donations to candidates for president (as well as for vice president, senator, congressman, and state legislator) hadn't been outlawed until 1907. And even after that, the statute had had little effect, since it placed no restriction on personal contributions from the corporations' wealthy stockholders and directors. Although he denied any quid pro quo, Roosevelt admitted that he had accepted the trusts' money. A former campaign official estimated that the corporate contributions in 1904 totaled more than $1.5 million, or 73 percent of all funds collected by the Republican national election committee.

In August, as the investigation was making headlines, Roosevelt had demanded to appear before the committee to clear his name. But Congress had been about to adjourn for the summer, and in the hiatus his enemies had published anonymous reports and rumors, which he had vehemently refuted during his cross-country barnstorming. On September 30, the committee had resumed calling witnesses, and just yesterday, J. P. Morgan had testified to contributing $150,000 to the 1904 campaign. But today, finally, the Colonel would get his chance, as he phrased it, to "put his cards on the table."

Senator Clapp called the session to order. Seven years older than the Colonel, he had a fleshy face hung with jowls and bags, and a huge walrus mustache concealing both lips. He began: "Colonel, were you a candidate for president in 1904?"

"I was."

"Mr. George B. Cortelyou was chairman of the New York campaign committee?"

"He was."

"And the late Cornelius Bliss was treasurer of that committee?"

"He was."

"Has your attention been called to the testimony given before this committee of John D. Archbold?"

"It has."

"You may state what, if anything," the chairman told him, "you knew at the time of the alleged contribution by Mr. Archbold to Mr. Bliss, of the fact of the contribution either being asked for or made."

The Colonel responded by reading letters he had written to Bliss, Cortelyou, and George R. Sheldon, another member of the Republican National Committee, in which he disavowed all knowledge of the contributions and gave instructions to return any money that might have been received from Standard Oil.

Senator Clapp continued, "In regard to what has become known as the Harriman fund—"

The Colonel interrupted. "I beg your pardon, Senator, but would you be willing that I should take up in succession the different charges made?"

The chairman indicated that he would. And thus the witness seized control of proceedings for the rest of the morning.

"In the first place," he said, "I want to call your attention to this fact, that there is no testimony against me except in the form of hearsay evidence, hearsay statements of men who are dead." As to the claim, published in *Hearst's Magazine*, that he had asked for a meeting with

Archbold, presumably to solicit a donation, he answered that he did recall seeing Mr. Archbold on two or three occasions, including once at Sagamore Hill. But, he said, he saw lots of men while in office. Speaking deliberately, he raised his fist to the committee. "I wish now to put this as explicitly as I know how: While I was President, if any man, trust magnet, labor leader, Socialist, prize fighter, lawyer, clergyman, had any business with me and wanted to see me, I always saw him and if I thought there was anything to be gained from the standpoint of the public service in seeing any men, then, without waiting for him to ask, I would send for him." A murmur of approval passed through the spectators.

"If I am elected President, a year hence if Mr. Rockefeller or anyone else wants to see me I'll see him; and, more than that, if I have anything to ask in connection with the public service of Mr. Rockefeller, or Mr. Gompers, or Mr. [John] Mitchell," another unionist, "or Mr. J. Pierpont Morgan, or anyone else, I will send for him myself and ask him about it. . . . And if I ever find that my virtue is so frail that it won't stand to being brought in contact with either a trust magnate or a Socialist or a labor leader, I will get out of public life."

At this point, Senator Paynter managed to make one of the few interjections of the morning: "Mr. President, one of your statements rather surprised me, and if you will pardon me for interrupting you."

"Certainly."

"You say you sent for John L. Sullivan. I did not know that you wanted anything to do with a has-been of a prize fighter."

"John L. Sullivan is a big fellow and a good fellow," the Colonel answered.

"I did not mean any reflection."

"And a man who has done valiantly. I do not expect him to last forever. I should say that I do not think I did send for Mr. Sullivan or for Battling Nelson, but each of them called upon me more than once. I saw both of them, and was glad to see them. There were some questions of public policy that they wanted to see me about."

There was laughter in the room.

"There may have been a little personality mixed up with it, too," the Colonel admitted, laughing himself. "But in Sullivan's case, I remember, he had a nephew in the Marine Corps, and that is why he wanted to see me.

"Now, about the Harriman business." His former secretary, William Loeb, was present during his conversation with Harriman, he said, and would confirm that Harriman's contribution was intended for the New York State Republicans, not for the Roosevelt campaign. "In Mr. Harriman's subsequent letters to me, and in his previous letters to me, and my letters to him, as laid before your committee, you can see that there is never a reference to getting aid from me in any shape or way."

The Colonel had been talking for an hour. "Now," he went on, sliding forward in his chair again, "I wish to take up the testimony of Mr. Archbold and Senator Penrose." He paused to glance at some papers before him, and the room hushed in anticipation. On Penrose's testimony before the committee, in which the senator claimed to have advised Archbold to contribute to the campaign or risk the consequences, the Colonel said: "Now, I want to call your attention to the fact that they could incur my hostility [as president] only if they violated the law. I could not be hostile to them, and I had no way of being hostile to them if they obeyed the law any more than a policeman can be hostile to any man here unless he disobeys the law." He paused for effect. "So that the purpose of Mr. Penrose in advising Archbold to have the Standard Oil make that contribution could only have been to secure it against Government action, taken because it had violated the law."

He leaned over the table. "I have been police commissioner. If it were proved to me when I was police commissioner that any policeman had done in reference to a law-breaking liquor seller or gambler what Senator Penrose admits he did—he, a Senator of the United States—in connection with the Standard Oil Company, I would have thrown the policeman off the force, and I hold that the Senate of the United States should throw Mr. Penrose out of the Senate on the admission that he has himself made before this committee."

Having just called for the expulsion of an elected member of the United States Senate, Roosevelt was about to press on, but Senator Pomerene asked to suspend for a moment. The Colonel began to rise from his chair. "Oh," he laughed, "I thought you asked me to stand a minute." During the short recess, he chatted with Senator Clapp and paced the room before retaking his seat.

"As for Archbold," the Colonel began after everyone was settled again, "he testifies that Mr. Bliss tried to blackmail him, and yet he testifies that he regarded Mr. Bliss as an excellent fellow. He evidently does not see that there is anything objectionable in what he alleges Mr. Bliss did. He has not a word of complaint to make against Mr. Bliss for attempting to extort from him a contribution—a contribution for improper purposes. His complaint is that he did not get anything for the contribution he made. The complaint is that nothing improper was done for him by the administration, . . . and he says that darkest Abyssinia has nothing to show comparable to the treatment administered to the Standard Oil Co. by the Roosevelt administration. I did administer the Abyssinian treatment to the Standard Oil Co. because it needed it; and if I ever were President again and the Standard Oil Co. or any other company acted in that way, I would give it the Abyssinian treatment again. . . .

"I would also like to call your attention to this fact: All of these men who testify against me testify that I refused to do or did not do anything improper in their interest, and they are now all opposing me; they are for one of the candidates against me—those of them who are left. They are all hostile to me."

When Senator Paynter assured him that the committee had no wish to single him out unfairly, the Colonel cut him off. "Our complaint is not that we are called here," he said, "but the men who make the charges were not called here first.... You can see it is hard on me to have to wait a month to answer Mr. Archbold's charges and then to have things so arranged that the attention of the country is riveted on the campaign expenses of the Progressive Party, while no attention is directed to the campaign funds of the other candidates."

Finally, after two hours, he concluded, "Now, gentlemen, it seems to me I have completed my statement. I want to reiterate that I asked no man to contribute to the campaign fund when I was elected President of the United States. I wish to reiterate that Mr. Bliss and Mr. Cortelyou explicitly assured me that no promise had been made and no obligation of any kind incurred in connection with any contribution; that it was on their explicit assurance that I issued my statement in response to Mr. Parker's accusation, and that their subsequent actions showed that their assurance was proper, for neither they nor anyone else having authority ever, either directly or indirectly asked me to act, or to refrain from acting, on any matter that came before me as President with any regard to the fact that any contribution had been either made or withheld."

There was a recess for lunch, and the committee reconvened at one thirty, when Senators Paynter and Pomerene took up the cross-examination. Paynter tried to make the witness admit he had known that the $125,000 had never been returned to Standard Oil, but the Colonel stood by his earlier testimony. Then Pomerene suggested that he must have realized that the trusts hoped for some consideration in exchange for their contributions, but Roosevelt pointed out that after his first administration, no sane person would have expected him to show the corporations any favoritism. "It is impossible for me to say that any man who gives a dollar does not expect to get something for that dollar. I do not know," he said. "But if I tell him he will not get anything for it then it is his own fault if he goes ahead and gives it." Gripping the arms of his chair, he rose to a crouch. "As a practical man

A triumphant Theodore Roosevelt leaving the Senate Office Building after his mastery of the Clapp Committee on October 4, 1912. "They couldn't ask me a question I wasn't ready to answer," he bragged.

of high ideals, who has always endeavored to put his high ideals into practice, I think any man who would believe that he would get any consideration from making a contribution to me was either a crook or a fool." The gallery applauded.

After two and a half hours of fruitless fencing, the witness was dismissed. He left the committee room beaming, to an ovation from the spectators. Then while William Loeb testified, substantiating the Colonel's claims, the ex-president went across town to the Smithsonian to view some of the big-game trophies he had brought back from Africa. At midnight he and his party boarded a train for New York.

The next morning, bemoaning the Colonel's utter domination of the senators, the *New York Times* editorialized: "The Clapp Committee behaved very well when it appeared before Col. Roosevelt on Friday. Evidently, it made a good impression on the witness. The Committee was unprotected, it did not even have that protection which a Judge in court sometimes, though rarely, extends to a witness under an examination by a bullying lawyer. Mr. Roosevelt addressed the Committee for two hours or so, and the Committee bore it with exemplary patience, which was rewarded, for when the Colonel scolded the Committee he did it mildly. Members of the Committee did venture to put a few questions, feeling, probably, that questions to a witness on the stand are not altogether out of place. But the questions were not troublesome, the answers for the most part were neither new nor illuminating."

The *Times* neglected to mention that even if the committee found no evidence of wrongdoing, or ever issued a report, it had already accomplished its purpose, of throwing Roosevelt's probity into doubt. But looking back over his performance, the Colonel was satisfied. "I think I wound up that Standard Oil affair," he chuckled. "They couldn't ask me a question I wasn't ready to answer."

After a few more days of rest and consultation at Oyster Bay, he would be ready to do what he did best, taking to the road and wooing voters.

—◆—

On the morning of October 4, as Theodore Roosevelt was preparing to testify before the Clapp committee, John Schrank awoke in the Sterling Hotel in Evansville, Indiana. Like most of the hotels where he'd stayed, the Sterling was a modest establishment located across the way from a railroad depot. Leaving Chattanooga several days before, Schrank had traced a desultory route, following the train lines and pausing briefly at Rome, Georgia, and Nashville, Tennessee. He'd reached Evansville at nine thirty on the evening of October 1. Walking into the Sterling's saloon, he was met by the comforting aroma he'd known since boyhood, the sweet scent of yeast mingled with the acrid odor of tobacco. He set behind the bar the umbrella he'd picked up when the weather had turned ugly. Then he ordered a cigar and a beer and asked the hotel's proprietor, Ira C. Wiltshire, for a room.

In the six days since leaving his suitcase in Charleston, Schrank had had his shirt laundered and bought new underwear. But his time on the road had begun to tell, and he looked unkempt and weary. To Wiltshire, the stranger behaved oddly, as though under the influence of some drug. The manager told him he didn't believe there was an empty room in the hotel, but that he would inquire. He went next door to the lobby and spoke to the night clerk, Ernest Slaton, who told him that Number 28 was free. Wiltshire returned to the bar and reported that there was a room available after all. But, he said, judging from the gentleman's appearance, he didn't think it would suit him, since it was on the third floor.

"Don't judge me by my appearance," Schrank told him. "All I want is a clean bed. I live in New York but just came from Nashville. I have been traveling around the country to see what I could learn."

At the front desk, he picked up a pencil and signed the register *John Flammang, Nashville.* He gave Slaton a half dollar for the room, collected the key, and went upstairs.

The next morning, it was still dark when Schrank came down to the lobby, a little after six o'clock. A stack of newspapers were waiting on the front desk, but he ignored them and exited the hotel without a word, not even to tell the staff whether to expect him for another night. At ten thirty that evening he appeared in the hotel's saloon and, standing at the end of the bar, drank five or six glasses of beer. Then he went to the lobby, laid another half dollar on the desk, and left it to Ernest Slaton to make the entry in the register.

Every day, it was the same. Mr. Flammang would disappear early in the morning, taking no meals in the hotel. Then he would return at night and assume his place at the end of the bar. He'd speak to no one unless spoken to, and even then would answer in monosyllables. Occasionally he would go to the saloon door and peer out, as though expecting someone. After half a dozen beers, he would pay his tab, never showing more than fifty cents. Then he'd give Slaton another half dollar and go to his room. One day, he varied his routine by asking the hotel barber, Joe Marx, for a shave; Marx was surprised when the stranger gave him a quarter and insisted he keep the change.

John Schrank had never given Evansville, Indiana, a thought in his life. But, situated in the southern part of the state, close to the borders with Illinois and Kentucky, the city afforded a central location to await the third termer's next move. Over the course of his enforced stay, as Schrank made his habitual rambles, he got to know the place. Set in a shallow bowl, on a sharp horseshoe of the Ohio River, Evansville counted a population of seventy thousand, a quarter of whom had either been born in Germany or had both parents born there. Coal was a major industry, and there were five mines within the city limits. But Schrank also noticed sawmills, gristmills, meat packers, and furniture makers. On First Avenue he discovered the Willard Library, a gothic brick building with an eccentric, oversized tower. On the city's east side was the Southern Indiana Hospital for the Insane, occupying a huge, rambling compound; once admitted, it seemed, you'd never find your way out again.

On three consecutive evenings—October 3, 4, and 5—Schrank followed the crowds to sober old Evans Hall for campaign rallies of the Progressives, Republicans, and Democrats, respectively. Afterward, when the Sterling's bartender, Charles Weir, asked for a report, Schrank didn't seem to want to talk about the gatherings. "They're all alike," was the most he would say.

Weir noticed that although there were always a couple of newspapers poking out of the stranger's coat pocket, he never seemed to read them. But during his long absences from the hotel, Schrank would pore over the papers, gleaning the third termer's activities and counting the days. Finally, Roosevelt launched his tour of the Midwest. His staff was being cagey, though. On his first campaign swing, the Republicans had shadowed him with "truth tellers" who rebutted his comments in public meetings of their own. The practice had irritated Roosevelt, and now, to keep the opposition off balance, the campaign was declining to publish all his stops in advance. But they couldn't keep the principal venues secret. And so it had been announced that the third termer would appear in Chicago on October 12 at the Coliseum, the same hall where he had contested the Republican convention and accepted the Progressive nomination. To John Schrank, it was perfect. Where better to fulfill his mission than the place where it had all begun, where King Roosevelt had offered himself as a martyr to the cause?

But the twelfth was still nearly a week away. In the meantime, he had nothing to do but wait, the task that was hardest of all. And as he prowled the streets of Evansville, he had ample time to think. There was time to brood about the fiasco in Chattanooga: He could still see the gleam of the automobile's radiator as it sped from the station and the ferocious smile on the third termer's face. And there was time to worry what would become of the valise and all the documents he'd left at the Moseley National House, where his room deposit had expired a week ago. He longed to have his papers back, but Charleston was seven hundred miles away, and, besides, he needed to travel light and quick. At last, Schrank read in his newspapers that Roosevelt had left New York's Grand Central Terminal on October 7, at 4:03 p.m., his private car coupled to the luxurious Twentieth Century Limited. Lingering on the *Mayflower's* rear platform, he'd shaken hands with well-wishers. "Never felt better in my life," he'd bragged. "I'm going to shake 'em up in the West."

Responsible for orchestrating the tour was Oscar King Davis, known to everyone as O. K. As a reporter for the *New York Sun*, Davis had covered the Spanish-American and Russo-Japanese wars and the Boxer Rebellion in China. He'd met the Colonel in 1898, when

Roosevelt was still at the Navy Department, and had become one of the president's trusted confidants among the press. He'd moved to the *New York Times*, where he'd been named Washington bureau chief. But earlier this year, when the Colonel threw his hat into the ring, Davis left the paper to become secretary of the Roosevelt National Committee. Then, after the bolt from the Republicans, Davis signed on as secretary of the Progressive campaign. Because of his newspaper ties, he also handled publicity, issuing daily releases to the capital press corps and weekly dispatches to two thousand newspapers across the country (sent as printer's plates, to encourage editors to run them). Davis hadn't accompanied the Colonel on his first tour, in September, but it had been decided he would travel with Roosevelt on this second swing.

The first event would come early the next day, at Detroit, followed by other stops in Michigan, Minnesota, Wisconsin, Illinois, Indiana, Kentucky, Ohio, Pennsylvania, Maryland, and New Jersey—states where Roosevelt could expect a warmer welcome than in the Deep South. He planned at least thirty addresses over eighteen days, and in order to conserve his voice, he announced that he would avoid whistle-stops along the route. All the more reason for John Schrank to plan their rendezvous for Chicago.

With a month to go until Election Day, the Colonel realized that he had to intensify his attack on Woodrow Wilson. Finally venturing out of the Governor's Cottage in Sea Girt, the Democrat had begun his own western tour. On October 10, he was scheduled to speak in Chicago, two days before the Bull Moose. Party patriarch William Jennings Bryan had been enlisted to campaign for Wilson, and the candidate would also call on Bryan at his home in Lincoln, Nebraska.

Thomas Edison, meanwhile, had come out for Roosevelt. "I'm a natural born Bull Moose," the sixty-five-year-old inventor told reporters. "I believe in change because all progress is the result of change. . . . The Americans are experimenters; we want to try experiments in government. . . . Roosevelt would win easily if there were not so many sheep in the world who won't think."

The Socialist candidate, Eugene Debs, was also on the road. Speaking to a crowd at Proctor's Theater in Schenectady, New York, he ridiculed Roosevelt's testimony before the Clapp Committee. "Just think of anybody dropping $100,000 in my campaign fund and I not know of it," he scoffed. "If men were not in mental childhood Mr. Roosevelt would not dare to attempt to palm off such an unmitigated untruth upon them."

President Taft was still secluded at his seaside retreat in Beverly, Massachusetts. But that didn't prevent him from making his own bitter attack on Roosevelt, charging that his former friend aimed "to become the head of a benevolent despotism" and make himself a "czar. . . . Mr. Roosevelt and his followers in their tendency would do away completely with the Constitution formed by the Fathers of the Republic," he warned. "They would wholly destroy all constitutional limitations and restrictions, and replace them with the unchecked will and emotions of a bare majority of the people. . . . That would be a monstrous form of despotism that quickly would utterly destroy our liberties and lead to the establishment of a monarchy—probably by a referendum of the people themselves." John Schrank had already expressed the same sentiments himself.

Roosevelt's train arrived in Detroit on October 8 at 9:15 a.m., two hours behind schedule. At noon he spoke at the armory, which was packed with workers because the city's factories had closed early for the occasion. "We cannot get better working conditions, shorter hours, the minimum wage for women, or general enforcement of employers' liability if we are to put into effect the vague ideas of Mr. Wilson," he told his audience. "As to Mr. Taft, he is even less definite and offers not the shadow of a solution to the industrial problem."

At one thirty, the Colonel left for Flint, Michigan, where he spent an hour shaking hands with workers at the Buick plant. That evening, in Saginaw, he spoke to several thousand people packed into the Light Guard armory, reminding them that justice for workers could not be achieved without government action, and calling for a living wage and better schools.

Traveling with Roosevelt was his clean-cut, square-jawed stenographer, Elbert Martin. Born in Manchester, New Hampshire, the thirty-one-year-old Martin had attended college and law school in Michigan. On August 16, the week after the Progressive convention, he'd walked into party headquarters in New York, applied for a job, and been hired. Now in Saginaw, Martin and the rest of the ex-president's party made the short walk from the hotel to the auditorium. The streets were crowded and poorly lit, and Martin felt on edge. Then a man rushed out of the throng with his hands outstretched. A former footballer, Martin threw himself between the stranger and the Colonel. He grabbed the man by the shoulders and flung him backward ten feet, into the gutter. But when it turned out the stranger was just another supporter looking for a handshake, Roosevelt took Martin aside and reprimanded him.

The next day, October 9, the Colonel stopped in Cheboygan, Michigan, and then crossed into the state's upper peninsula, where the large immigrant population was employed in mines and lumber camps. In Marquette, the crowd was so enthusiastic that Roosevelt was reminded of a football game. At his next stop, in Houghton, he kept up the attack on Wilson and his "sullen hostility to labor." To illustrate the point, he read passages from two of Wilson's speeches. In 1905 the Democrat had said, "The objection I have to labor unions is that they drag the highest man to the level of the lowest." And two years later, he had been even more pointed: "We speak too exclusively of the capitalistic class. There is another, as formidable an enemy to equality and freedom as it is, and that is the class formed by labor organizations and leaders of the country—the class representing only a small minority of the laboring men of the country, quite as monopolistic in spirit as the capitalist and quite as apt to corrupt and ruin our industries by their monopoly."

The campaign had resolved not to tire the Colonel with unplanned detours and whistle-stops, but they hadn't been able to resist the appeals of smaller towns, and so between Cheboygan and Houghton the candidate was called upon to speak at nearly every depot. On Thursday the 10th, he crossed into Wisconsin and stopped for an hour in Superior, before continuing into Minnesota.

In Duluth, where he spent most of the next day, the police couldn't control the crowd. At the station, the Colonel's men had to force their way from the *Mayflower* to his car, and at the hotel they managed to reach the lobby only by forming a circle around him. As the party battled up the hotel's main staircase, the throng tore off the Colonel's coat. When the visitors finally managed to slam the door to the room behind them, the crowd tried to break it down, yelling, "Teddy! Teddy! We want Teddy!"

That evening, he spoke to eight thousand in the Auditorium, with as many milling in the streets outside. Then, to accommodate the overflow, he did it all over again. In both speeches, he appealed to the foreign-born audience by attacking his opponent's derogatory statements toward immigrants, which had surfaced during the nominating campaign and which the Democrat had been trying to explain away ever since. Tonight, Roosevelt quoted Wilson's *History of the American People*, written while he was at Princeton, which characterized Eastern European immigrants as "multitudes of men of the lowest classes from the south of Italy and men of the meaner sort out of Hungary and Poland, men out of the ranks, where there was neither skill nor energy, nor any initiative of quick intelligence, and they came in numbers, which increased from year to year, as if the countries of Europe were disburdening themselves of the more sordid and hapless elements of their population." Roosevelt also quoted an earlier piece by Wilson published in *The Atlantic Monthly*, which described the insalubrious effects the newcomers were having on their adoptive country: "Our own temperate blood, schooled to self-possession, is receiving a constant infusion and yearly experiencing a partial corruption of foreign blood. Our own equable habits have been crossed with the feverish habits of the restless [Old] World. We are unquestionably facing an ever-increasing difficulty of self-command with ever-deteriorating materials, possibly with degenerating fibre."

That same day, Wilson arrived in Chicago, where more than ten thousand packed into the Seventh Regiment armory to hear him. It was the biggest, noisiest reception he'd received anywhere, and he was delighted. "This has been the red-letter day of my campaign," he told the crowd. "It has turned the Democratic tide into a Democratic cataract." Roosevelt could only hope that Chicagoans had reserved some of their enthusiasm for him, and that the Democratic cataract didn't become a Niagara.

On the eleventh, the day before the Colonel was to reach Chicago, the weather continued wet and cool. Turning south, he stopped in Oshkosh, Wisconsin. Since the city had no hall large enough to accommodate the crowd of ten thousand, a warehouse was pressed into service; despite a thunderstorm, thousands more stood outside. After speaking for two hours, the Colonel gave a second address in a nearby armory.

He bypassed St. Paul, since he had spoken in neighboring Minneapolis on his September trip. As he continued south, he found crowds waiting at Chippewa Falls, Thorp, Stevens Pointe, and other depots throughout the state's lumber region. Although he made brief appearances from the *Mayflower's* rear platform, he tried, under Dr. Terrell's urging, to conserve his voice for the major speech planned for Chicago the following evening.

— ∼ —

For millennia, people had been drawn to Chicago—not as a home, but as a place to pass through on their way somewhere else. Native Americans had portaged their canoes over its mudflats, which separated the great river to the west with the great lakes to the north and east. In 1673, French explorer Louis Jolliet recognized the location's strategic value as a link between Canada and New Orleans, but failed to interest the mother country. Then a century later, France lost its American colonies to Britain in the Seven Years' War, and the area called Chicago (supposedly from the Miami-Illinois *Shikaakwa,* for "Wild Onions") passed to the rival empire. In 1803 the newly independent United States built Fort Dearborn on the site, and within three decades the Native Americans had been expelled. By 1837, when Chicago received its charter as a city, the population had grown to four thousand. Eleven years later, a canal was opened over the old Indian portage, connecting the East Coast with New Orleans and the West, and finally realizing the potential that Jolliet had seen nearly two centuries before.

The railroads were quicker to grasp the value of Chicago's location. The first train came in 1848, and seven scant years later, the city was served by seventeen different lines and recognized as the crossroads of the nation. Thanks to the railroads, it had also grown into the greatest grain and livestock markets, slaughterhouse, and lumberyard in the world. In the decade before the Civil War, Chicago boomed with foundries, machine shops, steel mills, breweries, and dozens of other industries. During the war it thrived by supplying the Union army, and afterward by shipping material to rebuild the South. By 1870, Chicago's population had reached nearly three hundred thousand, and it had become famous for its fast-moving pedestrians, its slow-flowing traffic, its coal-polluted air, and its staggering murder rate. Rival metropolises took to calling it "the Windy City," not for the breezes off Lake Michigan but for its insufferable bluster.

In 1871, Chicago was devastated by fire, which destroyed seventeen thousand buildings, claimed some three hundred lives, and left a hundred thousand people homeless. But Chicagoans began a breakneck campaign to rebuild their city—bigger, better, more modern than before, and not of wood but of brick and stone. Many of the new buildings were skyscrapers, soaring more than ten stories tall. Industry flourished in Chicago, but as the disparity grew between rich and poor, labor peace proved tenuous. On May 4, 1886, erupted the notorious Haymarket Riot, in which half a dozen policemen and at least four protestors died after a bomb was hurled during a workers' demonstration. Though the perpetrator was never identified, four anarchists were hanged on flimsy evidence, and several others were sentenced to prison. A series of sometime-violent strikes—of meatpackers, teamsters, railroad workers—also shook Chicago, culminating in the Pullman walkout in 1894, which was quelled by federal troops (and for his role in which Eugene Debs was sent to the penitentiary).

It was raining when John Schrank reached Chicago. Leaving the Union Depot, he paused beneath the station's metal marquee, which had sheltered so many of his fellow immigrants. Then, snapping open his umbrella, he stepped onto Canal Street. It was just dusk, and Chicagoans were rushing home to their dinner. Head down, his brown suit coat pulled around him, Schrank picked his way one block south, until he came to Jackson Boulevard. Peering through the rain, he could see the skyscrapers of the Loop rising to his left. He turned right, toward a less exalted district. Several blocks to the north, near the corner of Randolph and Desplaines, was Haymarket Square, scene of the bombing and riot. On the corner of Halsted and Jackson, Schrank saw the New Jackson Hotel, a four-story brick building with a fire escape across the front. Though there was clearly nothing new about the place, he went in out of the rain and registered.

According to the Chicago newspapers, the third termer's train would arrive tomorrow at 9:30 a.m.

In the morning, the sky was still threatening. Leaving the New Jackson Hotel, John Schrank walked the few blocks to the North Western

Station, on Madison Street at Clinton. Opened the year before, the depot was a sober, gray stone building with two low clock towers and little in the way of ornamentation. As Schrank drew closer, he saw no crowd blocking the street. He passed through the stone columns and entered the vast waiting room, with its tall arched windows and high vaulted ceiling. But the only people he found were Saturday-morning travelers, waiting on the long wooden benches or hurrying for their trains. He approached a man and asked what time Roosevelt was due. There had been a change, the man told him; the Colonel would disembark at the Central Station, any minute now. Was the Central Station nearby? Not really—on Twelfth Street at the south end of Grant Park, next to the lake.

Schrank left the station and headed east on Madison Street. According to the papers, the third termer would be stopping at the La Salle Hotel, at La Salle and Madison, just a few blocks away.

~ ~ ~

The Colonel's train reached the Central Station at 9:20. There to meet him was a committee of fifty notables, including the social activist Jane Addams, founder of Chicago's Hull House, who had seconded his nomination at the Progressive convention. The Colonel shook hands all around, then strode under the clock tower and through the wide arch marking the station's entrance. He and the others climbed into waiting cars and, escorted by a troop of mounted police, turned up Michigan Avenue. As the motorcade entered a district of skyscrapers, the familiar streets were fringed with supporters, though the crowds were noticeably thinner than on his visit in August. As he passed the Karpen Building, site of Democratic headquarters, the assembled employees clapped politely; but up the street at the Auditorium, headquarters of the Republicans, the workers congregating on the balcony only watched in stony silence. At ten o'clock, the motorcade stopped in front of the La Salle Hotel, the city's finest, with twenty-two stories, a thousand rooms, and an opulent first floor shimmering in green and gold.

From the street, the hotel presented an intimidating stone front. Standing near the canopy that guarded the entrance, John Schrank watched the third termer arrive. He saw him raise himself in his car and heard him tell the crowd, "This demonstration speaks for itself. It apparently comes from the heart. It apparently means something. It comes from the people, and this is a fight for the people."

Schrank watched as though studying an insect under a glass. For nearly two weeks, he had thought of nothing but coming face-to-face with Roosevelt again. But this morning his vest pocket was empty of its accustomed metallic bulge; this morning he had left the Colt .38 in his room at the New Jackson Hotel. It had not been an oversight. He'd read in the paper of the "decent, respectable reception" the city was planning in Roosevelt's honor. And he'd decided it wouldn't be fitting to gun down their famous visitor at the moment of his arrival, before all these good people who had come out to welcome him. It would reflect badly on Chicago, a city toward which he bore no ill will. Better to bide his time, he told himself. He would find a better opportunity. That night, the third termer was scheduled to make not one speech but two.

———

The Colonel had been asked to ride in the Columbus Day parade to Grant Park, but when the Knights of Columbus had worried publicly that his appearance would politicize the event, he'd written to decline the invitation. And so the candidate spent an unexpectedly free afternoon in his hotel suite, conferring with aides and dictating speeches he would deliver during the rest of his tour. His next appearance wouldn't come until seven fifteen, when he would speak on the city's Near West Side, once a fashionable area but now a rough immigrant neighborhood.

Chicago was as much a city of foreigners as New York. Forty-six percent of Chicagoans had been born abroad, and more than two-thirds of the population counted at least a father (and often both parents) from overseas. Fifty-four percent of male citizens of voting age had been born outside the United States. To reach all these newcomers, the city's newspapers were published in ten languages.

It was on the immigrant-crowded Near West Side that Jane Addams had opened the first settlement house in the United States. In 1889 she had invested her inheritance in a rundown mansion once owned by real estate mogul Charles Hull. And with her companion, Ellen Gates Starr, she had launched a comprehensive program of social services benefiting two thousand people a week. Eventually the complex expanded to thirteen buildings, including a residence for women, a night school, a kindergarten, a kitchen, an art gallery, a coffeehouse, a gymnasium, a bathhouse, youth programs, music and drama programs, a library, a playground, and a summer camp. Guided by the nondenominational Social Christian philosophy, the institution concerned itself not with dogma or conversion but with good works, not so much with souls to be saved as with human spirits to be lifted.

For the Colonel's speech this evening, a large tent had been erected on the corner of West Twelfth and Ogden. Scheduled to begin only forty-five minutes before the evening's main event, the address across town at the Coliseum, this appearance was planned as a few brief comments, again focusing on Wilson's derogatory statements about immigrants. By the time the Colonel's car stopped on the Near West Side, the rain had cleared. But the weather had turned cold and blustery, not ideal for coddling a fading voice. The tent flaps were raised for the benefit of the overflow crowd outside, and in shouting to make himself heard, the candidate strained his vocal chords, causing Dr. Terrell to fret over the speech to be delivered later that evening.

Even before the Colonel had stepped onto the dais on the Near West Side, the Coliseum was filled to capacity and the doors had been barred. The site, on South Wabash between Fourteenth and Sixteenth Streets, had once been occupied by a Civil War museum housed in the infamous Libby Prison, which had been transported brick by brick from Richmond, Virginia, and reconstructed on the lot. But in 1899, when museum attendance had lagged, the building's owner, candy magnate Charles Gunther, had constructed the Coliseum, hoping to take advantage of Chicago's burgeoning convention business. In the intervening years, his investment had paid off, and the ungainly building, still incorporating part of the prison façade, had been the scene of innumerable meetings, including the Republican conventions of 1904, 1908, and 1912, and the Bull Moose convention of this past summer.

From the street, where John Schrank stood, the Coliseum's turrets and narrow windows gave the building a forbidding, feudal look. Arriving at seven thirty, Schrank had joined the crowd choking Wabash Avenue. He had pushed his way to the trolley tracks in the middle of the road, as close as he could manage to the main entrance. As he waited, he could feel in his vest pocket the reassuring heft of the Colt .38.

The audience inside the Coliseum sounded especially fervent. A women's chorus sang a medley of religious and patriotic songs. Then, at eight o'clock, the building's steel rafters rocked with a tremendous ovation. At first it seemed a preliminary speaker might have been introduced. But when the cheering continued for three, five, ten minutes, it was clear that only one man could command such a reception. Schrank was confused. Then he realized: Instead of bulling his way through the crowd in front of the auditorium, the third termer had stolen in through a side door, just as he had in Atlanta. And just as in Atlanta, John Schrank stayed with the crowd in the street and waited.

Even before the applause had quieted, the women's chorus broke into "Onward Christian Soldiers" and "There'll Be a Hot Time in the Old Town Tonight." At last the cheering stilled and the soft drone of a man's voice filtered down to the street. There was polite clapping.

Not Roosevelt, then. Maybe it was the evening's master of ceremonies, Charles Merriam, professor of political science at the University of Chicago and one of the founders of the Illinois Progressive Party. More restrained applause—another preliminary speaker—then another. Finally, the audience erupted. Standing in the dark street, Schrank could imagine the red bandanas waving, the third termer striding across the stage, his chin thrust forward, his square teeth flashing. But his weakened voice didn't filter down to the street, and only the cheers of the crowd were heard to punctuate the speech. Finally, the ovation rose to a frenzy, and the women's chorus swelled again. He had finished. A flurry of anticipation ran through the crowd, as they prepared for the Colonel's exit through the Coliseum's main door. As in Atlanta, it never came.

EIGHT

"I Want to Be a Good Indian, O. K."
Sunday, October 13, to Monday, October 14

THE FIRST METHODIST CHURCH IN EVANSTON, ILLINOIS, WAS uncommonly crowded on this seasonable October morning. The faithful occupied every pew, and the front steps and sidewalk teemed with the curious. It wasn't the promise of a stirring homily that had attracted the throng, but reports that Theodore Roosevelt would be here. According to the newspapers, the Colonel would spend Saturday night in Evanston with his friend the newspaper publisher John C. Shaffer, and then attend services this morning. But in the end, the Methodists' reaped a purely spiritual reward for their early rising. Worn out, the Colonel had decided to stay in Chicago and worship at Grace Reformed Church, on Jackson Boulevard.

He arrived with his cousin Philip Roosevelt, younger brother of George Emlen Roosevelt, who had accompanied the Colonel on his first campaign swing, in September. Twenty years old, lanky and fair, with a baby face and wire spectacles, Philip had graduated from Harvard just that spring and, like George Emlen, was acting as secretary to his famous relative. The Roosevelts sat in the second pew at Grace Reformed, in plain sight of the startled congregation, but the minister avoided mentioning them until just before the final hymn, when he asked his flock to remain in place so their guests could slip out undisturbed.

After church, the Colonel took advantage of the dry weather to make a driving tour of the Chicago parks, just coming into their peak of autumn color. In the afternoon, he received a few callers in his hotel suite. Among them was Ira Copley, newspaper publisher, streetcar and utility magnate, and Republican congressman now running for reelection on the Progressive ticket. At six o'clock, the Colonel dined in his room with Mr. and Mrs. Medill McCormick. Mr. McCormick's grandfather Joseph Medill had been part owner of the *Chicago Tribune* and later mayor of the city. Medill McCormick had also been an executive at the paper, and many supposed he would assume its management, but he'd decided to enter politics. A leader of the Progressive Republican movement, he was now a candidate for the Illinois assembly. Medill's wife, Ruth Hanna McCormick, was the daughter of Mark Hanna, the senator from Ohio who was widely considered the power behind William McKinley's throne (and who had reluctantly acceded to Roosevelt's vice-presidential nomination in 1900).

Also at dinner was the Colonel's daughter Alice Roosevelt Longworth, who had come up from her home in Cincinnati. Born just two days before the death of her mother, baby Alice had been left in the care of her Aunt Bamie while her father had gone to grieve in the Dakota Badlands. Nearly three years later, after Theodore had married Edith and resettled in Oyster Bay, Alice had gone to live with them and a growing brood of half-siblings. By the time her father was inaugurated, Alice had matured into a striking young woman, with flowing dark hair and arching eyebrows. Smart, witty, and mischievous, she was known for sneaking onto the White House roof for a cigarette, for betting on horses and cards, and for toting a live snake in her purse. "I can be President of the United States," her exasperated father told a friend, "or I can attend to Alice. I cannot possibly do both."

In Washington, Alice met Congressman and man-about-town Nicholas Longworth. Fourteen years her senior, Longworth was the son of a prominent Cincinnati family. He'd graduated from Harvard College and Cincinnati Law School, and then had been elected state legislator and state senator before being sent to the US House of Representatives in 1902. On February 17, 1906, he and the twenty-two-year-old Alice were married in a dazzling East Room ceremony that was proclaimed the social event of the decade. But sobriety and fidelity weren't Longworth's strong suits, and the couple drifted apart. Party loyalty was a different matter, though, and in 1912 Nick stuck by the Republicans and Taft, while Alice stuck by her father. In Cincinnati, the Progressives were challenging Longworth with their own candidate, who seemed to have an excellent chance of taking his seat. On this October night in Chicago, less than a month before the election, Nick Longworth did not join his wife and father-in-law for dinner.

It was a leisurely evening, since the Colonel had decided not to leave Chicago until the following afternoon. He'd been scheduled to make speeches in Gary, Hammond, and Indiana Harbor, Indiana; and Kenosha and Racine, Wisconsin. But with his voice still ragged from the open-air speech on the Near West Side, the campaign had canceled those events to save his strength for the major address planned for Milwaukee tomorrow night.

On Sunday morning, while Theodore Roosevelt was startling the congregation at Grace Reformed Church, John Schrank boarded a train for the ninety-mile journey to Milwaukee. At one o'clock in the afternoon, he stepped down at Union Station, the old brick depot on Everett Street where the third termer was due the following day. Exiting under the tall gothic clock tower, Schrank crossed the street and entered a tidy park, a block square and traced with walking paths. He took the sidewalk to his right and soon found himself on the corner of Third Street and Sycamore. On one side was the massive brick trolley terminal. Across the street was the Johnston Emergency Hospital, with its five pointed dormers; there was also a hotel, but he knew from his newspapers that Roosevelt would stop at the Gilpatrick, farther along on Third. Schrank kept walking.

The Gilpatrick Hotel, 223–225 Third Street, Milwaukee; a converted trunk factory, the Gilpatrick wasn't as lavish as some of the places Roosevelt stopped on his cross-country tour. COURTESY HISTORIC PHOTO COLLECTION/MILWAUKEE PUBLIC LIBRARY

In the next block he passed several more hotels—the Davidson, the Atlas, the Randolph, the Charlotte, and the Schlitz, the last of these set next to a welcoming beer garden. Crossing Grand Street, he saw a bookbinder, a sign painter, a brass workshop, a piano factory, a drug store, three movie houses, and the New Star Theater, but no more hotels. In the next block were the Milwaukee Lithographing & Engraving Company and the Riverside Printing Company, and a saloon. An alley bisected the street, and on the far side, in front of him, stood the Gilpatrick Hotel.

The narrow stone building, five stories tall, was more modest than the posh hotels the third termer usually favored. A fire escape snaked down the façade, and a short tower jutted from an upper corner, apparently meant to lend a touch of elegance. Mounted over the tower an electric sign flickered HOTEL GILPATRICK. Above the front door, rising over the sidewalk, was a square metal canopy supported by two thick columns.

Schrank continued up Third Street. At the next corner, Cedar, he turned east and entered a short, triangular block of West Water Street. To his right was a carpentry shop and a row of stores. Across the street, on the corner of the same alley that ran beside the Gilpatrick, he saw the Argyle Hotel. He noted the location.

The rest of the afternoon he spent roaming the streets of Milwaukee. The city was known as *Deutsch-Athen,* "German Athens," and everywhere Schrank could feel the influence of his countrymen—in the Teutonic architecture, the German-language newspapers, and the guttural accents overheard on the sidewalk. Milwaukee was home to 375,000 people, and it was said that half of them spoke German; in some neighborhoods the shops posted signs assuring patrons, ENGLISH SPOKEN HERE.

At ten fifteen that night, Schrank returned to the Argyle Hotel. Passing between two storefronts, he walked up a flight of stairs to a cramped office, where he found clerk Robert M. Lenten. Signing the register as Walter Ross, he paid in advance and was given the last vacant room, Number 1, located in the back of the building, overlooking the Milwaukee River. As Lenten showed him to the room, he joked that the gentleman had better stay away from the window if he didn't want to fall in. John Schrank laughed.

When the Colonel's train left Chicago on Monday afternoon, his evening's speech was already typed and ready. It was a fine speech. He only hoped he would have the chance to deliver it. Even after forty hours' rest, his voice was still weak, and barring a miraculous recovery, he might be able to make only a few introductory remarks tonight and then have to sit through the humiliation of someone else reading his words. Today he wouldn't appear at the whistle-stops but would have Congressman Cooper offer his apologies and make some remarks on his behalf. In Milwaukee, the schedule had also been pared down. Rather than parading from the station to a hotel, he would have a quiet dinner on the *Mayflower,* then go directly to the Auditorium.

As the train sped northward, the change in plans was proving contentious. In Chicago, Wheeler P. Bloodgood had come aboard. A member of the Wisconsin Progressive Committee, Bloodgood had traveled from Milwaukee to meet the Colonel and escort him to the city. Now when the committeeman heard the revised schedule, he pleaded with Cecil Lyon and Dr. Terrell that the Colonel go to the Gilpatrick Hotel as originally announced, so as not to disappoint his supporters. But Lyon and Terrell were adamant that Roosevelt stay on the *Mayflower.*

At Racine, twenty-five miles south of Milwaukee, a trim man with a handlebar mustache boarded. He was A. O. Girard, dispatched by the Milwaukee committee to deliver some documents. Girard had been a captain in the Rough Riders and had previously acted as the Colonel's bodyguard. Seeing his old friend, Roosevelt gave him a warm handshake and then asked him to stay by him for the rest of the afternoon and evening. Girard promised not to leave the Colonel's side.

⎯ ⌣ ⎯

The third termer was due at the Union Depot at five p.m. At three o'clock, John Schrank walked into Herman Rollfink's saloon at 215 Third Street, across from the Gilpatrick Hotel. He ordered the first of half a dozen beers, and as he drank, his customarily tight tongue began to loosen. He was a journalist "out on an investigating trip," he told bartender Paul Thume, pointing to the newspapers protruding from his coat pockets. Thume said that he was thinking of going out West to earn some cash, but Schrank told him the South was the place for men who wanted to make money. When Schrank asked where he could find a room, Thume mentioned a place, but Schrank complained that a dollar a day was too much to spend; he didn't want to pay more than seventy-five cents, he said.

After an hour, Schrank left the bar. He had no fixed destination in mind, but today above all days, he felt the urge to move. Heading down Third Street, he turned onto Wells and crossed the iron bridge that he could see from his hotel window. On the other side of the river, the roadway opened into a triangular plaza dominated by city hall and its square clock tower. In the center of the plaza was a round fountain, where carriage horses stopped to drink; rising above the basin was a bronze statue of an ordinary-looking man reaching down to scratch a dog's head.

Coming to wide, bustling Wisconsin Avenue, Schrank turned east, toward Lake Michigan. Ahead of him loomed the gray granite pile of the federal building, its pitched roof festooned with gargoyles and finials and surmounted by another clock tower. At the end of the street was a bluff overlooking the lake. Atop the cliff stood Lake Front Depot, a long, severe building with yet another clock rising above the train sheds. Across from the station he saw a park. He went in.

There were benches, but Schrank didn't sit. He'd been walking as though to outpace his thoughts, or his destiny. But now, standing a stone's throw from the great blue lake, he knew the hour was near. If only this cup could pass from him. But great sins had been committed. A president had been murdered. The sacred tradition of the third term had been broken. The nation was facing civil war and foreign occupation. For eleven years he had longed for a savior to step forward and end the wickedness. Then, belatedly, he'd understood that he, John Flammang Schrank, had been chosen as the instrument of divine vengeance. He would die in the act, of course. The mob would tear him to pieces. But his death would only underscore the necessity and justice of his deed. It would be an honor to give his life for his country and for the principle of republican government. God's will be done. A mighty fortress is our God.

Turning, he started toward the Gilpatrick Hotel.

———

At six o'clock, the Colonel's train pulled into the Union Depot, an hour behind schedule. Among the waiting dignitaries were Frank Cannon, secretary of the Citizen's Business League; former Governor George W. Peck; Oliver Remey of the Milwaukee Press Club; and Francis E. Davidson, chairman of the Progressive Party of Milwaukee County. Wheeler P. Bloodgood introduced Davidson to the Colonel.

"The boys are all anxious that you have your supper at the Hotel Gilpatrick," Davidson told him, "and we have made arrangements there so that you can rest. The hotel is not one of the best known hotels in Milwaukee, but it is a quiet and good place. The owner has been a great friend of the county committee, and it would please us all very much if you would come."

Taken aback, the Colonel said he'd planned to have dinner here on the *Mayflower*. Cecil Lyon, O. K. Davis, and Dr. Terrell murmured their agreement. But then Roosevelt asked Davidson whether the local boys would be disappointed.

"We do not want to do anything that will inconvenience you," Davidson answered carefully, "but I think they will be disappointed."

Summoning his authority as a physician, Dr. Terrell repeated that the Colonel needed his rest. O. K. Davis agreed, reminding him that he had a full schedule the next day, with stops at Indianapolis and Champaign, then a speech in Louisville on Wednesday night. But when the Colonel asked whether his absence would harm the party's chances in the city, the Milwaukee contingent urged him to go to the hotel. Davis said that the Colonel was too exhausted to push his way through unruly crowds. The Milwaukeeans countered that even now supporters were lining the streets and would already be wondering what was taking so long.

Finally, the Colonel looked at Davis and said, "I want to be a good Indian, O. K."

The committeemen made to leave, as if all had been decided. But Dr. Terrell wouldn't concede. What about police protection, he wanted to know. It was essential that the Colonel not have to fight through crowds either at the station or at the hotel.

Davidson assured him that there was ample protection. But he didn't mention that two days before, he had gone to discuss security arrangements with Milwaukee's longtime chief of police, John T. Janssen. The chief hadn't been in, and Davidson had met instead with an inspector, who had been disturbingly nonchalant. Davidson had started to leave headquarters afterward, then had gone back to underscore the importance of the assignment. But the inspector had only said he'd guarded the Colonel before and knew what to do. Now, on the *Mayflower*, Davidson assured Terrell and the others that the depot and the streets around the hotel and Auditorium would be kept clear. He only hoped that Milwaukee's finest wouldn't make a liar of him.

Finally, the Colonel put an end to the discussion. "I am going," he announced, and gave a salute with his right hand.

Dr. Terrell went back to get the Colonel's heavy army overcoat, and the party filed out of the *Mayflower*. With Davidson and Girard positioned on one side and Cecil Lyon on the other, the Colonel passed a marching band and a throng of well-wishers kept behind a tall wrought-iron fence. A newsboy named Howard Cunningham was allowed to trot alongside his hero, toting a bundle of papers under his arm. Police sergeant Robert Flood also walked with the candidate, wearing a long blue coat with stripes on the sleeve and a cavalry hat similar to the Colonel's own. Only one or two other policemen were in evidence.

Avoiding the depot's waiting room, the men exited through an inconspicuous side gate. Two open automobiles were waiting. The Colonel took a seat in the first and the others climbed into the second, larger car.

The streets en route to the Gilpatrick were jammed with cheering crowds, just as Davidson had said. The Colonel waved his hat but was too tired to stand or return their shouts. In a few minutes, the cars pulled up to the hotel's front door. Spectators had been kept back to the middle of the street, and the sidewalk was clear. But the good order seemed to owe more to the innate lawfulness of Milwaukeeans than to any effort by the police department, since just one patrolman was stationed in front of the building. Passing through the lobby, the Colonel tramped upstairs to his suite. With a few minutes to spare before dinner, he fell into a rocking chair and immediately nodded off. It was the first time O. K. Davis had ever seen him nap.

⁓

At 5:45, John Schrank was waiting with the crowd in front of the Hotel Gilpatrick. A little after six, he heard the cheers and saw two automobiles stop in front of the hotel. He watched the third termer and his men disappear inside. The cars remained in front, he noted.

At seven o'clock, he went back to Rollfink's saloon. Strangely agitated, he made more small talk with bartender Paul Thume. Then he asked the band to play "The Star-Spangled Banner," and they complied with the odd request. Odder still was the jig the portly stranger danced during the anthem. Afterward, he bought the musicians a drink and ordered a round for the entire bar. That seemed strange, too, for a man who didn't want to pay an extra twenty-five cents for a hotel room.

As it neared eight o'clock, Schrank went to the saloon door and peered into the darkness. The street was thick with people for more than a block in every direction. Stepping onto the sidewalk, he began to shoulder his way toward the hotel. Curious to get a look at the Bull Moose, Herman Rollfink followed. Schrank worked his way to the middle of the road. Knowing that the Colonel would come out at any moment, the crowd had pressed against the car. Schrank pushed his way to the second row, less than ten feet away.

The Colonel and his party had dinner in the hotel dining room, on the first floor. The room was closed to the public, and Captain Girard was stationed in a chair outside. About seven o'clock, a dark, clean-shaven man approached and said he had come from New York to see the Colonel. Girard told him that was impossible, but the man persisted. Finally, Girard forced him away. A little while afterward, the captain saw him make a purchase at the hotel cigar stand and then disappear.

Outside, a Progressive committeeman named Thomas Taylor sat behind the wheel of the lead car. Ten thousand people were expecting the Colonel at the Auditorium at eight o'clock, but it was later than that now. Beside the car, a man dressed in the rough clothes of a laborer was also standing, waiting.

It was time. After dinner, the Colonel and his aides returned to the suite for a few minutes. Slipping into his tan overcoat, the Colonel felt to make sure that his speech was in his breast pocket and his spectacles case was tucked into his vest. Then, just as the party was leaving, Dr. Terrell developed a nosebleed. He went into the bathroom, and O. K.

Davis stayed behind to help, along with one of the Colonel's stenographers, John McGrath. The others turned into the corridor and headed for the staircase.

From the driver's seat, Thomas Taylor saw the Colonel come down the steps to the lobby. A photographer's flash-lamp went off with a *whoosh*. Taylor started the engine.

◆ ◆

A. O. Girard was guarding the front door when the Colonel came out. The crowd had pressed onto the sidewalk, and now Girard and Sergeant Murray of the Milwaukee Police Department went ahead to make sure the way was clear. Cecil Lyon and Elbert Martin came next. Henry F. Cochems, member of the Wisconsin Progressive Committee, walked beside the Colonel, with Philip Roosevelt just behind. Fred Luettich, a big man who guarded the door at the Milwaukee party headquarters, was with them. As the men passed from the bright hotel into the dark street, they couldn't see the crowd distinctly, but they could hear the cheers.

Girard called for people to move away from the automobile. Ordinarily Martin or another aide would climb into the car first and stand on the side toward the crowd while the Colonel entered. But tonight, since the sidewalk was unobstructed, Martin stepped away from the open door to let the Colonel go ahead. The Colonel climbed in and took his seat, with no one between him and the throng, a few feet away. Cochems boarded next, then Philip Roosevelt, while Martin waited at the car door. Lyon was standing next to the driver, and Leuttich was in front, beside the bumper. The Colonel stood and waved his hat. As he did, he was silhouetted against the light spilling from the hotel door.

As Martin stepped into the car, he glanced toward the crowd. He saw a man, not a dozen feet away. The man removed his hand from his pocket and extended his arm. In his hand was a nickel-plated revolver. He leveled the pistol between the heads of two men standing in front of him. He fired.

NINE

"He Pinked Me, Harry"
Monday, October 14, evening

THE COLONEL WAS STANDING IN THE CAR, WAVING TO THE CROWD, when he saw the flash. There was the unmistakable retort of a gunshot. His knees buckled, and he clutched the upholstered seat back. He straightened himself, raised his hat again, and gave a reassuring smile. Then he slumped to the seat.

Even before the shot was fired, Elbert Martin was leaping from the car. He landed on the shooter as the revolver rose for a second round. Seizing the man by the shoulders, Martin threw him facedown onto the trolley tracks and planted his knee in the small of his back. The pistol's nickel barrel pointed up at him from beneath the assassin's shoulder. Martin wrenched the gun away. Then he dug his fingers into the man's throat as though to kill him.

Carl Leuttich had also seen the muzzle flash. Standing in front of the car, he'd flown over the hood and landed on Martin and the shooter, where a confused city policeman began beating him with a nightstick. Cecil Lyon was dancing from side to side, his own pistol drawn, looking to get a shot in.

A. O. Girard called to Martin, "Give me the man's revolver!"

Without taking his hands from the shooter's throat, Martin yelled, "I'll be damned if I do!"

Two more policemen drew near, and Lyon turned his gun on them. "If you advance another step I'll kill you both," he said. They retreated.

The crowd surged forward, and Lyon aimed his pistol at them. "Get back there!" he warned. They retreated as well.

An immigrant laborer named Frank Buskowsky had been standing to the right of the gunman. Seeing the pistol rise, he'd knocked it away just as the shot was fired. Then he'd jumped on the assassin, yelling, "Kill him! Kill him! Kill the damn scoundrel!"

Thinking Buskowsky meant Roosevelt, a policeman shouted, "What the hell is the matter with you?"

When Buskowsky's imperfect English failed him, the officer clubbed him over the head and dragged him away.

In the back seat of the automobile, Henry Cochems wrapped his arm around the Colonel and asked if he were all right.

The Colonel said, "He pinked me, Harry."

The crowd had taken up the cry, "Kill him! Kill him! Kill him!" But the Colonel pulled himself to his feet. "Don't hurt him!" he called. "Bring him to me!"

Martin jerked the man upright, still clutching the revolver in his other hand. With the help of Girard and the policemen, he hauled the assassin to the side of the car. Several people were grabbing for the gun, but ex-footballer Harry Cochems snatched it by the barrel and slipped it inside his overcoat. Martin twisted the shooter's face toward the Colonel.

It was a perfectly ordinary face, moon-shaped, clean-shaven. The Colonel peered into the heavy-lidded eyes, but the man said nothing.

The Colonel ordered, "Officers, take charge of him and see that no harm is done to him." Sergeant William Murray and detectives Louis Hartman, Harry Ridenour, and Valentine Skierawski seized the prisoner. Forming a flying wedge, they fought their way down the sidewalk to the Gilpatrick lobby and then raced through the dining room and into the hotel kitchen.

They searched the man for other weapons, but he told them, "My gun is gone. Your people took it away from me." Girard pushed him into a chair and held him there while a patrol wagon was called.

Upstairs, Dr. Terrell and John McGrath had been tending to the doctor's nosebleed when they heard the gun go off. McGrath rushed to the open window. "The Colonel's shot!" he yelled. The two ran downstairs and pushed their way through the crowd.

By the time they reached the car, the Colonel was seated again. He ordered Thomas Taylor to drive him to the Auditorium, but Terrell demanded to see the wound. Cochems told the Colonel he must go to the hospital and directed Taylor there. But the Colonel insisted he was fine and repeated his order to go to the Auditorium.

"No, Colonel," begged Cochems, "let's go to the hospital."

"You get me to that speech," the Colonel hissed. "It may be the last one I shall ever deliver, but I am going to deliver this one." Turning to the crowd, he said, "We are going to the hall. We are going to the hall." To Taylor he commanded, "Start the machine. Go ahead, go on."

O. K. Davis and Philip Roosevelt also beseeched the Colonel to go to the hospital, but they were no more successful than the others. Taylor put the car in gear, and it began to creep along the swarming roadway, with some of the Colonel's aides walking alongside. The crowd was still cheering, and as the men got farther from the hotel, they could see that the spectators had no idea what had happened.

In the car, Terrell insisted on seeing the wound. "No," the Colonel told him, "this is my big chance, and I am going to make that speech if I die doing it."

When they had rounded the corner onto Wells Street, Harry Cochems took the assassin's nickel revolver out of his overcoat and showed it to the Colonel.

"A Colt .38 has an ugly drive," the Colonel said.

John McGrath had taken a seat on the Colonel's right side. "Why, Colonel," he said, "you have a hole in your overcoat. He has shot you."

The Colonel answered, "I know it," and opened the heavy coat. His frock coat and black vest were covered with a seeping red stain. The Colonel's face went pale.

The aides implored him to go to the hospital. But he turned to Cochems and with a thin smile said, "I know I am good now; I don't know how long I may be. This may be my last talk in this cause to our people, and while I am good I am going to drive to the hall and deliver my speech." The sidewalks were filled with cheering crowds, but the Colonel didn't return their waves.

Fifteen thousand people jammed the streets outside the Auditorium. The car inched to a side door, and the Colonel gingerly climbed out. As he passed Elbert Martin, he told him, "I'm mighty glad it was one of our crowd that saved me, instead of an outsider."

Inside, Wisconsin committeeman Wheeler Bloodgood was waiting for them. Seeing that the two autos would be filled, he had made the short walk from the hotel to the hall. Now, with no inkling of the shooting, he asked the Colonel if he would mind waiting for a few minutes, while the donations were collected.

"Well, Mr. Bloodgood, I guess it's all right," the Colonel told him. "You know, I have been shot. I've got a bullet in me right now, but I'm going to make that speech if it's the last thing on earth I do."

He was ushered into a large dressing room. Ten thousand people had crammed the Auditorium, and their electric hum permeated the space. Then someone in the crowd started clapping impatiently, and others took it up.

The Colonel finally consented to have Dr. Terrell examine him. Unbuttoning the bloody frock coat and vest, Roosevelt exposed his shirt, the red stain even more shocking against the starched white cotton. He lifted the shirt and woolen undershirt. Just below the right breast was a jagged opening half an inch across.

O. K. Davis hurried to the stage, which was crowded with celebrities and committeemen. Going to Francis Davidson, the county chairman, he asked whether there were any doctors in the hall. When Davidson asked why, Davis told him that the Colonel had been shot. The chairman motioned to a man seated on the stage, Dr. Sayle, and two more in the audience, Drs. Stratton and Sorenson, and all rushed to the dressing room, where Dr. Terrell was still examining the wound.

The Colonel inhaled deeply but coughed up no blood. "It's all right, doctor," he said. "It didn't go through." He insisted he felt no pain. The physicians agreed that the bullet probably hadn't penetrated a lung, but they told him he must not give his speech.

The Colonel asked, "Has anyone a clean handkerchief?"

One was offered, and he laid it over the wound and buttoned his clothes. "Now, gentlemen," he said, "let's go in."

As the Colonel strode onstage, he was greeted by a tremendous roar. He and his party took their seats while Selden P. Delaney, dean of the Episcopal All Saints Cathedral in Milwaukee, gave the invocation: "Bless our land with honorable industry and purity of heart; defend our liberty, preserve our unity, and save us from all violence and discord."

When Delaney had finished, the Colonel leaned to Cochems and said, "You tell them, Harry."

Cochems rose. "We have with us a guest who embodies the Democratic qualities of Jefferson and the Republican qualities of Lincoln," he began in a quavering voice; "the one man who towers above all others in service to his country—the good citizen, the good father, the good civilian, but above all, the good soldier. Ladies and gentlemen, I have something to tell you, and I hope you will receive it with calmness. As he left his hotel, a dastardly hand aimed a revolver at the Colonel, and he will speak to you, though there is a bullet somewhere in his breast."

There was hissing from the crowd. "Fake! Fake!" a man shouted.

"Are you hurt?" called someone else.

The Colonel went to the front of the stage, where a table had been placed, and raised his hand for quiet. Before the shooting, his vocal chords had been so strained that he'd considered having someone else read his speech, but now his voice rang out. "No, it's no fake," he said with a smile. He opened his coat and exposed his bloody vest. There were gasps. Women screamed.

"Friends, I shall have to ask you to be as quiet as possible," he went on. "I do not know whether you fully understand that I have been shot, but it takes more than that to kill a bull moose." There was a huge ovation.

The Colonel reached into his breast pocket for the manuscript of his speech. When he pulled it out, he saw two ragged holes perforating every folded page. He hesitated, as though realizing for the first time how narrow his escape had been.

He raised the sheaf of papers for the crowd to see. "But, fortunately, I had my manuscript, so, you see, I was going to make a long speech. And, friends, there is a bullet—there is where the bullet went through—" he indicated the holes—"and it probably saved the bullet from going into my heart. The bullet is in me now, so that I cannot make a very long speech. But I will try my best."

As he'd started to speak, the Colonel's heart had begun to pound. There was little pain, but the wound felt hot. His breath was short and shallow, and he couldn't form lengthy sentences. Seeing that he was unsteady on his feet, aides moved to the floor in front of the stage, next to the reporters, the band, and color guard, in case he collapsed. The Colonel noticed them and took a step back from the edge.

He resumed. "First of all, I want to say this about myself: I have altogether too important things to think of to feel any concern over my own death; and now I cannot speak to you insincerely within five minutes of being shot. I am telling you the literal truth when I say that my concern is for many other things. It is not in the least for my own life. I want you to understand that I am ahead of the game, anyway. No man has had a happier life that I have led; a happier life in every way. . . . I am in this cause with my whole heart and soul. I believe that the Progressive movement is for making life a little easier for all our people; a movement to try to take the burdens off the men and especially the women and children of this country. I am absorbed in the success of that movement. ... I don't know anything about who the man was who shot me tonight. He was seized at once by one of the stenographers in my party, Mr. Martin, and I suppose is now in the hands of the police. He shot to kill. He shot—the shot, the bullet went in here—I will show you."

He unbuttoned his vest, revealing the bloodstained shirt.

A gray-haired woman in the audience called, "Mr. Roosevelt, we all wish you would be seated."

The Colonel looked at her. "I thank you, madam, but I don't mind a bit."

O. K. Davis slipped off the stage to telephone Progressive Party headquarters in New York and Chicago.

The Colonel went on: "I am going to ask you to be as quiet as possible for I am not able to give the challenge of the bull moose quite as loudly. Now, I do not know who he was or what party he represented. He was a coward. He stood in the darkness in the crowd around the automobile and when they cheered me, and I got up to bow, he stepped forward and shot me in the darkness.

"Now, friends, of course, I do not know, as I say, anything about him; but it is a very natural thing that weak and vicious minds should be inflamed to acts of violence by the kind of awful mendacity and abuse that have been heaped upon me for the last three months by the papers of not only Mr. Debs but of Mr. Wilson and Mr. Taft.

"Friends, I will disown and repudiate any man of my party who attacks with such foul slander and abuse any opponent of any other party; and now I wish to say seriously to all the daily newspapers, to the Republican, the Democratic, and the Socialist parties, that they cannot, month in and month out and year in and year out, make the kind of untruthful, bitter assault that they have made and not expect that brutal, violent natures, or brutal and violent characters, especially when the brutality is accompanied by a not very strong mind; they cannot expect that such natures will be unaffected by it.

"Now, friends, I am not speaking for myself at all. I give you my word, I do not care a rap about being shot; not a rap." More applause.

"I have had a good many experiences in my time and this is one of them. What I care for is my country. I wish I were able to impress upon my people—our people—the duty to feel strongly but to speak the truth of their opponents."

The Colonel appeared to stagger, and Dr. Terrell went to his side. "I am not sick at all," he told him. "I am all right. Let me alone." Terrell retook his seat.

"I cannot tell you of what infinitesimal importance I regard this incident as compared with the great issues at stake in this campaign, and I ask it not for my sake, not the least in the world, but for the sake of our common country, that they make up their minds to speak only the truth, and not to use the kind of slander and mendacity which if taken seriously must incite the weak and violent natures to crimes of violence. Don't you make any mistake. Don't you pity me. I am all right. I am all right and you cannot escape listening to this speech either." The crowd laughed.

"And now, friends, this incident that has just occurred—this effort to assassinate me—emphasizes to a peculiar degree the need of the Progressive movement. Friends, every good citizen ought to do everything in his or her power to prevent the coming of the day when we shall see in this country two recognized creeds fighting one another, when we shall see the creed of the 'Havenots' arraigned against the creed of the 'Haves.' When that day comes then such incidents as this tonight will be commonplace in our history. When you make poor men—when you permit the conditions to grow such that the poor man as such will be swayed by his sense of injury against the men to try to hold what they improperly have won, when that day comes, the most awful passions will be let loose, and it will be an ill day for our country."

A few aides approached, but he turned them away. "My friends are a little more nervous than I am. Don't you waste any sympathy on me.

I have had an A-1 time in life and I am having it now. . . . And now, friends, I shall have to cut short much of the speech that I meant to give you, but I want to touch on just two or three of the points."

Reading from his bullet-torn text, the Colonel assured his audience that the Progressives stood for all their fellow citizens, without regard to nationality or creed. He had been planning to answer Wilson's recent comments in regard to labor unions, he told them, but under the circumstances he would concentrate on his own record and plan.

Returning to the stage, Davis saw that the Colonel seemed pale and faltering. He approached and touched his arm.

The Colonel gave him a venomous look. "What do you want?"

"Colonel," Davis said, "I want to stop you. You have spoken thirty-five minutes. Don't you think that is long enough?"

"No, sir, I will not stop until I have finished this speech. You can't stop me. Nobody can stop me!" And he continued reading from his text.

A short time later, Dr. Terrell approached the Colonel again. They spoke briefly. Then turning to the crowd the Colonel said, "I know these doctors. When they get hold of me they will never let me go back, and there are just a few things more that I want to say to you."

He elaborated his strong record against the trusts while president. "I tell you, and I told you at the beginning, I do not say anything on the stump that I do not believe. I do not say anything I do not know. Let any of Mr. Wilson's friends on Tuesday point out one thing or let Mr. Wilson point out one thing he has done about the trusts as governor of New Jersey."

The Colonel laid his manuscript on the table while he made more impromptu remarks. Elbert Martin jumped to his feet and scooped up the pages, hoping to force the Colonel to quit. But Roosevelt demanded his text back. "Teach them not to grab," he said, and the crowd laughed again.

Addressing the people of Wisconsin, he cited the state's history in the progressive vanguard and asked them to join his national movement. "When I took office as president—" Turning to Dr. Terrell, he asked, "How long have I been speaking?"

The doctor looked at his watch. "Three quarters of an hour."

"Very well, I will speak for fifteen minutes more," the Colonel said. More laughter and applause.

He then turned his remarks to the Democrats and his erstwhile friends the Republicans—"not the Republican Party," he corrected himself, but "the bosses in control of the Republican party," who had stolen the nomination in August. "There are only two ways you can vote this year. You can be progressive or reactionary. Whether you vote Republican or Democratic it does not make any difference, you are voting reactionary."

The Colonel paused to take a sip of water, and the physicians pleaded with him again to stop the speech. He assured them, "It is getting better and better as time goes on." To the audience he said, "If these doctors don't behave themselves, I won't let them look at me at all." More cheers.

After eighty minutes, the Colonel was clearly spent. At last, he concluded: "I ask you to look at our declaration and hear and read our platform about social and industrial justice and then, friends, vote for the Progressive ticket without regard to me, without regard to my personality, for only by voting for that platform can you be true to the cause of progress throughout this Union. I appeal to you to join with us, to work, to fight, but with charity, with kindness, and with generosity, to bring about social and industrial justice." The audience roared, but he seemed not to hear. He dropped the last page of his speech to the floor and turned to Dr. Terrell. "Now," he said, "I am ready to go with you and do what you want."

TEN

"The Wound Is a Trivial One"
Monday, October 14, to Monday, October 21

THE COLONEL'S AIDES SOUGHT TO GUIDE HIM OFF THE PLATFORM, BUT the audience surged onstage, barring their route. Someone shouted, "Friends of Colonel Roosevelt, all stand back!" But the throng pressed forward, determined to shake his hand or touch his clothing. Forming ranks, the Colonel's men bulled their way to a pair of sliding metal doors. Two police officers fought off the crowd while the heavy doors were opened. In the scrimmage, Philip Roosevelt was separated from the others and barely managed to squeeze his slender frame through the doors as they slammed shut again.

The Colonel climbed into the back seat of his automobile. The three doctors and a few staff members tumbled after him, and the others scrambled into the second vehicle. As the car jounced through the dark streets, the Colonel tried to explain to O. K. Davis why he had been hell-bent on giving the speech. When this campaign had turned vicious, he said, he'd realized that a lunatic might try to kill him. But in Cuba, back in 1898, he'd decided that if he were ever wounded, he would carry on with his responsibilities as best he could. And the same held just as true in the present fight as in the Spanish-American War. Tonight, he hadn't known how seriously he was injured, and he hadn't wanted to know until he'd done his duty.

A few minutes later the cars squealed to a stop in front of the Johnston Emergency Hospital, across from Union Station. The hospital had been telephoned to expect the former president, and now his men helped him up the steep front steps, through the reception area reeking with disinfectant, and into the elevator. As they made their way to the upstairs operating room, the Colonel didn't cease talking. What messages had been sent about the shooting? he wanted to know. What had the press been told? Would he be able to keep tomorrow's engagements in Indiana and Illinois? Before the doctors could examine him, he dictated a telegram to Mrs. Roosevelt:

> *Am in excellent shape. Made an hour and a half speech. The wound is a trivial one. I think they will find it merely glanced on a rib and went somewhere into a cavity of the body. It certainly did not touch a lung and isn't a particle more serious than one of the injuries the boys used continually to be having. Am at the Johnston Emergency Hospital at the moment, but anticipate going right on with my engagements. My voice seems to be in good shape. Best love to Ethel.*

Mrs. Roosevelt already knew of the shooting. That evening she'd gone to see *The Merry Countess* at Manhattan's Casino Theater along with Laura Roosevelt, widow of Theodore's cousin J. West Roosevelt. When word of the attack reached the New York Progressive headquarters, via their direct telegraph line with the Chicago office, Laura's son Oliver was dispatched to the theater. The first report was that the Colonel hadn't been hurt, and so Mrs. Roosevelt remained smiling in her seat during intermission. But as the new act began, Oliver hurried back to say that the Colonel had in fact been wounded. Leaving the theater in tears, Mrs. Roosevelt rushed to Progressive offices at the Manhattan Hotel, on Madison Avenue and Forty-second Street, to wait for further bulletins. Ted Jr. had been notified by telephone, and he also hurried to the Manhattan. His sister Alice was at home in Cincinnati when she received a phone call from her friend Ruth McCormick; on hearing the news, Alice's first thought was, *It has come at last.* Although the family never discussed the threat of assassination, she worried about it, and she was certain the others did, too.

Alice liked to say that her father wanted to be "the bride at every wedding and the corpse at every funeral," and tonight in Milwaukee, first in the Auditorium and now in the Johnston Emergency Hospital, the Colonel was relishing his role of wounded warrior. In the brightly lit operating room, he wanted to sit in a chair for his examination, but the doctors insisted he lie on the table. "You've got the best of me now," he smiled. "I'll have to do as you say."

He was maneuvered onto the tabletop, a plain pine board set in an iron frame. "I don't care a damn about finding the bullet," he said, "but I do hope they'll fix it up so I need not continue to suffer."

As the diminutive hospital superintendent, Regina White, cut off his bloody shirt and undershirt, she asked if he planned to press charges against the man who had shot him. The Colonel answered in a sympathetic tone, "I've not decided yet, but God help the poor fool under any circumstances."

The doctors cleaned the wound with iodine. Dr. Stratton bandaged it, but Miss White didn't approve of his handiwork and ordered it redone, causing the Colonel to laugh.

"That's nothing," Dr. Sayle told him, "she's been bossing us doctors for the past twenty years!"

"Oh, please—not quite that long," protested Miss White.

"Well, we'll knock off two and make it eighteen," the Colonel compromised.

The doctors tried to convince him to stay in the hospital overnight, but he wouldn't hear of it.

"I know if Mrs. Roosevelt were here she would insist upon your staying," Miss White told him.

"Young woman," he answered with a glance at the four pretty nurses nearby, "if Mrs. Roosevelt were here, I'm certain she would insist upon my leaving immediately."

Phone calls and telegrams were already pouring into the hospital, from supporters such as Medill McCormick, George Perkins, and Lyman Abbott, and from strangers all over the country. Dashing the Colonel's hopes, O. K. Davis telegraphed Progressive committees from Illinois to New Jersey, telling them to cancel their scheduled events. Meanwhile, Elbert Martin, Harry Cochems, and other witnesses went to the Central Police Station to identify the would-be assassin.

Wheeler Bloodgood's brother Joseph Colt Bloodgood happened to be visiting from Baltimore, where he was on the surgical staff at Johns Hopkins. Wheeler telephoned him, and he hurried to the hospital and joined the other doctors in the operating room. After a while, he came out and took O. K. Davis aside. "Get him out of here just as quickly as you can," he whispered. "This is no place for him." Davis called Medill McCormick in Chicago, and they agreed to put the Colonel on a train that night; it was left to McCormick to arrange medical attention in that city.

In the operating room, Miss White tied around her patient a shirt embroidered *Johnston Emergency Hospital*. Nurse Elvine Kucko shook the Colonel's hand and apologized on behalf of Milwaukee. He told her not to worry, that the shooting could have happened anywhere. Miss White expressed relief that at least it had been a New Yorker and not a Milwaukeean who had pulled the trigger.

"You cruel little woman!" the Colonel teased, reminding her that New York was his hometown.

Miss White presented him with a sealed enveloped containing the studs and collar buttons they had taken from his shirt.

"No, you can't do that with me," he told her. "I want to see! I don't intend to get down to Chicago without the flat button for the back of my collar."

Laughing, Miss White tore open the envelope and made a show of counting each stud and button into the Colonel's palm. But the cherished back collar button was tangled with one of the others, and he insisted on a recount before accepting her tally.

When his metal spectacles case was retrieved from his vest pocket, it was found to have a neat round hole through one corner. That along with the thick, folded manuscript for his speech had apparently slowed the bullet and kept it from doing more damage. It seemed that the Colonel's myopia and long-windedness had spared his life. Said the national chairman of the Progressive campaign, Senator Joseph Dixon of Montana, "That must have been a great speech if it could stop a bullet that way."

A roentgenologist, J. S. Janssen, came to take some X-rays. "Oh, then you're Dutch," the Colonel said on hearing the name. "Well, I'm Dutch, too. The Dutch are a great race."

Janssen took him to the X-ray room, where two exposures were made. While the technician went to develop the films, the Colonel was helped to his automobile. The hospital staff fretted that his overcoat wasn't warm enough, but he assured them he would be all right. Escorted by a squad of detectives, he was driven to Union Station, just across the park.

A hundred people had gathered at the depot, and after the Colonel boarded, his private train was moved fifty yards down the tracks so he wouldn't be disturbed. It was decided that Dr. Sayle would accompany him to Chicago, equipped with rubber gloves, surgical instruments, and extra bandages in case the wound reopened. In the *Mayflower*, he and Dr. Terrell followed the Colonel to his stateroom and helped him undress.

The Colonel had the habit of shaving in the evening, and insisted on doing so tonight. As he waited for some hot water, he removed the studs from Miss White's envelope and inserted them in a clean shirt, in case he didn't have the strength to do it in the morning. Then, humming, he stood at the tiny mirror and performed his toilet. By the time he climbed into bed, his heart was pounding and his breath

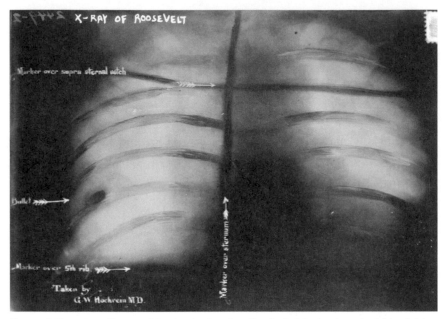

X-ray of Theodore Roosevelt's chest, showing the bullet lodged against his right rib cage.

was labored. But he gingerly rolled onto his good side and within two minutes had fallen asleep.

At eleven fifteen, Mr. Janssen arrived with the X-rays. The films were ambiguous, and he couldn't say whether the bullet had penetrated a lung or not. Drs. Terrell and Sayle believed it hadn't, while Harry Cochems and Philip Roosevelt feared it had. Feeling his responsibility as the only family member present, Philip ordered the Colonel taken back to the Johnston Emergency Hospital. Then he ran to the telephone room on the station's second floor to call Chicago headquarters and have noted surgeons John B. Murphy and Arthur Dean Bevan dispatched on the first train to Milwaukee. But Davis and Terrell had other ideas. At twelve forty-five, while Philip was making his call, they gave orders for the locomotive to start. Hearing the "All aboard!" the Colonel's cousin charged down the stairs four at a time, his woolen overcoat flapping and his fedora threatening to fly off his head. He leapt onto the rear of the *Mayflower* just as the car was leaving the platform.

While the Colonel was flirting with the nurses of the Johnston Emergency Hospital, his would-be assassin was causing an uproar at Milwaukee's Central Police Station. The drab brick building was located on the corner of Broadway and Oneida Street, three blocks east of the river and not far from the Argyle Hotel. Next door to the constabulary, and now a part of it, was an old stone armory, whose crenellations lent both buildings the air of a medieval dungeon. A mob of several hundred had chased the patrol wagon over the Oneida Street Bridge and now joined the crowd milling in front of the station. When the vehicle came into view, they began to chant, "Lynch him! Kill him!" As he was led out of the wagon and through a cordon of officers, the prisoner appeared relieved to gain the safety of the jail.

John Schrank after his arrest. "A man that wants a third term has no right to live," he told police.

He was taken to the main desk for booking, then upstairs to the sergeant's office. His clothes had been soiled in the fray; his hat and collar were missing, and his hair was disheveled. He sat facing Chief of Police John T. Janssen, whose dark handlebar mustache twitched as he began the questioning.

"What is your name?"

"Do I have to tell that tonight, sir?"

"Yes."

"I have to?"

"Yes."

"I have given the man below the promise that I will do that tomorrow, tell him all I know."

"Well, there is no reason for you to do that tomorrow," Janssen said. "If you do it this evening it will facilitate matters."

"I suppose I will inconvenience someone by not telling."

"Yes, you are helping a good deal by telling."

"Well, I come from New York."

"What is your name?" Janssen pressed.

"John Schrank."

"When did you come here from New York?" the chief asked. And so Schrank laid out the circuitous route that had brought him to Charleston, Augusta, Birmingham, Atlanta, Chattanooga, Nashville, Evansville, Louisville, Chicago, and Milwaukee. Among the bits of paper found in his pockets was a list of hotels where he had stayed in each city, written on a sheet of stationery from Nashville's Bismarck Hotel and Café.

"Why did you go to all those places?" Janssen asked.

"Because I wanted to meet that man."

"Well, what object did you have in mind to do when you went around in these different places?"

"I had in mind to meet him, and he escaped me every time; he escaped me in Atlanta and Chattanooga."

"What did he escape from? . . . Why did you want to meet him?"

"Because I wanted to put him out of the way. A man that wants a third term has no right to live."

"That is, you wanted to kill him?"

"I did."

"Have you any other reason in wanting to kill him?"

"I have."

"What is that?"

Schrank related his dream of eleven years before, when William McKinley had ordered him to avenge the president's murder. It was the first time he'd confided the visitation to anyone.

Had he ever met anarchists such as Emma Goldman or Leon Czolgosz? Janssen wanted to know.

"No, sir," Schrank answered. "I am not an anarchist or Socialist or Democrat or Republican; I just took up the thing the way I thought it was best to do."

In response to Janssen's questions, he gave the details of his birth in Bavaria, his journey to America, and his limited education.

"Ever been sick within the last year?" the chief asked.

"No, sir."

"Well, do you believe that that's a sane act that you committed this evening?"

"I believe it is my duty as a citizen to do; it's the duty of every citizen to do so."

"Have you ever been in trouble before?"

"No, sir; not that I remember."

"Ever been arrested for anything?"

"Not in my life."

"Have you ever been committed to an institution of any kind?"

"No, sir, never. I have always stayed out of trouble. I have never been in any trouble whatever, and this trouble I committed myself, now I am contented I did."

"You are not a bit sorry?"

"No, sir."

The Colonel's train arrived at Chicago's North Western Depot at 3:23 a.m., but instead of rushing their patient to the hospital, the doctors decided to let him sleep. At 5:12, John B. Murphy, chief of surgery at Mercy Hospital, came aboard, looking distinguished in his pinstripe suit, black bowler, and clipped gray beard. "Dr. Murphy reminds me of General Grant," the Colonel commented. "Grant was always the boss." To the doctor, he said, "You know, I have done a lot of hunting, and I know that a pistol slug will not kill a bull moose."

At 6:16, an ambulance pulled alongside the *Mayflower*. Assisted by Dr. Murphy, the Colonel made his way to the car's rear platform, where he had shaken so many hands and addressed so many supporters over the long campaign. Despite the early hour, some four hundred people were at the station to wish him well, and the city had sent forty policemen to keep them at a distance. The Colonel walked down the steps unaided and gave the reporters and police a cheerful good morning.

Someone called, "You had a pretty rough time last night, Colonel."

"We did have a middling lively time, didn't we?" he replied with a smile. Photographers' flash-lamps exploded, and everyone jumped. "Ah, shot again!" the Colonel said.

Cousin Philip stayed with him in the rear of the ambulance, while Dr. Murphy sat with the driver. Eleven minutes later, they reached Mercy Hospital, an impressive brick building on South Prairie Avenue. Founded in 1852, the institution was the first chartered hospital in the city, staffed by the Catholic order of the Sisters of Mercy.

As he entered, the Colonel tipped his hat to reporters and hospital staff. He was taken by wheelchair to Dr. Murphy's private suite, then, shortly before eight o'clock, to have more X-rays made. On the way, he read some telegrams and joked that he'd forgotten his pajamas. In the X-ray room, he thumbed through some magazines. Then he was settled in Room 314, where he promptly fell asleep.

When he awoke, he found waiting a breakfast of soft-boiled eggs, bacon, toast, and tea. He called in the reporters who had been traveling with the campaign. "Here they are, bless their hearts," he welcomed them. "They never deserted me."

The newspapermen crowded around the Colonel's narrow hospital bed, which seemed to barely accommodate him. How did he feel? one of the reporters asked.

"I feel as well as a man feels who has a bullet in him," he laughed before Dr. Terrell shooed everyone away. The Colonel waved as the newsmen filed from the room.

A hundred telegrams an hour were flooding the hospital. Dozens of books and floral arrangements arrived, which the Colonel ordered sent to other patients. Some jars of jelly and bunches of grapes were delivered and turned over to the police for inspection. The Colonel peppered the medical staff with questions, wanting to know the workings of each machine and the purpose of every medicine and procedure. "They'll be calling me Old Doc Roosevelt when I get out of here," he told them. Long-suffering Dr. Terrell tried to stem the flow of visitors, but when he reminded the Colonel that he must remain as quiet as possible, the patient ordered the doctor from the room.

Alice stepped off the train from Cincinnati, looking elegant as ever in a tailored black pinstripe suit and a dark-blue three-cornered hat graced with an ostrich feather. Medill and Ruth McCormick met her at the station; as she hurried from their car to the hospital, she was seen to wipe a tear from her cheek.

At four o'clock that afternoon, Mrs. Roosevelt left New York on the Twentieth Century Limited, along with Ted Jr., Ethel, and Alexander Lambert, the Colonel's personal doctor. "I am about the only person in the world who can make the Colonel abide by the instructions of his physicians," she said. "I am the only person who can manage him, and therefore I am going to his bedside."

At five o'clock, the patient's temperature began to rise, and the doctors feared an infection like the one that had killed William McKinley.

Alice Roosevelt Longworth *(left)* and her friend Ruth Hanna McCormick leaving Chicago's Mercy Hospital. On hearing of her father's shooting, Alice's first thought was, *It has come at last.*

Then, just as abruptly, the fever abated. The Colonel had a light supper and afterward read for a while, his head propped on three pillows. On his bedside table were the Bible, three copies of Lyman Abbott's magazine *The Outlook*, and Robert W. Chambers's *The Common Law*. In the evening, the Colonel asked for hot water and shaved himself in bed. He warned nurse Margaret Fitzgerald not to forget his breakfast. "And mind, I want a good one," he told her, "because I'm going to be hungry."

Mrs. Edith Roosevelt. "I am the only person who can manage him," she said, "and therefore I am going to his bedside."

At 9:15 on Tuesday morning, John Schrank was sitting on his cot in the Central Police Station.

Officer Conway appeared outside his cell. "Stand up, Schrank," he said. "Here is a man who wants to talk with you."

The morning found Schrank in a more belligerent mood than he'd been with Chief Janssen the night before. "Want to see the animal, do you?" he asked the reporter. "Well, here I am. Take a good look at me."

Conway asked if the prisoner wanted some breakfast.

"Well, I am not very hungry," Schrank said, "but I guess I better eat something."

The officer made him a sausage sandwich and a cup of coffee. Schrank drank the coffee but only picked at the food. "My appetite is not as good as I expected," he said. "I did not sleep very well. I am not accustomed to the bars."

"Did you worry about the act you committed?" the reporter asked.

"No. Why should I worry? My mind was made up about it, and I am not going to worry about it."

"Do you think of the punishment for your offense?"

"I haven't thought much about it, and I don't care much. I don't know what they will do with me, but I will take my medicine. I guess I will stand what they hand out to me."

"When did you last go to confession?"

"I think it was about sixteen years ago. It was so long ago I don't remember."

"Do you think your religion sanctions such work as this?"

"I refuse to answer," Schrank said, and began to pace.

When the reporter asked if he could take a photo, Schrank agreed, as long as it could be done in the hallway; he didn't want to be photographed behind bars.

The prisoner was fingerprinted. Then, at ten o'clock, Detective Hartman took him to the office of Inspector Lauberheimer, where his arrest warrant was read to him. Schrank listened intently but made no comment. On learning he was headed to court, he objected that he'd lost his hat in the scuffle last night. So an old hat was located in the station

John Schrank standing outside his cell, after refusing to be photographed behind bars.

John Schrank's Colt .38 revolver, purchased at a New York City gun shop for fourteen dollars.

for him to wear, and detectives Hartman and Skierawski escorted him to City Hall.

At 10:35, Schrank appeared in District Court before Judge N. B. Neelen. Two hundred people packed the courtroom. When Schrank's name was called, the spectators pressed against the rail for a better look and had to be held back by police.

Detective Hartman unwrapped the Colonel's bloody shirt and undershirt and held them up for the judge, along with Schrank's Colt .38.

District Attorney Winifred C. Zabel, young, handsome, and blonde, turned to Schrank. "You are charged with assault with intent to kill and murder," he said. "What do you plead, guilty or not guilty?"

"I plead guilty," Schrank answered.

The judge explained that the prisoner could ask for time to prepare his defense.

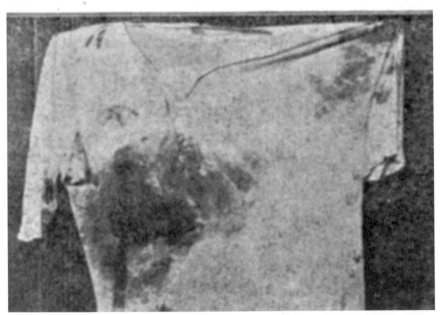
Theodore Roosevelt's bloody shirt (top) and undershirt, introduced as evidence in Milwaukee's District Court on October 15, the day after the shooting.

"I understand that," Schrank said. "I plead guilty, and I waive examination."

The maximum sentence was fifteen years. The judge levied bail of $7,500 and bound the prisoner over to the December sitting of the Municipal Court, so that the case would be heard after the election. He asked Schrank if that were acceptable, or if he'd like a faster hearing.

"No, I don't want one at once," Schrank said. "I wish to have some time."

"We will give you plenty of time," D.A. Zabel assured him.

For his own safety, the court considered transferring Schrank to the state penitentiary, seventy-five miles away at Waupun, but in the end he was remanded to the custody of William A. Arnold, an ex-newspaperman who two years before had been elected the first Socialist sheriff in the United States. Arnold ordered the spectators held in their seats until Schrank was led away, then the prisoner was taken across the street to the county jail.

As Schrank left, a reporter reminded Judge Neelen that President McKinley had died of blood poisoning. Wouldn't it be prudent, he suggested, to have the bullets from Schrank's gun examined for toxins? The judge agreed, and directed they be sent to Dean R. E. W. Sommers of Marquette University for a chemical analysis.

———

On Wednesday, the Colonel awoke feeling "like a bull moose." The courage he displayed after the shooting had only burnished the Roosevelt mythology, and nearly three thousand letters and telegrams had arrived at the hospital. After breakfast, he called in his stenographers, John McGrath and Elbert Martin, and dictated replies to some of the messages, which had come from world leaders such as Kaiser Wilhelm of Germany and King George V of England, as well as from political friends and foes and ordinary people.

Woodrow Wilson wrote, "Please accept my warmest sympathy and heartfelt congratulations that the wound is not serious."

President Taft wired, "I am greatly shocked to hear of the outrageous and deplorable assault made upon you, and I earnestly hope and pray that your recovery may be speedy and without suffering."

The Colonel considered a moment and then dictated a cool reply: "I appreciate your sympathetic inquiry and wish to thank you for it. Theodore Roosevelt."

Frank James, brother of the notorious Jesse, offered to form a hundred-man bodyguard if the Colonel resumed his campaign. The Colonel's old friend Bat Masterson declared, "The bullet has not yet been molded that can kill a man of your strength and character."

To Masterson the Colonel replied, "Bully for you, Bat."

But the letter the Colonel called "the bulliest" of all came from a Chicago boy, who had enclosed a ten-dollar bill:

Dear Mr. Roosevelt,

I hope you are getting on nicely. For I want you to be our President. If I was a man I'd help you, and work hard for you, and tell the people how good you are, but I am only 10 years old. Am sending money that I made selling flowers to help you, and I want you to keep it. I pray every night that you will soon be well, and I know that God is helping you. My brother, who is 5, prays too.

Yours truly,

Vincent Curtis Baldwin

Eighteen-year-old Mary Kelly, who was in the room directly above the Colonel, recuperating from an appendectomy, kissed a rose and had it delivered with a note: "I send you this red rose with my sincere wishes for a rapid recovery. . . . Lots of times I wake up in the night and wonder if you are resting well. I hope so."

Stenographer Elbert Martin, holding pages of Roosevelt's address. "That must have been a great speech if it could stop a bullet that way," said Senator Joseph Dixon of Montana.

The Colonel had the rose put in a vase on his bureau. "These little things touch me deeply," he said with a tear in his eye. "Poor little girl."

Newspapers around the world were condemning the attack and wishing the Colonel a speedy recovery. Wrote the *London Daily Mail,* "Mr. Roosevelt not only becomes the uncrowned king of America, but the most remarkable man in the world. He is the only politician whose words are less than his deeds." The assassination attempt "will not only win him the presidency," the paper predicted, "but will win for him for all time a place among the real heroes of this land."

The newspapers were eager to interview Elbert Martin, who abruptly found himself a national hero. "My regret is that I did not intercept the bullet that was meant for Colonel Roosevelt," he told a reporter. "When you work for Colonel Roosevelt, as I have done for the last six weeks, you come to feel such an enthusiastic devotion for the man that you could gladly die for him."

Martin's wife telegraphed, "I'm glad you did it, and I'm proud of you."

When Martin went to visit the Colonel in the hospital, Roosevelt refused to take his hand. "No, I will not shake hands with you," he told him. "I owe you a deeper debt of gratitude than a mere handshake can convey. I will shake hands with my other friends but not with you."

Martin blushed. "It really was nothing that I did," he said. "I saw the revolver gleaming in the light and instinctively I leaped from the automobile on the shoulders of the man who held it."

The Colonel kidded him that Cecil Lyon was holding a grudge against the stenographer. "You are the one who got in the way so Colonel Lyon couldn't shoot, too," he laughed.

Even his nurses became celebrities. Day nurse Welter received eleven proposals of marriage; night nurse Fitzgerald, nine.

Mrs. Roosevelt was due this morning, and the Colonel ordered his room straightened and his person primped. He sent out for toilet articles to be laid out for her. When the Twentieth Century Limited pulled in just before ten o'clock, Alice was at the station to meet it. On seeing her daughter, Mrs. Roosevelt said nothing but only peered into her electric-blue eyes. Alice told her, "There is no need for worry, Mother. He is all right." And then Edith broke into tears of relief.

Not long after, Nurse Welter gave a gentle knock on the Colonel's door and announced, "Mrs. Roosevelt." The Colonel grinned. "Fine, let her come in." Then the nurse withdrew so the couple could spend some time alone.

In the afternoon, Charles Merriam, Harry Cochems, and O. K. Davis were allowed a visit. Then, in her usual calm but determined manner, Mrs. Roosevelt gave instructions that the Colonel not be disturbed until five o'clock, when the children were to arrive. Ted, Ethel, and Alice stayed about an hour; Nick Longworth came, too, but he and his father-in-law did not discuss politics. The Colonel and Mrs. Roosevelt had a dinner of broiled squab, baked potato, bread, and tea, the first substantial meal he'd had since the shooting. Afterward, he lay in bed, with Mrs. Roosevelt sitting at his side, before turning out the light at eleven o'clock.

New X-rays, meanwhile, showed that the bullet had broken a rib. Dr. Terrell issued a statement that the patient was not yet out of danger, and that the crisis would most likely come on Friday, two days hence.

On Wednesday, Schrank awoke a little before seven o'clock. His appetite had returned, and for breakfast he ate five slices of bread with syrup and two cups of coffee. He sent for Sheriff Arnold and asked him to write to the Moseley House in Charleston, South Carolina, for his grip, but Arnold said that the police had already requested it. He also told Schrank that he could keep the rosary he was wearing around his neck, though the deputies wanted to remove it as a precaution against suicide.

"Now, Schrank," Arnold told him, "a number of people have asked to see you. Several newspapermen outside want to talk to you, and there is a man who wants to take your picture. Do you want to see them?"

"No," Schrank answered. "I have talked so much I am tired. I have told all I know, and I am not going to talk anymore. They have taken about forty pictures of me, and that ought to be enough for all the newspapers in the entire United States."

But Schrank said he would make an exception if any friends from New York came to see him.

"Are you expecting friends from New York?" asked Arnold quickly.

"No, but some might come."

"Who are those friends?"

"Oh, just some friends. I guess they won't come anyway, so it doesn't matter."

Schrank asked for paper and pencil and spent the morning writing feverishly in his cell.

Though he believed the defendant sane, District Attorney Zabel appointed a board of alienists to conduct an examination. When two of the doctors arrived that night, they found Schrank in an anxious state. But when a reporter came to interview him, the prisoner was composed.

"They're all trying to make me out crazy, as if I did it because I was out of my mind," Schrank complained. "That's not so. If Roosevelt hadn't been eager to get that third term he'd be alive now."

"Do you think he is dead?" the reporter asked. Since his arrest, Schrank hadn't inquired about the Colonel.

"I don't know anything about it," Schrank said. "What's more, I don't care a hang. They haven't told me if I killed him. I came here to do it, and if I didn't then anyhow, I did all I could. If he's alive, I made a bad job of it."

About the punishment waiting him, he said, "I don't care a damn about the electric chair. If they bring one in here now I'll sit in it, and they can go as far as they like."

Schrank's fellow prisoners had no doubt that he was in his right mind. Said James Clanton, charged with assault with intent to do great bodily harm, "I think he is sane. He may have been insane when he shot Roosevelt, but his is sane now. He jokes and laughs." Only once did Schrank mention the shooting, telling Clanton, "I am sorry I did it, but it is too late for that now. I must take my medicine. Anyway, this country can't stand for a third termer."

That same day, the laboratory announced that no trace of poison had been found on Schrank's bullets.

—⁓—

The Colonel slept well, and on Thursday morning he felt "hungry as a hunter." After breakfast with Mrs. Roosevelt, he read newspapers and answered another hundred letters and telegrams. Some bull moose steaks arrived from Montana and were stored in the hospital refrigerator. For lunch he ate chicken breast, baked potato, celery, beans, ice cream, and angel cake. "By George, I would like to go out for a good twelve-mile walk," he said. "You can't keep a squirrel on the ground."

As promised, Mrs. Roosevelt took an iron hand with visitors, prompting the Colonel to complain, "This isn't the rule of the people. This is boss rule." The couple spent most of the day reading and chatting, then the Colonel took a nap from three o'clock until four. The children visited twice, making the two-block trip from the apartment where they were staying. At five, Jane Addams was admitted briefly.

Shortly before six, a pair of twins were brought to the Colonel's room. On hearing of their births, the Colonel had said, "I would give anything to see the tots," and he had prevailed over Mrs. Roosevelt's objections. As the Colonel took one infant in each arm, both were squirming and one began to cry. "Tooty-too," he murmured, trying to calm them. "They are good Bull Moose timber," he ventured. "They aren't afraid to voice their protest against a situation or condition they believe unjust. Congratulate their mother for me." One of the boys was to be named Dominick after their father, the other, the Colonel learned, was to be called Theodore after him.

In the evening, the Colonel had no appetite and ate a light supper of only bread, milk, and a pot of tea. Shortly after ten, he turned out his light. At eleven forty-five, Mrs. Roosevelt looked in on him. "I am doing fine," he told her. "Don't worry."

Blood poisoning was no longer a threat, the doctors were saying. Tetanus, though still a possibility, was growing more remote with each passing day.

⸺

On Thursday morning, Schrank was feeling more relaxed. At ten o'clock, he finally grew tired of writing and strolled out of his unlocked cell.

"We should have a checkerboard," he announced to the other prisoners. "This is a fine game."

He enlisted another inmate to help him draw squares on a piece of cardboard with a pencil and to cut circles from sheets of paper. Fellow prisoner Walter Staszel played five games with him. After winning four, Schrank pushed away the board. "You should practice on this game, my friend," he said. "You are hardly interesting."

Sheriff Arnold had kept from Schrank any newspapers carrying accounts of the attack. But when a new prisoner named J. Bailey was brought in, Schrank asked him, "Is Roosevelt still alive?" Bailey answered that he was. Schrank walked back to his cell without comment, but the next day he inquired again about the Colonel. "Where did the bullet hit him?" he asked a deputy sheriff. "The bullet in Colonel Roosevelt is my property, and I want it back," he went on. "I am making my will, and I am going to give it to the New York Historical Society. That is my bullet. In after years, when I am regarded as a hero, that bullet will be valuable, and I want it to go to the New York Historical Society. I want the gun to go to it also, and I am putting that in my will. I am leaving my property to my relatives in the Old Country. But the bullet and the gun I want to be saved in this country."

That day Sheriff Arnold ordered Schrank to take a bath and to send out for some new clothes. When it was reported that some movie people were planning to post his bail so he could appear in a film, the court doubled Schrank's bond to $15,000.

—•—

On Friday, his fourth day in the hospital, the Colonel awoke at seven fifteen. When his breakfast of three soft-boiled eggs was presented, he complained, "That's nothing for a strong man. I want some fresh country sausage and peaches. Plenty of them, too."

The nurse glanced at Mrs. Roosevelt, who nodded her approval.

Grumbled the Colonel, "I didn't know who was boss. I do now."

For lunch he enjoyed stuffed wild duck. That afternoon he sat up for an hour, for the first time since the shooting. He didn't care if the bullet were ever removed, he said. "I would as soon carry it in my chest as in my pocket, and I am sure not to lose it where it is now."

On hearing that Schrank was demanding the bullet back, the Colonel countered, "I don't think such a claim will hold. According to law, when a man sends a letter to another, that letter belongs to the sender until it reaches the recipient, then no one can take it away from the recipient. Now that bullet belonged to Schrank when it was in his revolver and while it was on its way to me, but after it reached me, it was mine."

This was the day that Dr. Terrell had said the crisis would come, but the patient passed it without incident. On Saturday, the Colonel insisted on taking a more active role in his campaign, over the protests of his doctors and Mrs. Roosevelt, who seemed more exhausted with each passing day. Among the visitors was vice-presidential candidate Hiram Johnson, who had continued his own speaking tour. But now Johnson faced a dilemma. California law stipulated that if the governor were out of the state for more than sixty consecutive days, he would forfeit his office. For Johnson, that period would elapse on October 25, six days hence. He wanted to continue campaigning, but the Colonel demanded he go home. The two argued for half an hour, until Mrs.

Roosevelt stalked into the room and raised a warning finger. When Johnson persisted, she motioned to the policeman stationed in the hallway. Finally, the governor picked up his hat and excused himself.

Francis Heney, the ex–district attorney who had introduced the Colonel in San Francisco, stopped by to help draft a statement on the trusts. Six years earlier, Heney had been shot by a potential juror, and now the Colonel wanted to compare wounds. "Turn around, Heney," he said, "and let's see where the bullet got you. I think I have the advantage over you," he claimed, "for I still carry the bullet which struck me."

In the afternoon, an orderly named Aloysius Moravac asked to see the Colonel. Padding into the room, the big man broke into tears. "Everybody loves you, Colonel," he blubbered.

"Not everybody," the Colonel reminded him, "or I wouldn't have got this."

"Anyhow, all the good people love you," mumbled Moravac as he fled.

By nighttime, the Colonel was worn out from the constant activity, and even he had to admit that he had done too much.

—◦—

That same evening, Woodrow Wilson addressed large crowds in New York at the Brooklyn Academy of Music and at Carnegie Hall. Immediately after the shooting, he'd announced that he would suspend his appearances after fulfilling his current commitments. "I cannot cancel the engagements immediately ahead of me without subjecting those who have arranged them to very serious embarrassment and great unnecessary expense," his statement read, "but I shall cut the series at the earliest possible point. Mr. Taft has at no time taken an active part in the campaign, and I have no desire to be the single candidate on the stump engaged against no active antagonist." And so tonight's appearances were expected to be among Wilson's last before Election Day.

In the Academy of Music, prominent suffragist Maud Malone stood and demanded he explain his views on the vote for women.

Facing considerable opposition to women's suffrage within the Democratic Party, Wilson had avoided the issue during the campaign, calling it a matter best settled by the states. Now he reiterated this position, saying it was "not a question that is dealt with by the National Government at all." When Malone insisted, "I am speaking to you as an American, Mr. Wilson," she was arrested.

But at the end of his speech in Carnegie Hall, the candidate was nearly swept off his feet by jubilant supporters. A threat had been reported against Wilson's life, but he was fatalistic. "There is nothing that can be done to guard against such attacks," he said. "It seems to me that the police and Secret Service guards are useless if a madman determines to attack a man in public life." Being less sanguine, the Secret Service doubled the guard around President Taft.

Since the Colonel seemed to be getting little rest in the hospital, the doctors decided to send him home to Oyster Bay, where they hoped Mrs. Roosevelt could exert more control. And so on the evening of Sunday, October 20, he shook hands with all thirty-five nurses on the night shift. In his excitement, he managed to sleep only four hours, but the next morning he reported feeling "bully." By six a.m., he was having his sponge bath. After breakfast, he dressed and sat in his room, waiting. They came to collect him a little after eight. As he was wheeled through the corridors, his fellow patients waved goodbye through their open doors. Nurses Fitzgerald and Welter shook his hand, and he presented each with a Bull Moose pin.

"He was the best patient I ever had," said Miss Welter.

"He was consideration itself," added Miss Fitzgerald. "He never had a word of complaint all the time he was at the hospital, and his chief worry seemed to be that we were not comfortable. . . . He was never ill-humored or peevish, as many patients in a similar position are."

The block around Mercy Hospital had been cleared, and police were stationed on the roofs of nearby buildings. A limousine was pulled into the hospital courtyard and surrounded by thirty-five mounted and motorcycle police, who would see the Colonel to the depot. A squad of detectives waited on the train, with orders to accompany him to the Indiana state line.

A huge throng had formed at Union Station, but the Colonel's special train had been moved to the freight yards at Twelfth Street, half a mile from the hospital. A sizeable crowd was there as well, and as Assistant Police Chief Schuettler helped him onto the *Mayflower*, the Colonel waved to the well-wishers. "Goodbye and good luck!" he called.

But he wasn't ready to quit campaigning. His last scheduled event, a speech at Madison Square Garden, was planned for ten days from tonight. His doctors had urged him to cancel it, but he swore he would be there. "I am going to make the meeting anyway," he vowed, "even if I can speak only three words." It remained to be seen whether he would be able to mount the stage and utter even that many.

ELEVEN

"I Am Not a Lunatic"
Wednesday, October 30, to Monday, November 25

THE EVENING WAS UNCOMMONLY WARM FOR THE END OF OCTOBER. The sun had long set over the North River, and the electric lights had already winked on along the city's great avenues. At Twenty-sixth Street, Madison Square Garden's stately tower rose above its namesake park. The Garden was the largest auditorium in the world, with seats for sixteen thousand, but three times that many people were milling in the street outside. Scalpers dodged among the crowd, asking as much as seven dollars a ticket. Four hundred patrolmen and fifty detectives were on hand to maintain order—and to make sure what had happened in Milwaukee wouldn't be reprised in New York.

The program wouldn't begin for another hour, but half the seats were already filled, with more devotees streaming through the arcaded portals at every moment. On their chairs they found red bandanas and Bull Moose songbooks. Old Glory was draped from every balcony, the speaker's podium, even the ceiling girders. Opposite the stage hung an enormous banner sewn of bandanas from every US state and territory. Near the Fourth Avenue entrance stood a majestic stuffed bull moose, set on a pedestal and illuminated by a spotlight. While the audience waited, images flashed on a screen above the speaker's stand. One showed the tombstone of a factory girl who had supposedly succumbed from overwork. Another depicted the familiar Tammany tiger, who was said to feed on democracy—but this specimen sported the orange-and-black cap of Princeton University. There were also motion pictures of the Colonel's truncated western tour; whenever Roosevelt came into view, the crowd cheered his likeness.

The audience leapt to its feet when the preliminary speakers filed onto the stage. Among the dignitaries were Hiram Johnson, the vice-presidential candidate, and Oscar S. Straus, a German immigrant who had served as President Roosevelt's Secretary of Commerce and Labor and was now running for governor of New York. In the balcony, the band broke into "America," and the crowd joined in. Straus spoke first, reminding the faithful that they were embarked on the third great movement in the nation's history—after independence and abolition—"the struggle for social justice," spearheaded by their "great leader" Theodore Roosevelt. Then Johnson took the podium, announcing that "the victory is won, not alone the victory marked by the counting of the ballots, but the victory in the broader and higher sense of the crystallization of a public sentiment founded on a moral conception and forcing its way to fulfillment and achievement."

As the governor was speaking, cheers swelled in the street outside. A cluster of men appeared in the doorway beneath the stage. In another moment, the Colonel strode onto the platform. He was wearing a sober black suit, and his face seemed less ruddy than usual, his features more worn, his movements a little stiffer.

The crowd exploded. "We want Teddy!" they screamed. "Four, four, four years more!" They waved American flags and red bandanas. They made the strange low rumble meant to mimic the call of the bull moose, then they began to stamp their feet, until it seemed the old building would tumble down. Men danced in the aisles. Women climbed onto the seats of their chairs. A hatless man rushed the stage and came within feet of the Colonel before being knocked down and carried away. The band played "A Hot Time in the Old Town Tonight," "Onward, Christian Soldiers," "Dixie," and "Hail to the Chief." But

Theodore Roosevelt addressing sixteen thousand Bull Moosers at Madison Square Garden on October 30, 1912, two weeks after the shooting; his disciples cheered for forty-five minutes before allowing him to speak.

the instruments could scarcely be heard above the tumult, and instead of quieting the throng, the music seemed to inflame it.

The Colonel could only stand beside the flag-draped speaker's table and sing along. Spying friends in the audience, he gave a wave with his left hand. For five minutes the ovation went on, ten, fifteen. The candidate smiled and bowed stiffly to all sides. Twenty, twenty-five minutes. He waved for quiet, to no avail. When the noise slackened, he pounded his fist on the speaker's table, like a chairman gaveling a meeting to order, but the gesture only incited the crowd again. As time wore on, his smile grew fixed and grim, the look of a man in pain. Hiram Johnson and Senator Dixon went to his side, but he waved them away. Thirty, thirty-five minutes. By now the crowd was hoarse and covered with perspiration. Sweat also dotted the Colonel's face. As his impatience became unmistakable, the crowd began to quiet. After forty-five minutes, they finally let him speak. It was ten o'clock.

"Friends," he began, "perhaps once in a generation, perhaps not so often, there comes a chance for the people of a country to play their part wisely and fearlessly in some great battle of the age-long warfare for human rights." As he spoke, the hoarseness that had plagued him during his campaign tour was gone, and his explosive consonants and patrician vowels reverberated to the farthest reaches of the hall. But tonight he was a different man. Though he appeared even more passionate than usual, he didn't seem bitter or combative. He never mentioned his opponents by name. And there was gravity in his words, as though he believed this to be the last address he would ever give. It wasn't the call to arms the crowd had expected. It was, they realized, a valedictory.

Instead of arguments and plans, he gave them a simple statement of Progressive principles. Instead of the "I" they were used to hearing from his lips, they heard "we." The Progressives may have owed their existence to Theodore Roosevelt, but tonight, their founder looked beyond the impending election and spoke of the party's future. Tonight he was passing the baton. As they absorbed his message, the crowd grew pensive along with him.

"We must not permit the brutal selfishness of arrogance and the brutal selfishness of envy, each to run unchecked its evil course," he told them. "That end would be widespread disaster, for it would mean that our people would be sundered by those dreadful lines of division which are drawn when the selfish greed of the haves is set over against the selfish greed of the have-nots."

Only the Progressive Party stood against class division, and for social justice. "We war against the forces of evil, and the weapons we use are the weapons of right. We do not set greed against greed or hatred against hatred. . . . The doctrines we preach reach back to the Golden Rule and the Sermon on the Mount. They reach back to the commandments delivered at Sinai."

As he spoke, he jabbed his head for emphasis and waved his left hand, which gripped his speech. If he lost himself and raised his right arm, he winced and quickly lowered it to his side again. "We propose to lift the burdens from the lowly and the weary," he told his disciples, "from the poor and the oppressed. . . . We are for liberty. But we are for the liberty of the oppressed, and not for the liberty of the oppressor to oppress the weak and to bind burdens on the shoulders of the heavy-laden. . . . We intend to strike down privilege, to equalize opportunity, to wrest justice from the hands that do injustice, to hearten and strengthen men and women for the hard battle of life. We stand shoulder to shoulder in a spirit of real brotherhood. We recognize no differences of class, creed, or birthplace. . . . We firmly believe that the American people feel hostility to no man who has honestly won success. We firmly believe that the American people ask only justice, justice each for himself and justice each for all others. . . . Our people work hard and faithfully. They do not wish to shirk their work. . . . But there must be bread for the work. . . . When they grow old there must be the certainty of rest under conditions free from the haunting terror of utter poverty. . . . We are striving to meet the needs of all these men, and to meet them in such fashion that all alike shall feel bound together in the bond of a common brotherhood where each works hard for himself and for those dearest to him, and yet feel that he must also think of his brother's rights because he is in very truth that brother's keeper. . . . Surely there never was a greater opportunity than this. Surely there never was a fight better worth making than this. . . . I believe we shall win, but win or lose I am glad beyond measure that I am one of the many who in this fight have stood ready to spend and be spent, pledged to fight while life lasts the great fight of righteousness and for brotherhood and for the welfare of mankind."

He had promised Mrs. Roosevelt that he would speak for only half an hour, and now, having said what he had come to say, he stopped himself at thirty-five minutes—ten minutes shorter than the ovation that had welcomed him and forty-five minutes less than he had spoken in Milwaukee with blood still seeping from his lacerated chest. Sensing they had witnessed history, the crowd cheered, though not so wildly as before. The Colonel considered the event "the most enthusiastic and successful meeting of the campaign." In truth, it was the greatest reception in the long history of Madison Square Garden. But was the applause for the man or for the movement, for the Colonel's personality and courage, or for the power of his Progressive ideals? If this were a valedictory, could the party live without him?

The next evening, sixteen thousand screaming partisans were again gathered in Madison Square Garden. Not to be outdone by the previous night's crowd, they cheered and stamped and clapped for an hour and five minutes. It was ten fifteen before Woodrow Wilson was able to begin his remarks.

The Democrat was so touched by the outpouring that he abandoned his memorized speech and spoke extemporaneously. Whereas Roosevelt gesticulated to underscore his points, Wilson stood motionless on the podium, a center of calm in the surging auditorium. Sounding like a man already elected, he confessed to feeling a somber responsibility at the role he was about to assume. Then he directed his keen scrutiny to his opponents. The Republicans, he said, were afraid to venture any reforms, lest the monopolists turn on them with the tremendous power the party had given them. "We have builded a structure which we do not know how to change, and which we dare not touch," he averred, his sonorous tenor voice filling the hall. "We fear the men in whose interest we have builded, the men who control credit from one end of the country to the other."

Then he turned to the Progressives. Not deigning to mention their name, he would refer to them only as "the other branch of the Republican Party. I don't know how to characterize it," he confessed.

"Ninety-nine percent bull and one percent moose!" a man shouted.

The Progressives suffered from the reverse flaw of the Republicans, Wilson went on, not from lack of innovation but from a surfeit, advocating more radical change than the country needed. They were "adventurers," determined to "turn away from the old processes of law" and to burden corporations with unnecessary regulation. "I do not believe it is safe to put the disciplining of business in the hands of any officer of government whatever," Wilson said. "When business is once free it will not need the hand of discipline. It is now not free, and the great enterprise of politics in our day is to set the average businessman free again."

Unlike the Progressives, the Democrats wouldn't attempt to "bring about a forced cordiality and friendliness between all men, but to see to it that nothing more than justice is done. Our standard is not pity but justice. . . . Government is based on right, not on benevolence. . . . We are not proposing to go about with condescension; we are not proposing to go about with the helping hand of those who are stronger to lift up the weaker, but we are going about with the strong hand of government to see that nobody imposes on the weak. . . .

"The case is made up," he concluded. "The case is before the jury. I myself do not doubt the verdict. . . . You know that when a great engine runs free, as we say, its freedom consists in its perfect adjustment. All the parts are so assembled and united and accommodated that there is no friction, but a united power in all the parts. So I speak of political liberty—when we understand one another, when we cooperate with one another, when we are united with one another, then we are free. . . . I propose that men now forget their individual likes and dislikes, their individual sympathies and antipathies, and join together in a solemn act of a sovereign people and determine what the Government of the United States shall be." His words were met with another huge ovation, not of hope but of celebration. It was the roar of victory.

Socialist candidate Eugene Debs closed out his campaign with a massive rally in Chicago on November 2, replete with a parade and a fireworks display. For his part, President Taft made no great closing address, though he did issue several press statements, including one to the *New York Times* reminding voters that the Republican Party stood above all for "preserving our constitutional form of government" and warning that "a continuance of orderly government under the doctrines enunciated and limitations prescribed in the Federal Constitution is in danger." On October 30, the evening that Roosevelt spoke at Madison Square Garden, Vice-President James S. Sherman died after a long illness. Taft also happened to be in the city that day, for the launching of the battleship *New York*. He was reported riding down Fifth Avenue in an open automobile, dozing.

———

November 5, Election Day, broke sunny and crisp on Long Island. Newspapermen huddled outside Sagamore Hill, the rambling, brick-and-shingle house Theodore Roosevelt had built above the Sound. Nothing was seen of the candidate until noon, when he and the estate's seven male workers drove to the village to vote at the firehouse, where the Colonel cast ballot number 265.

Curiosity seekers motored by the house all day, but the Colonel didn't venture out again until just after three o'clock, when he and Mrs. Roosevelt took an hour's walk in the nearby woods. At 4:05, George Perkins arrived on the train from New York, conferred briefly with his chief, then returned to the city on the 5:15. At seven o'clock, the Colonel donned his dinner suit, as he did every night at Sagamore Hill.

A little after seven, a reporter stole onto the wide front porch and rang the bell insistently. Finally the door opened. It was the Colonel. "Is that you, Senator?" he called into the darkness. Then, recognizing the newspaperman, he said, "Please excuse me for the present. I can't say anything yet. You will have to return when I have had time to consider the returns and what they indicate."

The Colonel took dinner with Mrs. Roosevelt; Emlen Roosevelt, his first cousin, close friend, and financial adviser; Emlen's wife, Christine;

and Laura Roosevelt, the cousin who had been at the theater with Edith the night the former president was shot. The older Roosevelt children were gathered at Progressive headquarters in Manhattan, thirty miles away, to watch the returns firsthand. The Progressive National Committee had ordered a direct telegraph wire installed at Sagamore Hill so the Colonel could follow the voting, but he had canceled the line, preferring to receive the news by telephone. And so as the results trickled in, headquarters called and a servant relayed the bulletins to the candidate.

In New York, crowds had started to gather in hotel lobbies and at newspaper offices. A hundred thousand people clogged Times Square, outside the *New York Times*, where canvas screens were stretched over the windows and news flashes were projected in letters legible from five blocks away. In Princeton, Woodrow Wilson was having dinner at his Tudor-style home on Cleveland Lane, with his wife, daughters, extended family, and friends. He had voted just before eleven o'clock that morning, at Princeton's Chambers Street fire station, across from the boardinghouse where he had stayed as a student back in 1876. As he was leaving the polling place, a woman presented him with a rabbit's foot.

The Wilson home was fitted with a direct line to Democratic headquarters in New York. Dinner was interrupted by occasional bulletins, and as early as seven thirty, it appeared the Democrats would have something to celebrate. The guests were in a festive mood, but their host, seated at the head of the table, kept his emotions to himself. Just after ten o'clock, another wire was delivered. By then, Wilson and his guests had gathered in the parlor, around the fireplace, and Mrs. Wilson went to retrieve the message. In a moment she returned and put her hand on her husband's shoulder. "My dear," she said, "I want to be the first to congratulate you."

At ten thirty, the Democratic National Committee claimed victory. Fifteen minutes later, Wilson issued his own statement. On the Princeton campus, jubilant students paraded out of Alexander Hall and down Nassau Avenue. At eleven thirty, three hundred young men arrived outside the Wilson home. The president-elect went onto the front porch. "I have no feeling of triumph tonight," he told them, "but a feeling of solemn responsibility. I know the very great task ahead of me."

To William F. McCombs, Chairman of the Democratic National Committee, he telegraphed, "A great cause has triumphed. Every Democrat, every true progressive of whatever alliance, must now lend his full force and enthusiasm to the fulfillment of the people's hopes, the establishment of the people's rights, so that justice and progress may go hand in hand."

Across the Hudson in Manhattan, gloom descended on Republican headquarters in the Times Building. Party chairman Charles D. Hilles released a statement blaming the Bull Moose for the loss. "But for Mr. Roosevelt's action in deserting the Republican Party," he claimed, "Mr. Taft would unquestionably have been reelected."

The president received the long-expected news at his home in Cincinnati, and at eleven o'clock he issued a concession. But he warned: "The vote for Mr. Roosevelt, the third party candidate, and for Mr. Debs, the Socialist candidate, is a warning that their propaganda in favor of fundamental changes in our constitutional representative Government has formidable support. . . . It behooves Republicans to gather again to the party standard and pledge anew their faith in their party's principles and to organize again to defend the constitutional government handed down to us by our fathers. . . . Let us close ranks and march forward to do battle for the right and the true." To a friend, Taft confided, "I'll be very glad to ride down Pennsylvania Avenue with Governor Wilson. It wouldn't have been so easy if things had been different," if Roosevelt had won, "but I would have taken the ride just the same."

In Oyster Bay, residents had cast 510 votes for the Colonel, 218 for Wilson, and 67 for Taft. Now they stood in gloomy groups on street corners and in taprooms. At eleven o'clock, the telephone rang at Sagamore Hill, and the Colonel received the coup de grace. He dictated a terse telegram to the victor: "The American people, by a great plurality, have conferred upon you the highest honor in their gift. I congratulate you thereon. Theodore Roosevelt."

A little before midnight, still dressed in his dinner suit, the Colonel invited reporters into his library. A low fire glinted in the hearth, reflecting off the books and trophy heads lining the walls. The men chatted off the record like the old friends they were, then Roosevelt dictated a statement. He wasn't at all downcast by the results, he said. "Like all other good citizens, I accept the result with good humor and contentment. As for the Progressive cause, I can only repeat what I have already so many times declared, the fate of the leader for the time being is of little consequence, but the cause itself must in the end triumph, for its triumph is essential to the well-being of the American people." A few days later, he wrote to his friend James R. Garfield, son of the assassinated president, "We have fought the good fight, we have kept the faith, and we have nothing to regret."

When the ballots were tallied, Woodrow Wilson had received some 6.3 million votes to Roosevelt's 4.1 million and Taft's 3.5 million. Debs garnered just over 900,000, double what he'd earned in 1908 and, at 6 percent, the largest share ever won by a Socialist candidate for president. Wilson's proportion of the popular vote was just under 42 percent, but in the Electoral College he received a landslide—forty states and 435 votes. Roosevelt carried six states—California, Michigan, Minnesota, Pennsylvania, South Dakota, and Washington, with eighty-eight electoral votes. Taft won Vermont and Utah, for a total of eight electors, the weakest showing (in both the popular vote and the Electoral College) of any major-party candidate to that date. It was also the only time in American history that a third-party presidential candidate outpolled either a Democrat or a Republican. But if Schrank's attack had swung some voters to Roosevelt, as many observers had predicted, the trend wasn't enough to affect the result. Quipped the Colonel, "I got more bullets than ballots this time."

Republican Chairman Hilles's claim notwithstanding, it appeared that Wilson would have been victorious even if Roosevelt hadn't entered the fray, since many of the ballots cast for the Colonel would have gone to the progressive Democrat rather than to the conservative Republican. And since Roosevelt and Taft together polled 1.3 million more votes than Wilson, it was arguable that the Colonel, had he been the G.O.P. candidate, might have been elected, even though with Roosevelt on the ticket, the Republicans would have been divided between the progressive and conservative factions of their party.

But the *New York Times* entertained no alternate result. After congratulating the American people for their "soundness of judgment," the editorial writer ventured, "The victory of Wilson, the victory of the Democrats, was predetermined in our politics. It was time. . . . The Republican Party had betrayed its trust. It had come to be recognized not as a party of the people, but as an instrument of the business interests, of interests seeking special favors." As for Roosevelt, "only a small minority trusted in him, believed in him. To the great mass he was like Bryan, ambitious, unsteady, unsafe, but far more dangerous than Bryan because able, more fertile, more persuasive."

Wilson had asked for a Democratic Congress to implement his programs, and the people had heard him. In the House, the Democrats gained sixty-three seats, giving them 291 to the Republicans' 127 and the Progressives' 17. (One of those seventeen Progressive freshmen would be sent from Cincinnati, ousting the Colonel's Republican son-in-law, Nick Longworth, who lost by slightly more than a hundred votes.) In the Senate, Democrats took control for the first time in twenty years, with fifty-one seats versus forty-four for the Republicans and just one for the Progressives. Around the country, not one Progressive gubernatorial candidate was successful, though some 260 party members were elected to state legislatures. Judging from these results, it did appear that the tremendous excitement generated by the Progressive campaign had been for

Roosevelt and not for the party after all, for the man and not for his ideas. Now, with so few officeholders, the Progressives had no party machine to give them leverage. On both accounts, the election boded ill for their future.

⁓

On November 12, one week after the election, John Schrank sat in his cell at the Milwaukee county jail eating his breakfast, as he did every morning. But it was not to be a typical day. When a reporter reminded him, Schrank answered, "That's right, the trial is today, isn't it? Oh, it might as well be over. Now, I am not concerned with the outcome. My crime is a political crime, rather than a crime against humanity, and I guess with all the political crime that has taken place in the last few years they won't be very hard on me. However, if they do give it to me hard, why, I guess I can take my medicine."

In the municipal courtroom, 150 spectators were waiting, including twenty city detectives and as many deputy sheriffs. Schrank entered with a cheerful step, his chin up and his eyes straight ahead. He was more presentable today than at his last appearance. He had shaved, and his thin blonde hair was neatly parted and pasted. He had on a clean shirt, a white tie, and freshly shined shoes. Over his arm was a raincoat, in his hand a fedora. A white handkerchief peeked from the pocket of his new blue serge suit.

Presiding was Judge August C. Backus. Just thirty-five, Backus was boyishly handsome, with oiled hair and an expression kindly but firm. A deputy sheriff ushered Schrank before the judge, where District Attorney Winifred Zabel stood and read the charges against him.

"John Schrank, on October 14, with malice aforethought, did attempt to kill and murder Theodore Roosevelt. What do you plead to that, guilty or not guilty?" asked Zabel.

"I plead guilty to the shooting," Schrank answered uncertainly, as though the fact had already been established.

"Did you intend to kill Theodore Roosevelt?"

"I did not intend to kill the citizen Roosevelt."

"Did you intend to kill the candidate Roosevelt?"

"I intended to kill Theodore Roosevelt the third termer. I did not want to kill the candidate of the Progressive Party. I shot Roosevelt as a warning to other third termers."

"There we have it," interjected Judge Backus. He directed Schrank to take his seat.

The District Attorney had already appointed alienists to study Schrank's sanity, but the law dictated that the issue be settled by an impartial panel. Zabel now moved that the judge either appoint a board of experts to determine Schrank's mental competence or proceed to a trial by jury, who could also decide the question. The judge announced he would appoint a committee, to be named when the court reconvened at two o'clock. In the meantime, he ordered Schrank returned to the county jail across the street. "Let no man leave the courtroom until the prisoner has left the City Hall," he cautioned.

In the afternoon, Schrank resumed his place at the defendant's table. He watched with curiosity as the committee's five doctors stood to be sworn. Frank Studley was superintendent of a Milwaukee sanitarium; W. F. Becker had been director of the Northern Hospital for the Insane outside Oshkosh, Wisconsin; D. W. Harrington was a noted nerve specialist; William F. Wegge was former medical superintendent of the Northern Hospital; and Richard Dewey, the committee's chairman, was medical director of a sanatorium in Wauwatosa, Wisconsin. The judge set no deadline for the panel's report and ordered Sheriff Arnold to grant the doctors unfettered access to the defendant.

In appointing an expert committee, Judge Backus was deviating from standard procedure, which called for the prosecution and the defense to present their own experts and let the jury decide the defendant's sanity. But, said the judge, "In my experience I have never witnessed a case where the testimony of experts on one side was not directly contradicted by the testimony of as many or more experts on the other side. Where men especially trained in nervous and mental diseases disagree, how can it be expected that a jury of twelve laymen will agree?" He charged the panel with a single question: "Is the defendant John Schrank sane or insane at the present time?"

Schrank had earlier expressed hope that the victim would testify on his behalf. "Theodore Roosevelt is only human after all," he'd told a fellow prisoner. "He was shot and has recovered. Now that it is all over and he has had time for reflection, his better self surely has concluded that I should be pitied and not condemned. When McKinley was shot, he showed forgiveness. The entire case rests with Roosevelt. I know if he will come here and speak for me, and adopt a broad view of the matter, I will get a light sentence. His word will settle the whole matter. I should think he would come here when the case is tried."

But now, when a reporter asked Joseph Flanders, the respected Milwaukee attorney assigned to represent Schrank, if Colonel Roosevelt would be called as a witness, the counselor expressed his doubt. The sanity commission, he pointed out, had been asked to offer an opinion only on Schrank's mental state, not on the circumstances of the shooting, and Roosevelt wasn't qualified to testify on that issue.

On November 22, the alienists had completed their examinations and John Schrank was again before Judge Backus to hear their determination. The doctors had taken fifty typed pages to answer the judge's twelve-word question. As the report was read aloud, from shortly before ten o'clock until nearly noon, Schrank sat at the defendant's table, evincing little interest in the proceedings.

The document delved into his personal and family history; biographical facts such as age and occupation; data such as height, weight, eye color, and bowel habits; the acuity of his hearing, eyesight, and reflexes; personal tendencies such as smoking, drinking, and bedtime; and tests of his attention, memory, logic, judgment, insight, and state of excitement. Examples of his writings were appended.

The alienists were impressed by Schrank's command of English, which they found unusually strong for a nonnative speaker. In their interviews, the defendant had been helpful and seemingly honest in every regard, they reported. He had also shown himself confident, dignified, fearless, cheerful, calm, and courteous. But at no time did he demonstrate the slightest remorse. And they found that he had an inflated sense of his own importance; indeed, he believed himself an instrument of the Almighty, a modern-day Joan of Arc. The doctors concluded:

First—John Schrank is suffering from insane delusions, grandiose in character, and of the systematized variety.

Second—In our opinion he is insane at the present time.

Third—On account of the connection existing between his delusions and the act with which he stands charged, we are of the opinion that he is unable to confer intelligently with counsel or to conduct his defense.

After the report was read, District Attorney Zabel questioned the alienists, who confirmed the opinions expressed. Turning to the defendant, Justice Backus asked if he would like to make a statement before judgment was passed. Schrank consulted in whispers with attorney Flanders, who responded that the accused had nothing to say.

As Judge Backus read his decision, Schrank sat with his head bowed, his fingers twitching. "The court now finds that the defendant John Schrank is insane, and therefore incapacitated to act for himself. It is therefore ordered and adjudged that the defendant John Schrank be committed to the Northern Hospital for the Insane, near Oshkosh, in the County of Winnebago, state of Wisconsin, until such time when he shall have recovered from such insanity, when he shall be returned to this court for further proceedings according to law. And it is further ordered that all proceedings in this case be stayed indefinitely and until such recovery."

As Schrank was led back to the county jail, he complained to reporters, "Why didn't they give me my medicine right away, instead of making me wait? I did it, and I am willing to stand the consequences of my act." He added, "I had expected that they would find me insane, because it was in the papers two days ago. I want to say now that I am sane and know what I am doing all the time. I am not a lunatic and never was one. I was called upon to do a duty, and I have done it. The commission has sworn away my life. Each member went upon the stand and said I was incurably insane. They can bury me alive if they see fit. I don't care what happens now."

Meanwhile, Theodore Roosevelt had drawn his own opinion on Schrank's sanity. The would-be assassin "was not a madman at all," the Colonel wrote a friend. "I very gravely question if he has a more unsound brain than Senator La Follette or Eugene Debs. He simply represents a different stratum of life and temperament. . . . He had quite enough sense to avoid shooting me in any Southern State, where he would have been lynched, and he waited until he got into a State where there was no death penalty. I have not the slightest feeling against him; I have a very strong feeling against the people who, by their ceaseless and intemperate abuse, excited him to the action, and against the mushy people who would excuse him and all the other criminals once the crime had been committed."

One newspaperman was promoting a conspiracy theory, arguing that Schrank and his supposed victim were in cahoots. Writing in the *Ishpeming* (Michigan) *Iron Ore*, George A. Newett called the shooting a "put up job." The cartridge that struck the Bull Moose was loaded with nothing more than a dried pea, he claimed, as any independent X-ray of Roosevelt's chest could verify. As for Schrank's supposed insanity, that finding was also the product of corruption and collusion.

During Schrank's weeks in the county jail he had written a lengthy defense of his actions, on the assumption that he would be tried before a jury. This was the document he had scribbled for days, declining to reveal its contents. Now it was published as part of the alienists' report:

"I wish to apologize to the community of Milwaukee for having caused on October 14 last great excitement, most bitter feeling and expenses," it began. "I wish to apologize to you honorable men of the jury that I am causing to you this day unpleasantness in asking you to pass a verdict in a matter which should have been better tried by a higher than earthly court. . . .

"I am not here today to defend myself nor my actions. . . . I am here to defend the spirit of forefathers . . . . Tradition is above written statute, amended and ineffective. . . . Tradition is sacred and inviolable, irrevocable. . . . Gentlemen of the jury, the shot at Milwaukee, which created an echo in all parts of the world, was not a shot fired at the citizen Roosevelt, not a shot at an ex-President, not a shot at the candidate of a so-called Progressive party, not a shot to influence the pending election, not a shot to gain for me notoriety. No, it was simply to once and forever establish the fact that any man who hereafter aspires to a third presidential term, will do so at the risk of his life. If I cannot defend tradition I cannot defend the country in case of war. You may as well send every patriot to prison. . . .

"I hope that the shot at Milwaukee has awakened the patriotism of the American nation, that it has opened their eyes to the real danger and shown them the only safe way out of it as is proven by election returns in the great Democratic party the north, south, east and west is once more and more solidly united and proudly can we prove to the nations of the world that the spirit of 1776 is alive and shall never die, and that self-government is an established fact and a success. . . .

"Now, honorable men of the jury, I wish to say no more, in the name of God, go and do your duty. . . . Before me is the spirit of George Washington, behind me that of McKinley."

At eleven a.m. on November 25, the Monday before Thanksgiving, John Schrank was taken from the county jail. Because he'd been a model inmate, he was permitted to travel without handcuffs. "Goodbye, sheriff," Schrank said. "I hope I haven't caused you too much trouble while I have been here."

"Not a bit, Schrank," answered Sheriff Arnold. "You have been the best prisoner we have had here since I have been in office."

"I am glad to hear that, for I do not like to cause people trouble," Schrank told him. "I am not crazy, but as the doctors have said I am, I must go to the asylum. There is nothing else for me to do."

Schrank was bound for the Northern Hospital for the Insane, on the bucolic shores of Lake Winnebago, a few miles north of Oshkosh, Wisconsin. The facility had been founded in 1872, on the principles of the late Dr. Thomas Kirkbride, who had encouraged the "Moral Treatment" of the mentally ill. Like all Kirkbride buildings, the Northern Hospital had a central administrative section flanked by two long wings, one for men and one for women. Treatment emphasized fresh air, natural light, work in the building and gardens, and organized games and recreations. Each room had a view of the extensive grounds, with their landscaped parks and tidy plots for raising food. Schrank would be one of seven hundred inmates.

At one o'clock, the train stopped at Fond du Lac, a manufacturing city on the lake's southern shore, some sixty miles north of Milwaukee and twenty miles south of Oshkosh. A reporter for the local paper was on hand. "You still contend that you are sane, do you not?" he asked.

"Well, I guess that is for you to decide," Schrank answered. "The doctors say I am not, and I say I am. I'm not worrying though. The only thing I have to complain about is that they don't sell bottled beer on this train. I'm thirsty."

A crowd gawked at him through the train window, but the prisoner seemed to enjoy the attention. When an attractive woman stopped,

John Schrank with an unidentified police officer. "You have been the best prisoner we have had here since I have been in office," Sheriff William Arnold told the cooperative inmate.

he waved to her, but she went on her way without acknowledgment. Schrank chuckled at the snub.

The train jerked into motion again. Picking up speed, it passed the railroad's sooty car shops just north of the city. The tracks angled to the northwest, away from the lakeshore, and before long, the flat land was patched with farmers' fields. But in this season, the ground was barren, the oats and corn and buckwheat long gathered, the rows bristling only with tawny stubble.

In Oshkosh, the locomotive clanked to a stop in front of the long, narrow depot. Schrank and his guardian remained aboard, and in a few moments the train resumed its northward journey, again tracing the gentle curve of the lake. In just a few miles, the locomotive paused again, and this time the two men climbed down. The temperature was barely above freezing, and Schrank huddled in his new raincoat and fedora. Ahead of them rose a sprawling stone building with a pointed cupola and ornate iron balconies. Heading away from the tracks, they passed though a pair of anonymous stone plinths. A tree-lined driveway stretched before them, long and ruler straight. In time, their figures faded in the waning sunlight.

Epilogue

"I Have Already Lived and Enjoyed as Much of My Life as Any Other Nine Men I Know"

A CENTURY FURTHER ON, THE ELECTION OF 1912 IS STILL RECALLED as one of the most stirring in American history, with four exceptional candidates engaged in serious (if caustic) debate over the course of the nation. In many ways, the election marked the birth of modern presidential politics, with direct primaries; a longer campaign season; more travel by the candidates; an expanded role for the press; reduced influence of party bosses; and greater involvement of women, who campaigned for Roosevelt, the first American male politician of any stature to support women's suffrage. By Election Day 1912, six states—California, Washington, Idaho, Wyoming, Colorado, and Utah—had granted women the vote, and a million cast ballots that year. Most, however, wouldn't get the franchise until the ratification of the Nineteenth Amendment in 1920.

The election of 1912 proved a watershed for the candidates and parties involved. As William Howard Taft took that final ride down Pennsylvania Avenue on March 4, the outgoing president may have seemed the definition of *has-been*. But Taft's remaining years, following his lackluster administration and electoral drubbing, proved among the most productive and fulfilling of his life.

On leaving office, he accepted a position at Yale Law School, where he taught constitutional law for eight years. Then in 1921, he finally realized the ambition that had always been closest to his heart: On June 30, Republican president Warren G. Harding nominated him as Chief Justice of the Supreme Court, replacing Edward Douglass White, who had died in May. The Senate gave its confirmation that same day, by a vote of sixty to four. And so William Howard Taft became the only person in history to head two branches of the federal government, accomplishing what the *New York Times* called "a 'comeback' unprecedented in American political annals." As chief justice, Taft proved an effective, even revolutionary administrator, introducing a new efficiency in the workings not just of the Court but of the entire federal judiciary. After nine productive years on the bench, he retired due to poor health. He died a month later, on March 8, 1930, at the age of seventy.

Eugene Debs wasn't as fortunate as William Taft in the years following the election of 1912. In 1916, Debs ran for Congress from Indiana, but his Socialist beliefs proved too radical for his hometown constituency. Then two years later, after the United States had entered World War I, Debs's uncompromising views brought the wrath of the federal government upon him. In May 1918, at the urging of President Wilson, Congress had passed the Sedition Act, making it a federal crime to disparage the nation's war effort. In June, at a convention of the Ohio Socialist Party, Debs made a speech condemning American involvement and advocating resistance to the draft. Two weeks later, he was indicted for sedition, and in September he was convicted and sentenced to ten years in prison. One of two thousand antiwar protestors prosecuted (and one of nine hundred jailed), Debs began serving his term in April 1919, after the US Supreme Court upheld the verdict.

In 1920, though disenfranchised by his conviction, Debs ran as a write-in candidate for president. Without leaving his prison cell, he drew 919,000 votes, about as many as he had won in 1912 after a full season of cross-country campaigning (although this time his total represented slightly more than 3 percent of ballots cast, versus nearly

6 percent in 1912). The following January, though the war was won and Debs was in declining health, Woodrow Wilson pointedly refused to pardon him, branding him "a traitor to his country." In December of that year, President Warren Harding finally commuted the sentence, and Debs went free after serving just less than two years. He died on October 20, 1926, of a heart attack, aged eighty.

For Debs's party, the campaign of 1912 remained a high-water mark, yielding the greatest proportion of popular votes the Socialists would ever receive. In subsequent years, their more-radical members would defect to the Communist Party, even as more-centrist supporters were alienated by the Socialists' opposition to World War I and their perceived association with the Russian Revolution. The party fell outside the American mainstream, and for the next century and more, "Socialist" would remain an epithet hurled at anyone left of center, even as it had been aimed at Theodore Roosevelt in 1912.

***

Following his inauguration in March of 1913, Woodrow Wilson launched one of the most ambitious and productive domestic programs in American history. Working closely with the Democratic Congress (and coaxing along his party's conservative members), he signed legislation reducing the tariff, authorizing a federal income tax, and creating the Federal Reserve to regulate the nation's money supply. To rein in the corporations, he approved laws strengthening the Sherman Anti-Trust Act and forming the Federal Trade Commission.

Less than two years into his administration, in August 1914, Wilson's wife, Ellen, died of Bright's disease, the kidney disorder that had claimed Theodore Roosevelt's first wife, three decades before. Wilson fell into a period of profound grief, which he sought to ameliorate with nonstop work. Then in December 1915, he married stylish widow Edith Gault. About that same time, his legislative program assumed an even more progressive tenor, and over the course of the next year he signed into law such reforms as government loans to farmers, restrictions on child labor, workmen's compensation for government contractors, an eight-hour workday for interstate railroad employees, and higher taxes on the wealthy.

By the time he was campaigning for reelection, Wilson had enacted every major plank of the 1912 Progressive Party platform. Said the president, "I am a progressive. I do not spell it with a capital *P*, but I think my pace is just as fast as those who do." In truth, he had discovered that the relatively limited federal government he had espoused as a candidate was not sufficient to curb the trusts. And so as chief executive, he would time and again adopt measures more akin to Theodore Roosevelt's "New Nationalism" than to the "New Freedom" on which he himself had campaigned.

In 1916, Wilson ran against the progressive Republican Charles Evans Hughes, associate justice of the US Supreme Court and former governor of New York. But voters who had supported Roosevelt four years earlier now turned out for Wilson, and by one of the narrowest margins in US history, he became the first Democratic president to receive a second consecutive term since Andrew Jackson in 1832. True, Wilson could seem aloof and even arrogant, but the economy had recovered from the recession of 1913, and citizens appreciated his unflagging efforts to maintain neutrality in the First World War and to bring the conflict to a just and sustainable end. As their campaign slogan, the Democrats adopted "He kept us out of war."

Then in January 1917, Germany announced the resumption of unrestricted submarine warfare against neutral countries. In early April, scarcely a month after Wilson's inauguration, the United States finally joined the hostilities. And so Wilson's second term was dominated not by any domestic agenda but by war, the protracted treaty negotiations, and the struggle to launch his brainchild the League of Nations, the forty-two-member organization dedicated to mediating international disputes and maintaining world peace.

In September 1919, the president launched a coast-to-coast tour to promote America's membership in the League, but exhausted and in failing health, he was forced to cut the journey short. On October 2, in Washington, he suffered a devastating stroke that left him an invalid, secluded in the White House while the First Lady covertly managed the executive branch. In the coming months, he gradually regained some strength and resumed more of his presidential duties. But when the US Senate hesitated over the clause in the League covenant that committed signatories to protect other members from external aggression, Wilson refused to consider any compromise language. As a result, the Senate declined to ratify the Treaty of Versailles, the document ending the war and establishing the League of Nations. (The United States finally signed a separate accord with Germany in June 1921 but never did join the League, which was disbanded in 1946 and succeeded by the United Nations.)

In 1920, even if Wilson had been fit to run for a third term, his reelection would have been doubtful. The once-robust economy was sputtering again, with high inflation, widespread unemployment, and violent strikes. To succeed Wilson, the Democrats nominated progressive Ohio governor James M. Cox (along with his running mate Assistant Secretary of the Navy Franklin D. Roosevelt), but in a landslide, voters chose the conservative Republican Warren G. Harding, who promised a "Return to Normalcy." In December of that year, Wilson was awarded the Nobel Peace Prize for the crucial role he played in founding the League of Nations. After leaving the White House, he and Edith settled into a comfortable home in Washington, where the former president lived quietly until his death on February 3, 1924, at the age of sixty-seven.

⌒⌒

Like the Socialists, the Progressives reached their apogee in 1912. The party had been forged from an amalgam of disparate groups including farmers, urban factory workers, small-town professionals, and socially minded millionaires, and the delicate alliance never recovered from the defeat of Theodore Roosevelt. In 1914, their weak party organization managed to elect only five members to the House of Representatives (out of 138 candidates) and to reelect one governor (Hiram Johnson of California). "The fundamental trouble," concluded Roosevelt, was "that the country was sick and tired of reform." In the recession of 1913, Americans had "felt the pinch of poverty; . . . and compared with this they did not care a rap for social justice or industrial justice or clean politics or decency in public life." By 1916 the Progressive prodigals were eager to return to the Republican fold, with Roosevelt as the fusion candidate for president; but still bitter over the Bull Moose debacle, the G.O.P. refused a merger. At the Progressive convention that summer, the party nominated the Colonel, who stunned them by refusing to make another third-party run. When O. K. Davis read Roosevelt's telegram in the convention hall, William Allen White recalled, "For a moment there was silence. Then there was a roar of rage. It was the cry of a broken heart such as no convention ever had uttered in this land before." It was also the party's death throes; before long, most Progressives, including Roosevelt, were Republicans once more.

But even after the Progressives' demise, their ideas would prevail in American politics for decades, championed by Woodrow Wilson's Democrats. And beginning in 1932, with the election of Franklin D. Roosevelt, the Democratic Party would expand progressive programs to unimagined horizons. Now calling themselves "liberals," they would institute the sweeping political and economic reforms known as the New Deal, in the process "redefining the social contract," as FDR said, and surpassing even Theodore Roosevelt's vision of a powerful executive promoting universal justice. In later years, the liberal mantle would be taken up by other Democratic presidents such as John F. Kennedy and Lyndon B. Johnson, perpetuating the debate over the size of government and its proper role in society that still divides Americans today.

Theodore Roosevelt didn't waste much time replaying the what-ifs of his Bull Moose campaign. Rather, as he had after leaving the presidency in 1909, he escaped overseas. In October 1913, along with his son Kermit (now twenty-four), the Colonel embarked on an expedition to Brazil to chart an Amazon tributary with the daunting name Rio da Dúvida, River of Doubt. Roosevelt was only four years older than when he and Kermit had made their celebrated safari, but conditions in Amazonia were brutal compared to those of the African savannah. When reminded of the dangers before the journey, the Colonel assured Frank Chapman of the American Museum of Natural History, "I have already lived and enjoyed as much of my life as any other nine men I know; I have had my full share, and if it is necessary for me to leave my remains in South America, I am quite ready to do so." The comment nearly proved prophetic. Though the party did manage to map the river (now called Rio Roosevelt), the Colonel contracted debilitating fevers and a nearly fatal leg infection, returning home fifty pounds lighter and in permanently diminished health. (Schrank's bullet, which Roosevelt would carry for the rest of his life, apparently played no role in these maladies.)

Politically, the Colonel remained as active and bellicose as ever. After the outbreak of war in 1914, and especially after the sinking of the British luxury liner the *Lusitania* in May of the following year, with the loss of 128 American lives, the ex-president became a voluble advocate of American preparedness and intervention and a bitter, unrelenting critic of Woodrow Wilson. Even after the United States entered the conflict, Roosevelt disparaged Wilson's prosecution of the war and condemned the Sedition Act (though, unlike Eugene Debs, he wasn't imprisoned for his critiques). At the heart of Roosevelt's condemnation, it has been suggested, was not so much a difference in policy as envy that it had fallen to Wilson, and not to him, to lead the country in a time of war and crisis.

On April 10, 1917, just four days after America finally joined the Allies, the Colonel went to the White House and, shrugging off his earlier criticism as mere "dust in a windy street," petitioned the commander in chief for approval to lead an American division to France. Calling his rival "a great big boy," Wilson confided to his personal secretary, "I was, as formerly, charmed by his personality. There is a sweetness about him that is very compelling. You can't resist the man." But the president did resist the application. Though the ostensible reasons were Roosevelt's age, poor health, and lack of recent military experience, the Colonel suspected that the real motives were personal enmity and a desire not to advance the political career of a perennial rival.

All four of the Roosevelt sons enlisted, and daughter Ethel served as a nurse in France. Ted and Archie were wounded, and in July 1918 their younger brother Quentin, a pilot in the 95th Aero Squadron, was lost over the Marne. Though devastated by Quentin's death, the Colonel wrote a friend: "It is bitter that the young should die, but there are things worse than death; for nothing under heaven would I have had my sons act otherwise than as they acted. They have done pretty well, haven't they?"

America's belated entry into the war seemed to vindicate Roosevelt's long, loud calls for military preparedness, even as his unstinting criticism of radicals at home and abroad reassured citizens alarmed over the rise of Communists and Bolsheviks. Reconciled with Republican leaders, including his old friend William Howard Taft, the Colonel emerged as the odds-on favorite for the party's nomination in 1920. The third term that had eluded him in 1912 finally seemed within his grasp.

But Roosevelt's health continued to deteriorate, and he was plagued by rheumatism, hardening of the arteries, and other complaints. He was hospitalized for six weeks in November and December of 1918; by the time he was released for Christmas, he could barely walk and his normally ruddy complexion had turned ashen. On the evening of January 5, 1919, he reported "a curious feeling," but a doctor called to Sagamore Hill found nothing. At four o'clock that morning, the Colonel died peacefully in his sleep, of a pulmonary embolism. His son Archie telegraphed his brothers Ted and Kermit, still with the Army in Europe, "The old lion is dead."

As the autumn of 1912 deepened into winter, John Schrank settled into life at the Northern Hospital for the Insane. He enjoyed daily walks to the train station and began writing his memoirs. He refused to mix with the other inmates, and they seemed to want nothing to do with him. Still, Schrank said, "I am satisfied. My food is good; my clothing comfortable. What can any man like me want? I am of no further use to the world. I have fulfilled my destiny. That I failed to accomplish that on which I had set my heart is not my fault. It was merely an unfortunate combination of circumstances."

Determined to reclaim his confiscated revolver, Schrank wrote to officials in Milwaukee, assuring them he had "made all the arrangements to turn the weapon over to the board of trustees of the Metropolitan museum in New York." But the following April, Judge Backus entrusted the pistol to Elbert Martin, to be delivered to Oyster Bay after the Colonel's return from South America.

In the same letter, Schrank took the opportunity to complain about the injustice of his treatment, writing, "It is a disgrace that a man with such high intellect as I be locked in an asylum as a dangerous maniac when I am far more sane than my keepers." On February 18, 1914, he was transferred to a new facility, the Central State Hospital for the Criminally Insane, at Waupun, Wisconsin. His mental health continued to decline, and by summer of that year, Judge Backus publicly doubted that Schrank would ever be competent to stand trial. Even so, the would-be assassin was a model inmate. The hospital's acting director, R. A. Remley, found him "a very good patient. He was pleasant and cooperative, and he never gave us a problem."

Schrank still pored over the newspapers. After the outbreak of World War I, he followed the fighting avidly, marking on a map each shift in the Western Front. And he continued to brood over the events of October 1912. According to Dr. Remley, "Several times he said that he believed himself to have been insane at the time of the attack on Roosevelt. At other times he sought to justify the attack." In January 1919, Schrank learned of the Colonel's death. "A good man gone," he said. "Personally I admired his greatness."

In the new decade, Warren Harding was succeeded in the White House by two more Republicans, Calvin Coolidge and Herbert Hoover. Riding the cultural and economic effervescence of the Roaring Twenties, the nation soared like a bubble escaping from a (prohibited) champagne cocktail, before crashing spectacularly to earth on October 29, 1929. In November 1932, during the worst of the Great Depression, Theodore Roosevelt's distant cousin Franklin was elected president, pledging "a New Deal for the American people." Four years later, after the country had made its first, halting steps toward recovery, voters put their faith in FDR again. Then in November 1940, as a new world war raged in Europe, John Schrank read in his newspapers that Franklin Roosevelt had become the first American president ever elected to a third term. According to Dr. Remley, Schrank "was worked up, and said that if he was free he would take a hand in the matter. He believed his mission in life was doing anything to avert a third term as president for anyone."

By then, Schrank was suffering from hardening of the arteries, and beginning in 1943 he was confined to bed. On Wednesday, September 15 of that year, at nine thirty p.m., he died of pneumonia, at the age of sixty-seven. When no one claimed his remains, they were shipped to

Marquette University in Milwaukee, where they were dissected by medical students.

Over the thirty-one years of his confinement, John Schrank never had a visitor, never received a single letter. By the time of his death, he had drifted from the headlines, and only a dwindling few recognized his name or recalled that, during that crowded autumn of 1912, the great Bull Moose had nearly been brought down by a vengeful hunter.

Author's Note

THIS IS A WORK OF NONFICTION. THE EVENTS PORTRAYED IN THESE pages actually happened. All the characters are real, and no names have been changed. Every word within quotation marks (or in italics, in the case of thoughts) was said or written by the person indicated, or at least reported by a witness—though not necessarily at the same point in the narrative that it is cited here.

In the name of dramatic presentation, I have made some assumptions. In a few places, the thoughts ascribed to characters are based on my understanding of their mental state at the time. I believe these assumptions are reasonable, even obvious, and are easily identified by the reader. I've also assumed, for instance, that the working conditions of John Schrank's "fiancée," Elsie Ziegler, were typical of cap makers in her time and place. I've assumed that in a strange city, with a fixed destination, John Schrank would take the most direct route on major streets. For the interested reader, all such conjectures are detailed in the Sources. Any item not identified in the Sources as my supposition is part of the historical record, down to the clothing the characters wore and the gestures they made.

In my research, I discovered significant factual discrepancies among various sources—for example, on John Schrank's family background. The text of candidates' speeches can also vary significantly as reported in various newspapers. Accordingly, I have tried to choose my sources with care, and in the Sources I point out some cases where sources disagree. The Sources also include some updates on subsequent events, for instance, the future political career of TR's son-in-law Nick Longworth.

Finally, this book is a work of narrative, not biography or historical analysis. I have sought to include enough background to enhance the story, but not so much as to overwhelm it. Readers who would like more context on this fascinating and pivotal period of American history may wish to consult the works listed in the Bibliography; please see the notes at the beginning of that section for suggestions for further reading.

Acknowledgments

I'D LIKE TO EXTEND MY DEEP APPRECIATION TO THE 2011 CLASS OF the Columbia Publishing Course, of the Columbia Graduate School of Journalism, who suggested the idea for this book. Every summer for the past decade, it has been my privilege to work with the course's expert and committed faculty; the director, my dear friend Lindy Hess; and one hundred gifted publishing-professionals-in-training. Every year I return home certain that I have learned more from all of you than you have from me.

My thanks to the staff of the following institutions, whose dedication and professionalism permitted the extensive research required by this project: Atlanta-Fulton Public Library System; Biblioteca Pública, San Miguel de Allende, Mexico; Charleston County (SC) Public Library; Chattanooga Public Library; Chicago History Museum; Chicago Public Library; Digital Library of Georgia, of the University of Georgia; Fond du Lac (WI) Public Library; Library of Congress; Milwaukee Public Library; Nashville Public Library; National Climatic Data Center at NOAA; New York Public Library; B. S. Ricks Memorial Library (Yazoo City, MS); and Willard Library (Evansville, IN).

Thank you to Garry Beene of Signal Research Services, Signal Mountain, Tennessee, for your thorough and timely assistance.

My special acknowledgment to my hundreds of unseen colleagues— the authors, journalists, artists, and photographers whose efforts, as detailed in the Sources and Bibliography, gave me a glimpse into the world of 1912; without your work, mine would have been impossible.

Thanks again to my editor at Lyons Press, Keith Wallman, for your enthusiasm and commitment to this project and for your sure editorial hand. As always, it's been a pleasure.

My warm thanks to my friend and agent, Deirdre Mullane of Mullane Literary Associates. As we enter our second decade of collaboration, I appreciate your wise counsel more than ever.

Finally, my most profound gratitude is reserved for my wife of thirty-six years, Teresa Nicholas, my partner in writing and in life, to whom I owe more than words can say.

Sources

I have listed below the sources where I discovered the information cited; please note that in many cases the same material can also be found elsewhere. In general, I haven't given sources for readily available, noncontroversial information, unless I thought the reader might want to consult those publications directly. Under each subheading, I have tried to list the sources from most germane to least.

In the text, quotations from written sources (such as letters) are reproduced with any original idiosyncrasies in spelling and punctuation; in quotations that were originally spoken (such as speeches), I have occasionally modernized spelling and punctuation in the interest of readability.

Prologue: "Avenge My Death!"
ix.   Schrank's dream: Remey, pp. 93, 119, 122, 203; *New York Times*, September 15, 1901. The description of McKinley's burial suit is from a photo taken of him as president. A few other details, such as the presence of flowers, are my supposition.
ix.   McKinley's activities at the Pan-American Exposition, shooting, aftermath, and death: S. Miller.
x.   McKinley quotation "No one would wish to hurt me": S. Miller, pp. 4 and 5.
x.   Czolgosz's background and activities leading up to the assassination: S. Miller.
xi.   American political climate in 1901: S. Miller.
xii.   Bryan quotation "The extremes of society": Morris 2001, p. 37.
xiii.   McKinley quotation "Don't let them hurt him": S. Miller, p. 302. Some other sources quote the same sentiment in various ways, such as, "Go easy on him, boys."
xiii.   Czolgosz quotation "I done my duty": S. Miller, p. 301.
xiv.   Text of telegram to TR: Morris 2001, p. 3.
xiv.   TR quotation "If it had been I who had been shot": Morris 2001, p. 4.
xiv.   McKinley quotation "God's will be done": S. Miller, p. 320.
xv.   That Schrank expected to see Czolgosz is my supposition; also that he sat up in bed, that his breathing was ragged, and that he lay awake until dawn.

Chapter One: "We Stand at Armageddon"
3.   Weather in New York: National Climatic Data Center (ncdc.noaa.gov).
3.   Schrank's excursion to buy newspapers: Schrank was an inveterate reader of newspapers, but it is my supposition that he went out to buy them on this particular morning.

3. Physical description of John Schrank: Remey, pp. 115, 193; *New York Times*, October 16 and 17, 1912.

3. New York City at turn of the century, including statistics on millionaires and corporations: Reitano, pp. 79–84.

5. White House Hotel proprietor Gustav Jost: Remey, p. 121.

5. Jost's previous dealings with Schrank: *New York Times*, October 15, 1912.

5. Schrank's tenure at the White House Hotel: Remey, p. 121.

5. Rent of two dollars per week: Morris 2010, p. 237.

5. Address of the Flammangs' apartment and saloon: Remey, p. 118.

6. Schrank's age at immigration: *Index to Petitions for Naturalization Filed in New York City, 1792–1989* (available, for a fee, on ancestry.com). Remey gives Schrank's age as twelve, but this is incorrect.

6. Schrank's family and upbringing in Erding: Remey, pp. 124, 127, 192; *New York Times*, October 17, 1912. It's my supposition that he would have shared a bed with at least one sibling in Erding.

6. Biographical data on Dominick and Annie Flammang: 1900 US Census (available, for a fee, on ancestry.com).

6. Schrank's life with the Flammangs: Remey, pp. 118, 129, 195.

6. More than a quarter million New Yorkers born in Germany, and the city had more German speakers than any other but Berlin or Vienna: Burrows, p. 1111.

6. Characteristics of German immigrants: Schneider.

7. Schrank's education, poetry, newspaper reading, admiration of George Washington: Remey, pp. 124, 129, 152–53, 157–58, 188, 192, 195, 208, 209. It's my assumption that the historically minded Schrank would have hung on Civil War veterans' stories.

7. Date of Schrank's naturalization: *Index to Petitions for Naturalization Filed in New York City, 1792–1989* (available, for a fee, at ancestry.com).

7. *General Slocum* disaster: Ellis; *Brooklyn Daily Eagle*, June 23, 1904. The sinking was the greatest loss of life in New York City until September 11, 2001.

7. Biographical details of Elsie Ziegler: US Census (available, for a fee, on ancestry.com).

7. Working conditions of a cap maker: Schneiderman.

8. Schrank was planning to marry Elsie: Remey, p. 97. Schrank claimed that he and Elsie were engaged, but her neighbors and family later denied it; the romance may have been a delusion on his part. The names of their neighbors are from the 1900 US Census (available, for a fee, on ancestry.com).

8. Quotation from *Brooklyn Daily Eagle*: Edition of June 23, 1904.

9. Schrank identified Elsie's body: *Brooklyn Daily Eagle*, June 17, 1904

9. Schrank would sit at the monument in Tompkins Square Park: There is no record of Schrank having done this, but I believe the monument would have been an irresistible destination for someone of his obsessive, brooding personality.

9. Schrank quotation "That wouldn't be right to Elsie": *New York Times*, October 16, 1912.

9. Changes in Little Germany after the *Slocum* disaster: Binder, pp. 96–97; Burrows, p. 1117.

9. Dominick Flammang's retirement and his and Annie's purchase of tenement in Yorkville: Remey, p. 195; *New York Times*, October 16, 1912.

9. Deaths of the Flammangs: *New York Times*, August 8, 1913. These dates differ from those in Remey, p. 195, but I believe the later, more specific *Times* account is correct.

10. Schrank hadn't kept up with his family in Germany: Remey, p. 126; *New York Times*, October 17, 1912.

10. Schrank had no friends: According to a note found in his suitcase, as quoted in the *Charleston News and Courier*, October 16, 1912.

10. Schrank was a fallen Catholic: Remey, pp. 192 and 233.

10. Schrank stored his belongings: Remey, p. 182.

10. Schrank's activities after the death of his aunt and uncle, job in Brooklyn, attitude of neighbors, lawsuit: *New York Times*, October 16 and 17, 1912. The state of Schrank's finances in this period is uncertain; acquaintances remembered him talking about his money problems, but after his arrest he told police that he had an income of $800 per year from the tenement, enough to live on as long as he watched expenses (Remey, p. 121). I'm inclined to believe that he was in financial straits, which would explain why he sought work as a bartender. Also, he stopped paying the mortgage on the tenement on July 1, 1912 (according to *New York Times*, August 8, 1913); since this was before he decided to hunt TR, it seems to suggest that he was short of funds.

10. Schrank's letter to Judge Strahl: *New York Times*, October 17, 1912. Strahl had destroyed the letter, and the wording given is from his memory.

11. Schrank's habits at the White House Hotel: *New York Times,* October 16, 1912.

11. Schrank's poetry, walks, and newspapers: Remey, pp. 152, 195, 209.

11. TR quotation that he was "fit as a bull moose": This has been widely cited.

11. Progressive convention: Gould, *Four Hats*, p. 183ff; Morris 2001, p. 220ff; Donald, p. 249ff.

12. TR's family background and pre-presidential political career: Morris 1979.

12. TR author of dozens of books: Before his death, he would publish more than thirty volumes; later ones included his autobiography and *Through the Brazilian Wilderness*.

12. TR quotation "the wealthy criminal class": Morris 1979, p. 193.

13. TR's mother's and Alice's deaths and TR quotations "There is a curse on this house" and "The light has gone out": Morris 1979, pp. 229–30.

14. TR quotation "There were all kinds of things I was afraid of": National Park Service website (nps.gov).

14. Edith Carow Roosevelt: For more, see the website of the National First Ladies' Library (firstladies.org).

15. Harrison quotation that TR "wanted to put an end to all evil": Pringle, p. 86.

15. TR quotation that Harrison was "cold-blooded, narrow-minded": Morris 1979, p. 439

15. TR as police commissioner: Morris 1979.

15. Policemen called their profession "the business"; illicit revenues of $10 million per year; Byrnes's fortune; $2 million in bribes from saloonkeepers; 15,000 saloonkeepers; German and other immigrant opposition to dry law: Morris 1979, pp. 491, 499–500, 513ff.

16. Liquor dealers voted Democratic: Remey, p. 155.

16. Sunday-closing crackdown: Pringle, p. 98ff; Morris 1979, p. 512ff.

16. Nearly a quarter of the city's barkeepers were close to bankruptcy: Morris 1979, p. 501.

16. Germans' protest parade; their hostile reception of dry laws; "Teddy's Folly" quotation; German voting statistics: Morris 1979, pp. 504, 506, 509; Jeffers, pp. 135–36.

17. TR called King Roosevelt I: Harbaugh, p. 85.

17. McKinley considered TR too excitable: Morris 1979, p. 578.

17. Spanish-American War: S. Miller, p. 85ff.

17. TR quotation "I rather hope that the fight will come soon": This comment, from a letter to Henry Cabot Lodge, has been widely cited.

18. Sending the *Maine* was like lighting a candle near an open cask of gunpowder: From Walter R. Herrick's *The American Naval Revolution*, quoted in S. Miller, p. 104.

18. Board of inquiry found that the *Maine* had been sunk by a Spanish mine: It is now generally accepted that the *Maine* was sunk when one of its munitions stores exploded accidentally.

18. Rough Riders and their role in battle of San Juan Heights: S. Miller, p. 188ff; Spanish-American War Centennial website (spanamwar.com); Yockelson; Auchincloss, pp. 28–32.

18. Leonard Wood: A surgeon by training, Wood would become Army chief of staff under Taft and later a candidate for the Republican presidential nomination (in 1920) and governor-general of the Philippines (1921–27).

18. TR quotations "my crowded hour" and "the great day of my life": These have been widely cited.

19. Augustus Van Wyck biography: *New York Times*, June 9, 1922.

19. TR's governorship and accomplishments in office: Morris 1979.

19. "Boy governor": Morris 1979, p. 692.

19. TR quotation on "the combination of business with politics": Roosevelt 1913, p. 217.

19. TR quotation "All together, I am pretty well satisfied": Morris 1979, p. 735.

19. TR as vice president: Morris 1979.

20. TR as president: Morris 2001; Donald.

20. TR quotation on "great corporations": Morris 2001, p. 73.

20. Pennsylvania Coal Strike: Donald, p. 147ff; Morris 2010, p. 131ff.

21. Panama Canal: Morris 2001; Donald, p. 159ff.

21. Cost of the Panama Canal: Website of the Panama Canal (micanaldepanama.com).

21. Adams quotation "Theodore thinks of nothing": Donald, p. 178.

22. Renovation of the Executive Mansion and name change to the White House: Gould 2003, pp. 16–17. The First Lady played a leading role in the changes.

22. Buildup of American navy: Donald, p. 200–201.

22. Russo-Japanese War peace negotiations: Morris 2001, pp. 399–414.

22. Tillman quotation that TR was "the most popular president" and Twain quotation that TR was "the most popular human being": Morris 2001, pp. 430–31.

23. TR quotation on "the wise custom which limits the President to two terms": Morris 2001, p. 364.

23. TR quotation on the "still, small voice": Morris 2001, p. 490.

23. Taft not beholden to Wall Street: Morris 2001, p. 482.

23. It was hoped that Taft could unite progressive and conservative Republicans: Chace, p. 32.

23. Taft quotation "My ambition": Auchincloss, p. 86.

24. TR quotation "Of course, if I had conscientiously felt": Morris 2001, p. 540. Note the spelling of *thoroly*; TR was an avid proponent of the simplified spelling movement, and in 1906 ordered the Government Printing Office to use simplified spellings of 300 selected words; faced with popular and Congressional opposition, he later rescinded the directive.

24. Africa far from reporters: Chace, p. 12.

24. J. P. Morgan quotation "Wall Street expects every lion": O'Toole, p. 15.

24. TR received as "something more than a king": Morris 2010, p. 49.

24. Quotation from *Le Temps* "Never since Napoleon": Morris 2010, p. 76.

25. TR quotation "I felt if I met another king": Morris 2010, p. 68.

25. TR's reception in New York: Donald, p. 237; Gardner, p. 169; Morris 2010, pp. 80–87; O'Toole, p. 92.

25. TR's conflict with Taft and decision to run for a third term: Gould, *Four Hats*; Brands; Morris 1979.

25. The tariff: Gould, *Four Hats*, pp. 8–11; Cooper 2009, p. 187.

25. Percentage of federal income derived from tariffs: *Historical Statistics of the United States, 1789–1945* (available online at census.gov).

26. Tariff raised retail prices between 5 and 75 percent and cost average worker $115 per year, $16 of which found its way to treasury: O'Toole, p. 207.

26. Average worker's earnings in 1912 ($592): Gould, *Four Hats*, p. 8.

26. Farmers' population and problems: Chace, pp. 83–84; Morris 2001, p. 36; Kelly, p. 45.

26. Payne-Aldrich Tariff Act: Gould, *Four Hats*, pp. 8–11.

26. Taft quotation "the best tariff bill that the Republican Party ever passed": This has been widely cited.

27. Taft as president: Morris 2010; Gould, *Four Hats*.

27. Taft letter about being called "Mr. President": Morris 2010, p. 13.

27. Poem from *Life* magazine: Gould, *Four Hats*, p. 1.

27. TR quotation "conflict between the men who possess more than they have earned": Gardner, p. 189.

27. TR quotation "What a floppy souled creature he is": Gardner, p. 210.

28. TR quotation "The fight is on and I am stripped to the buff!": This widely quoted comment was made on February 21 to a reporter in Columbus, Ohio. It appears in a slightly different form in Gould, *Four Hats*, p. 56.

28. TR quotation "Frequently when asked to take another cup of coffee": Brands, p. 698.

29. TR's nomination campaign: Gardner, p. 230ff.

29. TR was 66 percent ahead of Taft among Republicans: Morris 2010, p. 176.

29. TR's performance in primaries: Gould, *Four Hats*, Appendix B.

29. Effects of primary elections: Gould, *Four Hats*, pp. 24 and 86.

29. Statistics on primary campaign contributions and Turner quotation on "the underwriting of presidential candidates": O'Toole, p. 171.

29. Taft quotation that TR was a "dangerous egoist": *New York Times*, May 14, 1912, quoted in Morris 2010, p. 187.

29. TR quotation that Taft was a "fathead": Morris 2010, p. 187.

29. Taft quotation "Roosevelt was my closest friend": Brands, p. 707.

29. Taft quotation "Sometimes I think I might as well give up": Gardner, p. 258.

30. Republican convention: Gardner, p. 236ff; Gould, *Four Hats*, p. 124ff.

30. Delegates needed to nominate, delegate counts for TR and Taft, number of contested delegates and number of contested delegates awarded to TR and Taft: Gardner, p. 236; Gould, *Four Hats*, p. 67.

30. Root quotation "I care more": Auchincloss, p. 120.

31. TR's claim that nomination was stolen: The consensus is now that the great majority of TR's contested delegates were in fact specious and that the nomination was not "stolen." (See Gardner, p. 243.)

31. TR quotation "We are fighting for honesty against naked robbery": Gould, *Four Hats*, p. 70.

31. Final delegate count: Chace, p. 122.

31. Formation of Progressive Party: Gould, *Four Hats*, p. 125ff; Chace, p. 161ff.

31. Depew quotation "The only question now is which corpse": Gardner, p. 252.

32. Schrank was a member of no party, had no love of Republicans: Remey, pp. 131, 155.

32. Theodore Rex: As related in Morris 2001 (p. 370), the jibe was coined by Henry James.

32. *NY World* quotation that TR was "the most cunning and adroit demagogue": Gardner, p. 254.

32. Quotations from TR's speech before Progressive convention: *New York Times*, August 7, 1912.

33. The beginning of mob rule, just as the editors of the *World* had warned: Morris 2010, p. 167.

33. Schrank's written rebuttal to TR's confession of faith: Remey, pp. 201, 224–234. It's not clear when this rebuttal was written.

35. Schrank's statement that Abraham Lincoln said, "War is hell": This expression is actually attributed to William Tecumseh Sherman.

36. Schrank quotation "This is my murderer and nobody else!": Remey, p. 199.

Chapter Two: "God Has Called Me to Be His Instrument"

38. Details of TR's arrival in Oakland and San Francisco: Van Smith.
38. For a period map of San Francisco, see Chevalier; available online at davidrumsey.com.
38. The text of his speech was in TR's breast pocket: This was his habitual place for it.
38. TR had been lulled onto the defensive: Morris 2010, p. 238.
38. TR had forsaken the usual whistle-stops: Tiller, September 15, 1912.
38. TR's western tour as president: Morris 2001, pp. 214–35.
39. TR's campaign swing from New England to California: Gould, *Bull Moose.*
39. TR would have logged 10,000 miles: Morris 2010, pp. 236, 238.
39. TR quotations "Parties of privilege" and "a crooked alliance": Gould, *Bull Moose,* p. 61.
39. TR quotation "dared to go forward for righteousness' sake": Gould, *Bull Moose,* p. 70.
39. TR the heir of Lincoln, fighting for freedom: Cooper 2009, p. 155.
40. Taft quotation "I have been told I ought to do this": O'Toole, p. 205.
40. Taft would rely on interviews, advertisements, etc.: Gould, *Four Hats,* p. 126.
40. Sherman's ill health: Gould, *Four Hats,* p. 156.
40. Quotations from Taft's acceptance speech: Gould, *Four Hats,* p. 127.
40. Differences among TR, Taft, and Wilson on the tariff (including quotations): O'Toole, pp. 207–8; Cooper 2009, p. 187; Chace, p. 206.
41. Extent of Wilson's campaign journeys: Cooper 2009, pp. 165–66.
41. Wilson's biography and career: Cooper 2009 and Cooper 1983.
42. Princeton's curriculum was notoriously unchallenging: Cooper 2009, pp. 117–18.
42. Wilson quotation on his "brightest dream": Cooper 2009, p. 35.
42. Wilson quotations that the law was "antagonistic to the best interests of the academic life" and "No man can safely enter political life": Cooper 2009, p. 40.
43. TR quotation that Wilson was "a perfect trump,": Cooper 2009, p. 79.
44. Wilson quotation "What we need is not a square deal": Cooper 2009, p. 92.
44. Progressive mood of the nation: Chace, p. 100; Milkis, p. 1.
45. Wilson quotation "We have begun a fight": Cooper 2009, p. 126.
45. Wilson quotation that his win was "a victory of the 'progressives'": Cooper 2009, p. 127.
45. Wilson quotation "After dealing with college politicians": Cooper 2009, p. 117.
45. Wilson's ill health and romantic liaison: Gould, *Four Hats,* pp. 77–78.
46. TR quotation "no evidence could ever make the American people believe": Gardner, p. 270.
46. Wilson seen as overly friendly to cities and to industry: Cooper 2009, p. 150.
46. Advantages of Wilson's short tenure: O'Toole, p. 214.
46. Wilson was a fresh face: Gould, *Four Hats,* p. 77.
46. Democratic Party's strategic shift to the left: Gould, *Four Hats,* p. 80ff.
47. Characterization of Oscar Underwood: Chace, p. 125.
47. Characterization of Champ Clark: Chace, p. 147.

47. Wilson quotation "It begins to look as if I must merely sit on the sidelines": Cooper 1983, p. 184.
47. Wilson's primary results: Gould, *Four Hats*, Appendix A.
47. Clark and Wilson's delegate counts entering the convention: Gould, *Four Hats*, p. 88.
47. Vote counts on first ballot: Cooper 2009, p. 155.
47. Democrats' convention fight: Gould, *Four Hats*, pp. 89–93; Cooper 2009, pp. 155–58; Chace, pp. 146–58.
48. Wilson's nomination one of the great upsets: Lewis L. Gould has called it "one of the great dramas in American political history" (Gould, *Four Hats*, p. 76).
48. Wilson quotations "a sort of political miracle" and "I feel the tremendous responsibility": Cooper 1983, p. 186.
48. Comparison of TR to John the Baptist: Donald, p. 251.
48. TR's reception in Reno: Ogden (UT) *Evening Standard*, September 14, 1912.
49. TR's reception in Blackfoot, Idaho: *New York Tribune*, September 14, 1912; *Washington Times*, September 14, 1912; *New York Sun*, September 14, 1912.
49. TR's reception in Pocatello, Idaho: *San Francisco Call*, September 14, 1912; *New York Sun*, September 14, 1912.
50. TR was perhaps the most skilled campaigner the country had ever seen: Morris 2010, p. 221.
50. TR quotation "Pure Barnum and Bailey": Gould, *Four Hats*, p. 133.
50. TR's health issues: Morris 2001, pp. 376–77.
50. His aides saw that he was becoming stale: Morris 2010 p. 238.
51. Sherman quotation "It was essential": Gould, *Four Hats*, p. 125.
51. Taft quotation "a long hard fight": Cooper 2009, p. 167.
51. Consideration of TR's chances and challenges: Gould, *Four Hats*, p. 155ff.
51. TR quotation "be able to give the right trend to our democracy": Cooper 1983, p. 189.
52. TR's reception in Oakland: Van Smith.
52. Statistics on the San Francisco earthquake: Website of the US Geological Survey (earthquake.usgs.gov).
53. Carl Olson incident: *New York Times*, September 15, 1912. At least one other source spells Olson's name differently.
53. TR carried a revolver and sometimes escaped the Secret Service: Morris 2001, pp. 117, 122.
53. Assassination attempt at Sagamore Hill: Morris 2001, p. 266.
54. Members of TR's party: Van Smith.
54. Fog in San Francisco Bay: *San Francisco Call*, September 14, 1912, p. 25.
54. Francis Heney biography: "Francis J. Heney (1859–1937)," *Oregon Encyclopedia* (oregonencyclopedia.org).
55. Hiram Johnson biography: Gould, *Four Hats*, p. 133.
55. TR's late arrival: *San Francisco Call*, September 14, 1912, p. 1; *Tacoma Times*, September 14, 1912.

57. TR's reception at the Coliseum: Van Smith; Tiller, September 15, 1912; *Washington Herald*, September 15, 1912; *New York Tribune*, September 15, 1912; *New York Times*, September 15, 1912. For a photo of the exterior of the Coliseum in 1912, see the website of the San Francisco Public Library (sfpl.org).

57. Text of TR's speech in the Coliseum: Gould, *Bull Moose*, pp. 108–17.

58. Text of Wilson's speech on September 9: This has been widely cited.

58. Wilson's remarks seemed to indicate that he hadn't fully converted to progressivism: Cooper 2009, p. 165.

58. Differences between TR and Wilson on the role of the federal government: Cooper 1983, pp. xiii, 180, 184, 192–96, 212–16, 219–20; Cooper 2009, pp. 162–64, 176–78; Gould, *Four Hats*, pp. 162–65; Chace, pp. 99, 194–96.

58. Louis Brandeis: In January 1916 President Wilson nominated Brandeis to the Supreme Court; in June, after rancorous, unprecedented public hearings, the Senate overcame the nominee's perceived radicalism and his Jewish faith and confirmed his appointment.

60. Schrank's activities, thoughts, and writings: Remey, pp. 92–93, 159, 161–62, 186, 189, 200, 210–11.

Chapter Three: "We Want No King"

64. Weather in New York: *New York Sun*, September 22, 1912, p. 15.

64. Schrank's bankroll: Remey, p. 202.

64. Schrank borrowed money from Herman Larunger, and contents of letter to Larunger: *New York Times*, October 17, 1912.

64. Canal Street scene: This is my supposition.

64. *Tribune* and *Sun* headlines: From their front pages of September 21, 1912.

65. Geography of Lower Manhattan: Throughout this chapter, I have used the Bromleys' *Atlas of the City of New York, Borough of Manhattan*, and *Atlas of the Borough of Brooklyn, City of New York*, available online from the New York Public Library (digitalgallery.nypl.org); see Bibliography for full citation.

65. History of Five Points: Christiano.

66. Schrank had determined not to act in New York: Remey, p. 201.

67. Schrank's purchase of pistol, familiarity with guns: Remey, pp. 122, 179, 181–83, 202; *Charleston News and Courier*, October 16, 1912.

67. Sullivan Act: *New York Times*, October 21, 1912; Duffy; Walsh. For the text of the Sullivan Act, see New York State Penal Code (full citation in the Bibliography).

68. Estimated 5,000 illegal pistols sold: *New York Times*, October 21, 1912.

68. Text of TR's speech in Topeka: Gould, *Bull Moose*, p. 121ff.

68. TR's travels through California: Tiller, September 16, 1912; *San Francisco Call*, September 16, 1912.

69. TR in Los Angeles: *New York Times*, September 17, 1912; *San Francisco Call*, September 16 and 17, 1912.

69. TR's travels through Arizona, New Mexico, Colorado, Nebraska, Kansas: *Washington Times*, September 17, 1912; *San Francisco Call*, September 18, 19, and 21, 1912;

Bisbee Daily Review, September 18 and 19, 1912; Tiller, September 20 and 21, 1912; *New York Tribune*, September 21, 1912.

70. TR quotation that Taft was "a dead cock in the pit": *New York Tribune*, September 21, 1912.

70. Incidents in Oxford, Nebraska: *New York Tribune*, September 21, 1912.

70. TR's breakfast of four eggs, etc.: O'Toole, p. 180.

70. Quotation from TR's Omaha speech: *San Francisco Call*, September 21, 1912.

71. Interruption in Topeka speech: Tiller, September 22, 1912.

71. Perkins was charming, soft-spoken, and beautifully tailored: William Allen White, quoted in O'Toole, p. 159.

71. George Perkins biography: Gould, *Four Hats*, p. 130; O'Toole, pp. 159–60.

71. Penrose scandal: Gould, *Four Hats*, pp. 148–49; Cooper 1983, p. 42; Macoll; O'Toole, p. 214.

72. Penrose quotation "I believe in the division of labor": This has been widely cited.

72. La Follette's assertion on 140 v. 10,000 trusts: O'Toole, p. 214.

73. Wilson's travel schedule in September: Davidson; on the same journey, Wilson continued into Pennsylvania and New England.

73. Wilson quotation "not to take you out of the hands of the men": Gould, *Four Hats*, p. 168.

73. Wilson quotation "The Bull Moose appeals to their imagination": Gardner, p. 268.

74. Reed quotation "I never met a man": Cooper 1983, p. 238.

74. TR's London letter: *New York Times*, September 21, 1912.

74. TR quotation "If they'll specify the person": *New York Times*, September 22, 1912.

74. Debs itinerary: Chace, pp. 223–24; Gould, *Four Hats*, p. 159.

75. Taft refused an invitation to debate Debs: *San Francisco Call*, September 21, 1912.

75. Debs accused TR of stealing his ideas: Gould, *Four Hats*, p. 158.

75. Socialist platform: Chace, p. 186.

76. Debs and the Socialist Party: Gould, *Four Hats*, p. 103ff.

76. Debs quotation "Let us make this our year": Gould, *Four Hats*, p. 36.

76. Debs biography and his union activities: Salvatore. (Note that Salvatore discounts the traditional version that Debs was converted to socialism by his reading of Marx and other writers while in prison.)

77. Great Railroad Strike of 1877: S. Miller, pp. 80–82, 107–9.

78. Pullman strike and aftermath: Salvatore, pp. 126–39; Samuel Gompers Papers website, sponsored by the University of Maryland at College Park (history.umd.edu).

79. Debs quotation "I am for Socialism": Salvatore, p. 161.

79. Lincoln was Debs's hero: Chace, p. 81.

79. TR's activities in Emporia and characterization of the town: White, pp. 493–96; Tiller, September 21, 1912; Morris 2010, p. 238; *San Francisco Call*, September 23, 1912; *New York Sun*, September 23, 1912.

79. Biography of William White: White.

80. White quotation "I was afire with the splendor of the personality": White, p. 297.

80. White found rift with Taft "heartbreaking": White, p. 444.

81. White quotation "sinister figure": White, p. 459.

82. White quotation re TR's "rough bass": White, p. 494.

82. For more on "Red Rocks," see the website of the Kansas Historical Society, kshs.org.

82. TR quotation "considering the cosmos": White, p. 494.

82. Making of TR's recordings, including quotations: Sooy.

83. Text of TR's recordings: Library of Congress's National Jukebox (loc.gov/jukebox). They are also available on other websites.

85. A photo of TR with the White family at "Red Rocks" is available on the website of the Kansas Historical Society (kshs.org).

85. TR's farewell remarks and crowd reaction in Emporia: *New York Sun*, September 23, 1912.

85. That Schrank would have walked to Pier 36 is my supposition.

85. SS *Comanche*: *New York Times*, August 21 and December 1, 1895. For a photo of the *Comanche*, see website of Encore Editions (encore-editions.com). For an illustration of the Clyde Line flag, see the website of CRW Flags, Inc. (crwflags.com).

86. Weather in New York: *New York Sun*, September 21, 1912, p. 1.

86. It is my supposition that Schrank had never sailed on the North (Hudson) River before.

86. Schrank's suitcase was new and cost about three dollars: This was the assessment of E. H. Moseley, as recounted in the *Charleston News and Courier*, October 16, 1912.

86. Contents of Schrank's suitcase, including quoted writings: Remey, pp. 128, 185; *Rock Hill Evening Herald*, October 16, 1912.

Chapter Four: "A Perfect Stranger"

89. SS *Comanche* arrived late afternoon: Remey, p. 165.

89. Details of Charleston: *Charleston, South Carolina* (see Bibliography for full citation); Horton; 1911 *Encyclopedia Britannica* (available online at 1911encyclopedia.org).

90. Progressive campaign released schedule for the rest of the month: *Thomasville Daily Times Enterprise*, September 23, 1912, p. 1.

90. Schrank's plans and activities in Charleston and decision to go to Atlanta: Remey, pp. 117, 125, 165–66, 191. It is my supposition that he bought a newspaper at the ship terminal. Also, in his later interrogation, Schrank appeared confused about when he had stopped at Birmingham. At one point he told police he went to Birmingham before Atlanta, but another time he said he traveled from Augusta directly to Atlanta, and on his list of hotels Atlanta appears before Birmingham. It's my interpretation that he stayed in Atlanta twice, once en route to Birmingham and again when TR was in Atlanta.

91. Weather in Charleston: National Climatic Data Center (ncdc.noaa.gov).

91. Schrank's route to the Moseley House is my supposition.

91. Schrank thought of himself as "a perfect stranger" in Charleston: Remey, p. 166.

92. Moseley House: Remey, pp. 94 and 165 (where it is misspelled *Mosley*); *Charleston News and Courier*, October 16, 1912. For a photo of the Moseley House, see *Charleston Evening Post*, November 25, 1969, on the occasion of the building's demolition.

92. Moseley's impression of Schrank and conversation with him: *Charleston News and Courier*, October 16, 1912. It is my supposition that Schrank had only a slight accent, based on the assessment of his English in Remey and the fact that he came to America at age thirteen.

92. Schrank registered under his real name and prepaid: Remey, pp. 125 and 127.

92. TR awoke feeling recharged; TR at Arcadia, Liberal, and nearby towns: Tiller, September 23, 1912.

93. TR at Pittsburg, Kansas: *El Paso Herald*, September 23, 1912; *Tacoma Times*, September 23, 1912.

93. TR at Lamar and Springfield, Missouri: Ogden (UT) *Evening Standard*, September 24, 1912; *New York Sun*, September 24, 1912.

94. Hadley's role in nomination and election campaigns: Hahn; Ogden (UT) *Evening Standard*, September 24, 1912. Hadley eventually gave Taft his halfhearted endorsement; in the general election, the state voted for Wilson, with TR a distant third.

94. TR's relations with blacks and his Southern strategy: O'Toole, pp. 193–96; Chace, pp. 163–65, 201; Gould, *Four Hats*, pp. 27, 47, 134–36.

94. Brownsville incident: In 1972, President Richard Nixon pardoned the black soldiers and awarded them honorable discharges.

95. Frequency of lynching: Gibson.

95. Black population and voter rolls ca. 1912: O'Toole, p. 193.

95. Democratic Party longtime advocate of segregation and white supremacy: Gould, *Four Hats*, p. 29.

95. TR was determined to crack the Solid South: Gould, *Four Hats*, pp. 134–35; Tiller, September 23, 1912.

95. Wilson and blacks: Cooper 2009, pp. 79–80, 109; Gould, *Four Hats*, p. 155.

96. Taft and blacks: Gould, *Four Hats*, p. 29.

96. TR in Joplin: Ogden (UT) *Evening Standard*, September 24, 1912; *Washington Herald*, September 24, 1912; Pratt, September 24, 1912; *New York Sun*, September 24, 1912; Blair, p. 104.

97. George W. Johnson anecdote: *San Francisco Call*, September 24, 1912.

97. Schrank mailed a postcard to Gustav Jost: *New York Times*, October 16, 1912.

97. Charleston weather: National Climatic Data Center (ncdc.noaa.gov).

97. That Schrank consulted a train schedule and walked to the depot, as well as the route he took, are my suppositions.

97. Schrank worried over his luggage, had no check for it: Remey, 125–27, 183.

97. Inventory of effects Schrank carried with him: Remey, pp. 92–94, 183, 191.

98. Schrank sliced open his vest pocket: Remey, p. 171.

98. For a photo of Charleston's Union Station and plaza, see the numerous period pictures available online. It's my assumption that Schrank bought a ticket before boarding the train.

98. Schrank's thoughts en route to Augusta and his route from the station to the Planters Hotel are my supposition.

99. For a detailed period map of Augusta, see the Sanborn Fire Insurance Map of that city (full citation in the Bibliography).

99. Schrank at the Planters Hotel: Remey, pp. 94 and 166. Period photos of the Planters Hotel are widely available online; its floor plan is available on the Sanborn Fire Insurance Map of Augusta, 1904, available online at the Digital Library of Georgia (dlg.galileo.usg.edu).

99. The reason that Schrank gave his real name in Charleston was to avoid a problem in reclaiming his luggage: Schrank implies this in his police interrogation (Remey, p. 125) but doesn't say so explicitly.

99. Clerk didn't comment that Schrank had no luggage: Remey, p. 126.

99. TR in Little Rock: Tiller, September 25, 1912; *New York Sun*, September 26, 1912; Pratt, September 26, 1912; *New York Tribune*, September 26, 1912; *El Paso Herald*, September 25, 1912; *Thomasville Daily Times Enterprise*, September 25, 1912; *Caldwell Watchman*.

100. TR in Memphis: *San Francisco Call*, September 26, 1912; Tiller, September 26, 1912; *New York Tribune*, September 26, 1912.

100. Vardaman quotation "coon-flavored miscegenist": This has been widely cited.

101. The Teddy Bear and Billy Possum: Brinkley; Morris 2001, pp. 171–74.

101. Schrank's decision to intercept TR in Atlanta: Remey, pp. 125 and 165.

102. TR in New Orleans: *Daily Picayune*, September 27 and 28, 1912; *San Francisco Call*, September 28, 1912; Tiller, September 27 and 28, 1912; *Richmond Times Dispatch*, September 28, 1912; *New York Sun*, September 28, 1912; *Thomasville Daily Times Enterprise*, September 27, 1912.

102. For more on New Orleans in the period, see 1911 *Encyclopedia Britannica* (available online at 1911encyclopedia.org) and *Rand McNally New Commercial Atlas of New Orleans* (full citation in the Bibliography).

102. TR's battered black Stetson and weather in New Orleans: *Daily Picayune*, September 28, 1912.

104. Background on Cecil Lyon: Texas State Historical Association website (tshaonline.org).

104. Winter Garden Theater: *Daily Picayune*, October 23, 1910.

105. John M. Parker: In 1920, Parker was elected governor of Louisiana.

105. New Orleans's potential benefit from the Panama Canal: Kaufman.

105. Text of TR's speech in New Orleans: Gould, *Bull Moose*, pp. 136–42.

107. Schrank at Atlanta's Child's Hotel: Remey, p. 94. The building still stands; for more information, see the City of Atlanta website (atlantaga.gov).

107. Schrank signed guest book as Walter Ross: Remey, p. 125. In Milwaukee, according to Remey (pp. 97 and 109), Schrank signed as Albert Ross. In other cities, reports conflict regarding whether he used Walter or Albert Ross.

107. Schrank's decision to intercept TR in Birmingham: Remey, pp. 117, 166–67. The specifics of his reasoning are my supposition. Also, as noted above, Schrank appeared confused during his interrogation about when he had stopped at Birmingham. He told police he went to Birmingham before Atlanta, but another time he said he traveled directly from Augusta to Atlanta, and his list of hotels shows Atlanta before Birmingham. It's my interpretation that he stayed in Atlanta twice, once en route to Birmingham and again when TR was in Atlanta.

108. TR in Montgomery: Tiller, September 28, 1912; *Thomasville* (GA) *Daily Times Enterprise*, September 28, 1912; *The Day Book*, September 28, 1912.

108. For more on the New Exchange Hotel, see Davis, Oscar King 1925; also Davis, Paul; numerous period photos of the hotel are available online.
109. TR in Chehaw: Tiller, September 28, 1912.
110. TR's schedule for September 28: *Milledgeville News*.
110. Schrank at the Plaza Hotel in Birmingham: Remey, p. 94.
111. Schrank rushed back to Atlanta with little time to spare: *San Francisco Call*, October 16, 1912.

Chapter Five: "I'm Not a Fancy Fencing Match"
112. Union Depot: Caldwell, pp. 277–79; see photos widely available online.
113. Quotation that Auditorium and Armory was "ideal for nothing" is from Atlanta Mayor William B. Hartsfield, quoted in Craig. Photos of the Auditorium and Armory are widely available online.
113. Schrank arrived in Atlanta slightly before TR: *San Francisco Call*, October 16, 1912.
113. Schrank's reaction to seeing TR is my supposition.
114. Scene in the Auditorium: *Washington Herald*, September 29, 1912; Tiller, September 29, 1912; *Chicago Examiner*, September 29, 1912.
114. Text of TR's speech: Gould, *Bull Moose*, pp. 144–45.
116. M. T. Floyd incident: *Atlanta Constitution*, October 16, 1912.
116. Schrank's wait in front of the Auditorium and TR's exit through side entrance: Remey, p. 118. Schrank's specific actions during the wait are my supposition.

Chapter Six: "It Was a New Thing to Me"
118. Atlanta weather: *Atlanta Constitution*, Sunday, September 30, 1912; Weathersource (weathersource.com).
118. TR's visit to Roswell: Tiller, September 29 and 30, 1912. TR's specific actions in the car and state of mind are my supposition.
119. For more on the Bulloch family and homestead, see the websites of Roadside Georgia (roadsidegeorgia.com) and Historic Roswell Convention and Visitors Bureau (visitroswellga.com); also Cleland.
119. Civil War service of James and Irvine Bulloch: Auchincloss, p. 10.
120. TR quotation "It has been my very great good fortune": This has been cited widely.
121. Schrank's thoughts and feelings in Atlanta are my supposition.
121. The third termer's schedule had changed again: Tiller, September 30, 1912.
121. TR's travels through Tennessee: Tiller, September 30 and October 1, 1912; *Washington Herald*, October 1, 1912.
122. TR's visit to Dalton: *Chattanooga Daily Times*, September 29 and 30, 1912.
124. For more on Ben W. Hooper, see *Tennessee Encyclopedia of History and Culture* (tennesseeencyclopedia.net).
124. For more on Mr. Facing-Both-Ways, see Johnson.
125. Information on the W&A RR, including quotation: Southeastern Railway Museum website (srmduluth.org).
125. For more on the Great Locomotive Chase, see the extensive website greatlocomotivechase.com.

126. Schrank's thoughts en route to Chattanooga and while waiting for TR are my supposition. From the schedules, it appears that the train the crowd tore through looking for TR would have been the same one that Schrank was on, but I can't verify this.

126. For more on period Chattanooga, see the 1911 *Encyclopedia Britannica* (available online at 1911encyclopedia.org).

126. Chattanooga geography: Stern.

126. For a photo of Chattanooga's Union Station and Auditorium (and other historical photos of the city) see the Chattanooga Public Library's online photo database (lib.chattanooga.gov).

126. TR's arrival and activities in Chattanooga: *Chattanooga Daily Times*, September 29 and 30, 1912; Tiller, September 30, 1912.

127. Schrank's confrontation with TR in Chattanooga: Remey, pp. 174–77, 179, 187. Some of Schrank's specific actions and thoughts are my supposition.

128. Background on the Hotel Patten, including quotations: Shearer.

128. Man approached Lyon with a song: *Tacoma Times*, September 30, 1912.

128. Schrank's route from the depot to the Redmon Hotel is my supposition.

128. Appearance of the Redmon Hotel: Chattanooga Encampment Association (see Bibliography for complete citation). For a map of the neighborhood around the hotel, see the Sanborn map of Chattanooga, 1917 (full citation in the Bibliography).

129. Schrank's thoughts while at the Redmon Hotel are my supposition.

129. Schrank quotation "It was a new thing to me": Remey, p. 176.

129. Schrank decided he'd have a better opportunity elsewhere: Remey, p. 176.

129. TR's campaigning in Tennessee and North Carolina: *New York World*, October 1, 1912; Tiller, September 30 and October 2, 1912; *El Paso Herald*, October 1, 1912; Ogden (UT) *Evening Standard*, October 2, 1912; *Richmond Times Dispatch*, October 1 and 2, 1912, p. 7; *New York Sun*, September 30, 1912; *San Francisco Call*, October 1, 1912.

132. TR quotation "I want to reserve my fire": Tiller, September 30, 1912.

Chapter Seven: "A Decent, Respectable Reception"

135. For more on the Senate Office Building, see Senate Historical Office website (senate.gov).

135. Washington weather: *Washington Times*, October 4, 1912, p. 1.

135. TR's arrival in Washington and activities before testimony: Tiller, October 4, 1912. For more photos of TR on that day, see the Library of Congress American Memory collection online (memory.loc.gov).

136. Background on John W. McGrath: *The Guardian*; *New York Sun*, March 29, 1916.

136. Willard Hotel: Website of the National Park Service (nps.gov).

137. TR's testimony before Clapp Committee: Macoll; Annin; *San Francisco Call*, October 5, 1912; *New York Tribune*, October 5, 1912. The Clapp Committee continued to meet until October 26, 1912, calling 80 more witnesses (111 in all, over a period of nine months). It eventually published two volumes of testimony but never issued a report.

144. *New York Times* editorial: *New York Times*, October 6, 1912.

145. TR quotation "I think I wound up that Standard Oil affair": *Washington Herald*, October 8, 1912.

145. Schrank's route from Chattanooga to Evansville: Remey, p. 94. According to Remey, the list of hotels found in Schrank's pocket included the Third Avenue Hotel in Rome, Tennessee, but the hotel was actually located in the much larger (and more easily accessible) city of Rome, Georgia; I suspect that Schrank's memory was mistaken, since he didn't start keeping the list until halfway through his journey, but it's possible that someone made the error in transcribing Schrank's note.

145. For more on period Evansville, see 1911 *Encyclopedia Britannica* (available online at 1911encyclopedia.org).

146. Schrank bought new underwear: Remey, p. 191. That he would have had his shirt laundered is my supposition.

146. Schrank's activities in Evansville: *Evansville Journal-News* and *Evansville Courier*.

147. Schrank had never given Evansville a thought: This is my supposition, as are his thoughts while roaming the city.

148. TR's activities after leaving Washington: *Washington Herald*, October 7 and 8, 1912; *Washington Times*, October 7, 1912; *New York Tribune*, October 7, 1912.

148. Background on O. K. Davis: Davis, Oscar King 1925; O'Toole, pp. 159 and 165.

149. Edison's endorsement of TR: *New York Sun*, October 7, 1912.

150. Debs quotation "Just think of anybody dropping $100,000": *New York Sun*, October 7, 1912.

150. Taft quotation "to become the head of a benevolent despotism": *Washington Times*, October 6, 1912.

150. TR's travels through Michigan, Wisconsin, and Minnesota: *Washington Times*, October 8, 11, and 12, 1912; *New York Tribune*, October 9, 10, 11, and 12, 1912; Pratt, October 12, 1912; *New York Sun*, October 13, 1912; *Washington Herald*, October 9, 1912; Davis, Oscar King 1925, p. 361ff.

151. Background on Elbert Martin: *Milwaukee Journal*, October 16, 1912; *Chicago Examiner*, October 16, 1912; *New York Times*, October 16, 1912; *Amsterdam Evening Reporter*.

151. Wilson quotations showing hostility to labor and immigrants: Gould, *Bull Moose*, pp. 152 and 158.

152. Wilson's derogatory attitude toward immigrants and attempts to explain it away: Chace, pp. 135–36.

153. Wilson reception in Chicago: *Salt Lake Tribune*; *San Francisco Call*, October 11, 1912.

154. For more on period Chicago, see Pacyga and 1911 *Encyclopedia Britannica* (available online at 1911encyclopedia.org).

155. Chicago weather: *Chicago Examiner*, October 12, p. 1; National Climatic Data Center (ncdc.noaa.gov).

155. New Jackson Hotel: The hotel is still in operation; numerous photos appear online.

155. Schrank's activities in Chicago: Remey, pp. 117, 122, 125, 163, 167–69, 171. His conversation in the North Western Station is my supposition, as is his route from the station to the La Salle Hotel.

156. TR's activities in Chicago: *New York Tribune*, October 13, 1912; *Chicago Examiner*, October 11, 12, and 14, 1912; *Washington Times*, October 13, 1912; *New York Times*, October 13, 1912; *San Francisco Call*, October 13, 1912; *Washington Herald*, October 13, 1912; Davis, Oscar King 1925, p. 365ff.

157. La Salle Hotel: Period photos are available online. In 1946, the hotel burned, killing more than sixty people.

157. TR quotation "This demonstration speaks for itself": *New York Sun*, October 13, 1912.

157. Schrank's desire not to disturb TR's "decent, respectable reception": Remey, pp. 169 and 171.

158. Chicago immigration figures: 1911 *Encyclopedia Britannica* (available online at 1911encyclopedia.org).

158. For more on Jane Addams and Hull House, see the website of the Hull-House Museum (ulc.edu).

159. Period photos of the Chicago Coliseum are readily available online.

159. Schrank's activities outside the Coliseum: Remey, p. 122. His thoughts are my supposition.

159. TR's appearance at the Coliseum: *Richmond Times Dispatch*, October 13, 1912; *Washington Herald*, October 13, 1912.

160. TR's voice didn't reach the street: Having damaged his voice at the earlier appearance that night, TR could barely speak above a whisper in the Coliseum and was forced to cut his speech short: Davis, Oscar King 1925, pp. 366–67.

Chapter Eight: "I Want to Be a Good Indian, O. K."
161. TR's activities in Chicago and environs on October 13: *Chicago Examiner*, October 14, 1912; *Lake Shore News*.

161. Chicago weather: *Chicago Examiner*, October 13, 1912, p. 1; National Climatic Data Center (ncdc.noaa.gov).

162. Medill McCormick was elected to the Illinois assembly in 1912, to the US House of Representatives in 1916, and to the US Senate in 1918. He committed suicide in 1925 at the age of forty-eight.

162. TR quotation "I can be President": This has been widely cited.

163. TR's schedule for Indiana and Wisconsin: *Chicago Examiner*, October 14, 1912.

163. Schrank's arrival in Milwaukee and activities on October 13: Remey, pp. 97, 109, 126. His walking routes through the city are my supposition.

163. For detailed period maps of Milwaukee, see 1910 Sanborn maps (full citation in the Bibliography).

165. Gilpatrick Hotel: The hotel opened in 1907 and closed in 1932; the building was razed in the early 1940s, and the location is now the site of a Hyatt Regency hotel.

165. German influence in Milwaukee: From the website of the television series "The Making of Milwaukee" (themakingofmilwaukee.com). That Schrank would have felt this influence is my supposition.

165. Milwaukee population: US Census (census.gov).

165. Schrank at the Argyle Hotel: Remey, pp. 97, 109, 126.

166. TR's travels from Chicago to Milwaukee: Davis, Oscar King 1925, p. 371; Remey, pp. 133–34.
167. Schrank's activities on the afternoon of October 14: Remey, pp. 107–8, 164, 175–77. Schrank discusses walking to the Lake Front Depot, but his exact route there is my speculation, as are his specific actions and his thoughts in the park (though he expressed some of these ideas in various writings reproduced in Remey).
167. The statue of the man petting the dog is still in place; it depicts Henry Bergh, founder of the American Society for the Prevention of Cruelty to Animals.
168. TR's decision to go to the Hotel Gilpatrick: Davis, Oscar King 1925, pp. 371–73; Remey, pp. 133–34.
168. Exchange between TR and Davidson: Remey, p. 135.
169. TR quotation "I want to be a good Indian, O. K.": Davis, Oscar King 1925, p. 371.
169. Davidson's visit to police headquarters: Remey, p. 144.
169. TR quotation "I am going": Remey, p. 135.
169. TR's arrival in Milwaukee and activities before leaving hotel: Davis, Oscar King 1925, pp. 371–74; Gores; Remey, p. 145. For a photo of TR's arrival, see Gores.
171. Man approached Girard outside hotel dining room: Remey, pp. 139 and 141.
171. Events in TR's party leading up to shooting: Remey, pp. 108, 141; Davis, Oscar King 1925, pp. 374–75. TR's speech and spectacles were in his pockets, but it is my supposition that he would have checked to see if he had them.

Chapter Nine: "He Pinked Me, Harry"
173. Details of the shooting and immediate aftermath: Remey, pp. 15–17, 19, 91, 141–43, 145–49, 151; Davis, Oscar King 1925, pp. 372–79; Davis, Oscar King 1913; Thompson, pp. 147–48; *Milwaukee Journal*, October 15, 16, and 17; *New York Times*, October 16, 1912; Gores; Roosevelt 1954, p. 705. These accounts vary slightly in their details.
173. Girard quotation "Give me the man's revolver," Martin quotation "I'll be damned if I do," and Lyon quotations "If you advance another step" and "Get back there": Thompson, p. 148.
174. Buskowsky quotation "Kill him": Remey, p. 149.
174. Policeman quotation "What the hell": Remey, p. 151.
174. TR quotations "He pinked me, Harry" and "Don't hurt him": Remey, p. 16.
174. TR quotation "Officers, take charge": Remey, p. 17.
174. Quotation "My gun is gone": Remey, p. 142.
175. McGrath quotation "The Colonel's shot": Davis, Oscar King 1925, p. 377.
175. Cochems quotation "No, Colonel" and TR quotation "You get me to that speech": Davis, Oscar King 1925, p. 378.
175. TR quotation "We are going to the hall": *Milwaukee Journal*, October 17, 1912.
175. TR quotation "No, this is my big chance": Davis, Oscar King 1925, p. 379.
175. TR quotation "A Colt .38" and exchange between TR and McGrath: Remey, p. 17.

176. TR quotation "I know I am good now": Remey, p. 19.
176. TR quotation "I'm mighty glad": Thompson, p. 148.
176. Milwaukee Auditorium: Period photos are widely available online. It is still in use and is called the Milwaukee Theatre.
176. Events at Auditorium: Remey, pp. 19–49, 138–39; Davis, Oscar King 1925, pp. 379–86; *Milwaukee Journal*, October 15, 1912; Roosevelt 1954, p. 705. These accounts vary slightly in their details.
176. TR quotation "Well, Mr. Bloodgood": *Milwaukee Journal*, October 15, 1912.
177. TR quotation "It's all right, doctor": Davis, Oscar King 1925, p. 380.
177. TR quotations "Has anyone a clean handkerchief?" and "Now, gentlemen, let's go in": Remey, p. 19.
177. Delaney invocation, TR quotation "You tell them, Harry," and Cochems quotation "We have with us a guest": *Milwaukee Journal*, October 15, 1912.
177. TR quotation "No, it's no fake": Remey, p. 20.
178. Text of TR's speech in Milwaukee: Gould, *Bull Moose*, pp. 175–84.
179. TR's exchange with gray-haired woman: Davis, Oscar King 1925, p. 383.
180. TR's exchanges with Terrell and Davis: Davis, Oscar King 1925, p. 384.
181. TR quotation "Teach them not to grab": Remey, p. 39.
182. TR quotations "It's getting better and better as time goes on" and "If these doctors don't behave themselves": Remey, p. 42.
182. TR quotation "Now I am ready to go with you": Davis, Oscar King 1925, p. 385.

Chapter Ten: "The Wound Is a Trivial One"

183. Events in Auditorium after speech: *Milwaukee Journal*, October 15, 1912, p. 12.
183. TR's explanation of why he insisted on speaking: Davis, Oscar King 1925, p. 387.
184. Events at Johnston Emergency Hospital and on the *Mayflower*: Remey, pp. 51–63; Davis, Oscar King 1925, pp. 385–92; *Milwaukee Journal*, October 15, 1912; *Chicago Examiner*, October 15 and 16, 1912. For a period photo of the Johnston Emergency Hospital, see the website of the Milwaukee Public Library (mpl.org).
184. Telegram to Mrs. Roosevelt: *Chicago Examiner*, October 15, 1912.
184. Events with the Roosevelt family in New York: *New York Times*, October 15, 1912.
184. Events with Alice Roosevelt Longworth in Cincinnati: *Chicago Examiner*, October 15, 1912.
184. Alice Roosevelt Longworth quotation "It has come at last": *Chicago Examiner*, October 16, 1912.
185. Alice Roosevelt Longworth quotation "The bride at every wedding": This has been widely cited, in slightly differing words.
185. TR quotation "You've got the best of me": *Chicago Examiner*, October 15, 1912.
185. TR quotation "I don't care a damn about finding the bullet": Remey, p. 62.
185. TR quotation "I've not decided yet": Remey, p. 58.
185. TR's exchange with Dr. Sayle and Nurse White: Remey, p. 61.
186. Bloodgood quotation "Get him out of here": Davis, Oscar King 1925, p. 389.

186. TR exchanges with Miss White about New York and buttons: Remey, pp. 58–59.
187. Dixon quotation "That must have been a great speech": *New York Times*, October 15, 1912.
187. TR exchange with J. S. Janssen: *Milwaukee Journal*, October 15, 1912.
189. Schrank in police custody and in court: Remey, pp. 92–103, 112–14; *Milwaukee Journal*, October 16 and 22, 1912; *New York Times*, October 16, 1912; *Chicago Examiner*, October 16 and 17, 1912.
190. John T. Janssen's interview with Schrank: Remey, pp. 117–31.
192. Events on the *Mayflower* in Chicago and at Mercy Hospital: Remey, pp. 64–81; *Milwaukee Journal*, October 15, 16, 17, 18, and 19, 1912; *Chicago Examiner*, October 16, 18, 19, 20, and 23, 1912; *New York Times*, October 16, 17, 18, 20, 21, and 22, 1912; Montague.
192. TR quotation "Dr. Murphy reminds me of General Grant": *New York Times*, October 17, 1912.
192. TR quotation "You know, I have done a lot of hunting": *Chicago Examiner*, October 17, 1912.
192. TR's exchange with reporters at North Western Depot: Pratt, October 16, 1912.
192. History of Mercy Hospital: Mercy Hospital website (mercy-chicago.org). The hospital is still in operation. For a period photo, see Wikipedia entry "Mercy Hospital and Medical Center."
193. TR quotations "Here they are" and "I feel as well": *Chicago Examiner*, October 16, 1912.
193. TR quotation "They'll be calling me Old Doc Roosevelt": *New York Times*, October 17, 1912.
193. Mrs. Roosevelt quotation "I am about the only person in the world": *New York Times*, October 16, 1912.
195. TR quotation "And mind, I want a good one": *Milwaukee Journal*, October 16, 1912.
195. Schrank's exchanges with Officer Conway and reporter, and his court appearance: *New York Times*, October 16, 1912.
199. Maximum penalty was fifteen years: *Milwaukee Journal*, November 25, 1912; Remey, p. 98.
199. William Arnold background: *Office of the Sheriff, Milwaukee County, Wisconsin* (full citation in Bibliography).
199. TR awoke feeling "like a bull moose": *Chicago Examiner*, October 18, 1912.
199. TR's courage after the shooting burnished his mythology: Donald, p. 254.
200. Wilson telegram: *Chicago Examiner*, October 16, 1912.
200. Taft telegram: *New York Times*, October 16, 1912.
200. TR's response to Taft telegram: *Chicago Examiner*, October 18.
200. Frank James and Bat Masterson telegrams and TR's reply: *Chicago Examiner*, October 17, 1912.
200. Vincent Curtis Baldwin's letter and TR's response: Gores.
200. Mary Kelly's letter and TR's response: *Chicago Examiner*, October 17, 1912.

201. Quotation from the *London Daily Mail*: Reprinted in the *Milwaukee Journal*, October 16, 1912.
202. Elbert Martin quotation and telegram from his wife: *Chicago Examiner*, October 16, 1912.
202. Martin's exchange with TR: *Milwaukee Journal*, October 16, 1912.
202. Alice Roosevelt Longworth quotation "There is no need for worry" and exchange between Welter and TR: *Chicago Examiner*, October 17, 1912.
203. Exchange between Arnold and Schrank: *Milwaukee Journal*, October 16, 1912.
204. Exchange between Schrank and reporter "They're all trying to make me out to be crazy": Pratt, October 17, 1912.
204. Clanton quotation: *Milwaukee Journal*, October 22, 1912.
205. TR quotations "hungry as a hunter," "By George," and "You can't keep a squirrel": *New York Times*, October 18, 1912.
205. TR quotations "This isn't the rule of the people," "I would give anything," and "Tooty-too," *Chicago Examiner*, October 18, 1912.
205. TR quotation "They are good Bull Moose timber": *New York Times*, October 18, 1912.
206. TR quotation "I am doing fine": *Chicago Examiner*, October 18, 1912.
206. Schrank's checker playing: *Milwaukee Journal*, October 17, 1912.
206. Schrank quotation "Is Roosevelt still alive?": *New York Times*, October 19, 1912.
206. Schrank quotation "Where did the bullet hit him" and demand that bullet be returned: *Milwaukee Journal*, October 18, 1912.
207. TR exchange with Mrs. Roosevelt and nurse about breakfast: *Milwaukee Journal*, October 18, 1912.
207. TR quotation "I would as soon carry it in my chest": *Chicago Examiner*, October 19, 1912.
207. TR response to Schrank's request to get bullet back: *Milwaukee Journal*, October 19, 1912.
208. TR quotation "Turn around, Heney": *Chicago Examiner*, October 19, 1912.
208. TR exchange with Aloysius Moravac: *New York Times*, October 20, 1912.
208. Wilson quotation "I cannot cancel the engagements": *Chicago Examiner*, October 16, 1912.
209. Democrats' opposition to women's suffrage: Cooper 2009, p. 252.
209. Exchange between Wilson and Maud Malone: Cooper 2009, p. 171.
209. Wilson's speeches in New York: *New York Times*, October 20, 1912.
209. Wilson quotation "There is nothing that can be done": *Chicago Examiner*, October 16, p. 4.
209. TR's departure from Chicago: *Milwaukee Journal*, October 21, 1912; *New York Times*, October 21 and 22, 1912.
209. TR was feeling "bully": *Milwaukee Journal*, October 21, 1912.
209. Welter quotation "He was the best patient" and Fitzgerald quotation "He was consideration itself": Remey, p. 63.
210. TR quotation "Goodbye and good luck": *Milwaukee Journal*, October 21, 1912.
210. TR quotation "I am going to make the meeting anyway": *New York Times*, October 21, 1912.

Chapter Eleven: "I Am Not a Lunatic"

211. New York weather: *New York Sun*, October 31, 1912, p. 15.

211. For period photos of Madison Square Garden, see Wikipedia online entry "Madison Square Garden (1890)."

212. TR's appearance at Madison Square Garden: *New York Times*, October 31 and November 1, 1912; O'Toole, pp. 220–22. TR appeared again at Madison Square Garden on November 1, to address a meeting of the New York Progressives.

214. Text of TR's Madison Square Garden address: Gould, *Bull Moose*, pp. 187–92.

216. TR quotation "the most enthusiastic and successful meeting": *New York Times*, November 1, 1912.

216. Wilson's Madison Square Garden appearance, including excerpts: *New York Times*, November 1, 1912.

217. Debs's closing address: *Tacoma Times*, November 2, 1912.

218. Taft quotation that the Republican Party stood for "preserving our constitutional form of government": *New York Times*, November 3, 1912.

218. Taft was seen dozing in an automobile: O'Toole, p. 222. It was Alice Longworth Roosevelt who reported seeing this.

218. Election Day weather on Long Island: *New York Sun*, November 5, 1912.

218. Election Day events at Oyster Bay: *New York Times*, November 6, 1912; Morris 2010, p. 251ff; O'Toole, pp. 223, 227.

218. Exchange at door between TR and reporter and Election Day scene in New York City: *New York Times*, November 6, 1912.

219. Election Day events in Princeton, Mrs. Wilson quotation "My dear," Wilson quotations "I have no feeling of triumph" and "A great cause has triumphed," events at Republican Party headquarters, Hilles's quotation "But for Mr. Roosevelt's action," and Taft quotation "The vote for Mr. Roosevelt": *New York Times*, November 6, 1912.

220. Taft quotation "I'll be very glad": *New York World*, November 6, 1912.

220. Oyster Bay vote and reaction, TR's telegram "The American people," TR's meeting with reporters and his quotation "Like all other good citizens": *New York Times*, November 6, 1912.

221. TR's letter to James Garfield "We have fought the good fight": Gardner, p. 280.

221. Presidential vote tallies: Gould, *Four Hats*, pp. 176–77, Appendix C; Chace, pp. 238–39.

221. Taft showing was weakest in history for any major-party candidate: Gould, *Four Hats*, p. vii.

221. TR quotation "I got more bullets than ballots": Gould, *Four Hats*, p. 180.

222. Possible election results if TR had not run or had been nominated by the Republicans: Chace, pp. 238–39; O'Toole, p. 228; Gould, *Four Hats*, p. 179; for the argument that TR would not have beaten Wilson in a two-man race, see Cooper 2009, pp. 175–76.

222. *New York Times* editorial about Americans' "soundness of judgment": *New York Times*, November 6, 1912.

222. Nonpresidential election results: Gould, *Four Hats*, pp. 176–77; Chace, p. 239.

222. Nick Longworth lost by slightly more than 100 votes: O'Toole, p. 232. He was elected to Congress again in 1914 and eventually became Speaker of the House.

222. Significance of election results to Progressives' future: Chace, p. 239.

223. Schrank quotation "That's right, the trial is today": *New York Times*, November 13, 1912.

223. Schrank's November 12 court appearance: *New York Times*, November 13, 1912; Remey, pp. 99–103. (Remey gives the court appearance as November 13, but this is incorrect.)

223. Judge Backus: For a photo, see Remey, p. 110.

223. Schrank's exchange with Zabel and Backus: Remey, pp. 101–2.

224. Backus quotation "Let no man leave the courtroom": Remey, p. 102.

224. Members of the insanity commission: Remey, p. 103. For photos, see Remey, p. 170.

224. Backus quotation "In my experience": Remey, pp. 235 and 237.

225. Backus quotation "Is the defendant John Schrank sane or insane": Remey, p. 238.

225. Schrank quotation "Theodore Roosevelt is only human": *New York Times*, November 2, 1912.

225. Joseph Flanders: For a photo, see Remey, p. 236.

225. Alienists' report: Remey, pp. 192–212.

226. Backus quotation "The court now finds": Remey, p. 105.

227. Schrank quotation "Why didn't they give me my medicine": Remey, p. 106.

227. Schrank quotation "I had expected": *New York Times*, November 23, 1912.

227. TR quotation that Schrank "was not a madman": Rauchway, p. 198.

227. Newett quotation that the shooting was a "put up job": *Keowee Courier*, November 26, 1912. Just before Election Day 1912, Roosevelt sued Newett for an article in the *Iron Ore* calling TR a profaner and a drunkard. The case came to trial the following year; when it was decided in TR's favor, he waived punitive damages and was awarded nominal damages of six cents. He had spent forty thousand dollars to bring the case. (For more, see O'Toole, pp. 239–42.)

228. Schrank's defense, beginning "I wish to apologize": Remey, pp. 213–34.

229. Schrank's exchange with Arnold and "I am not crazy" quotation: *Milwaukee Journal*, November 25, 1912.

229. Northern Hospital for the Insane: Website of the J. Farrow Museum (dhs.wisconsin .gov). For a photo, see Kirkbride Buildings website (kirkbridebuildings.com).

229. Thomas Kirkbride: Kirkbride Buildings website (kirkbridebuildings.com).

229. Schrank's stop in Fond du Lac, including dialogue: *Fond du Lac Reporter*, November 25, 1912.

231. Weather in Oshkosh: National Climatic Data Center (ncdc.noaa.gov).

Epilogue: "I Have Already Lived and Enjoyed as Much of My Life as Any Other Nine Men I Know"

232. Influence of the election of 1912: Gould, *Four Hats*, pp. xi, 182–83; Chace, p. 8; Milkis, pp. 1–2.

232. Six states with women's suffrage: Gould, *Four Hats*, p. 26.

232. A million women would vote in 1912: O'Toole, p. 206.

233. Taft's tenure on Supreme Court: Post.
233. *New York Times* quotation "a 'come-back'": *New York Times*, March 9, 1930.
233. Debs was one of 2,000 prosecuted and 900 imprisoned: O'Toole, p. 361.
233. Debs's results in 1920 election: Chace, p. 259; Gould, *Four Hats*, p. 185.
234. Wilson quotation that Debs was "a traitor to his country": Chace, p. 275.
234. Future of the Socialist Party: Gould, *Four Hats*, p. 180; Chace, p. 277.
234. Wilson's domestic agenda: Cooper 2009, pp. 213–36; Cooper 1983, pp. 232–36; Gould, *Four Hats*, p. 177; Gould 2003, p. 41; Gardner, p. 326.
234. Death of Ellen Wilson: Cooper 2009, pp. 260–61.
234. Edith Gault and her courtship and marriage to Wilson: Cooper 2009, pp. 280–84.
234. Wilson's more radical domestic agenda: Cooper 1983, p. 251.
235. Wilson had enacted every major Progressive plank: Cooper 1983, pp. 209, 252–53.
235. Wilson quotation "I am a progressive": Cooper 2009, p. 351.
235. Wilson's policies resembled New Nationalism more than New Freedom: Gould, *Four Hats*, p. 183; Milkis, p. 271; Cooper 1983, pp. 211–13.
235. TR voters turned to Wilson in 1916: Cooper 1983, pp. 255–56.
235. Wilson's 1916 election was one of the narrowest votes in US history, and Wilson was the first Democratic president since Andrew Jackson to be reelected: For more on the voting, see Cooper 2009, p. 358.
235. Economy had recovered: Cooper 2009, p. 335.
235. Wilson's efforts to avoid war and achieve sustainable peace: Cooper 1983, p. 262ff.
236. Wilson's stroke and aftermath: Cooper 2009, p. 530ff.
236. League of Nations: Cooper 2009, p. 506ff.
236. The economy was sputtering: Cooper 2009, p. 546.
236. Progressive Party uneasy amalgam with weak organization: Milkis, pp. 257, 260, 262; Morris 2010, p. 212; O'Toole, p. 202.
237. TR quotation "The fundamental trouble": Cooper 2009, p. 274.
237. White quotation "For a moment there was silence": Chace, p. 252.
237. Future of the Progressive Party and its influence in later years: Gould, *Four Hats*, pp. 185–86; Milkis, pp. 286–89; Cooper 2009, pp. 179–80; Chace, pp. 278–81; Gable, p. 250.
237. FDR quotation "redefining the social contract": Milkis, p. 289.
238. TR quotation "I have already lived": This has been widely cited.
238. TR's South American journey: Millard.
238. TR was envious that Wilson had been called to lead the nation in a time of war and crisis: Cooper 1983, pp. 284–87, 307.
239. TR quotation "dust in a windy street" and Wilson quotation "a great big boy": Cooper 2009, p. 394.
239. The reasons, alleged and suspected, of Wilson's refusal of TR's World War I commission: Cooper 1983, p. 325.
239. TR quotation "It is bitter that the young should die": Auchincloss, p. 135.
239. TR's reputation improved, and it appeared he would be nominated and elected in 1920: Cooper 1983, p. 261.
239. TR's final illness and death: O'Toole, pp. 402–4; Chace, p. 265.
240. Archie Roosevelt quotation "The old lion is dead": This has been widely cited.

240. Schrank's daily life in mental hospital: *New York Sun*, January 19, 1913; *Washington Times*, June 28, 1918; *New York Times*, September 17, 1943.

240. Schrank quotation "I am satisfied": *New York Sun*, January 19, 1913.

240. Schrank's letter that he had "made all the arrangements": *San Francisco Call*, April 26, 1913.

240. Pistol put in safekeeping of Elbert Martin: *St. Paul Appeal*.

240. Schrank quotation "It is a disgrace": *San Francisco Call*, April 26, 1913.

240. Schrank's move to new facility: *Day Book*, February 19, 1914; *Milwaukee Journal*, September 16, 1943.

241. Backus's doubts that Schrank could stand trial: *New York Times*, July 25, 1914.

241. Remley quotations: *Milwaukee Journal*, September 16, 1943.

241. Schrank quotation "A good man gone": *New York Times*, September 17, 1943.

241. Schrank's illness and death, lack of visitors and letters: *Milwaukee Journal*, September 16, 1943; *New York Times*, September 17, 1943.

BIBLIOGRAPHY

Readers wishing to delve more deeply into the election of 1912 would do well to consult Lewis L. Gould's meticulous *Four Hats in the Ring* and James Chaces's highly readable *1912*. Those looking for contemporaneous documents on the assassination attempt, including Schrank's writings, eyewitness reports, police interrogations, and court documents, will find a great deal of interest in *The Attempted Assassination of Ex-President Theodore Roosevelt* by Oliver E. Remey, et al., which is available free of charge online. For more about the life of TR, see Edmund Morris's exhaustive three-volume biography, *The Rise of Theodore Roosevelt*, *Theodore Rex*, and *Colonel Roosevelt*. Or, for more on TR's life after the White House, see Patricia O'Toole's elegantly written *When Trumpets Call*. As a biography of Roosevelt's political nemesis, I recommend John Milton Cooper, Jr.'s Pulitzer Prize-nominated *Woodrow Wilson*. For more about the complex political and personal rivalry between Roosevelt and Wilson, see the same author's masterful study *The Warrior and the Priest*. Readers curious about the geography of American cities in the past should seek out the maps prepared for fire insurance companies by Sanborn and other publishers; the maps, many of which are available online, are astonishingly detailed, showing individual buildings with their dimensions, uses, and other features. Readers seeking a different kind of glimpse into a vanished world might want to consult the Library of Congress's online collections, which include archives of thousands of American newspapers across a wide temporal and geographic sweep, and thousands of historical photographs. Much interesting period data can also be found in the 1911 edition of the *Encyclopedia Britannica*, which is available without charge online.

Below are the books and articles that I found helpful in my research. Virtually all are cited in the Sources. Publications with a byline are alphabetized under the author's name; those without a byline appear under the title of the publication. If only a date is given under a newspaper's name, it means that the article had no headline. For newspaper articles I have given page numbers where available, but online sources do not always provide these references; in general, the numbers refer to the page where the story begins and do not include any jump to another page.

Amsterdam Evening Reporter, October 17, 1912, p. 6.

Annin, Joseph A., "Colonel Comes Through Ordeal with Colors Up," *Washington Herald*, October 5, 1912, p. 1.

Atlanta Constitution, "Mercury Drops to Lowest Mark," September 30, 1912.

———, "Did Schrank Try to Shoot Here?" October 16, 1912, p. 2.

Auchincloss, Louis. *Theodore Roosevelt*. New York: Times Books, 2001.

Binder, Frederick M., and David M. Reimers. *All the Nations Under Heaven: An Ethnic and Racial History of New York City*. New York: Columbia University Press, 1996.

Bisbee (AZ) Daily Review, "Col. Roosevelt Receives Cold Hand at Tucson," September 18, 1912.

———, "Indians of New Mexico Listen to Colonel Roosevelt," September 19, 1912.

Blair, Emily Newell. *Bridging Two Eras: The Autobiography of Emily Newell Blair, 1877–1951*. Edited by Virginia Jeans Laas. Columbia: University of Missouri Press, 1999.

Brands, H. W. *TR: The Last Romantic*. New York: Basic Books, 1997.

Brinkley, Douglas. "The Great Bear Hunt," *National Geographic* website, May 5, 2001 (nationalgeographic.com).

Bromley, George W., and Walter S. Bromley. *Atlas of the Borough of Brooklyn, City of New York*. Philadelphia: G. W. Bromley and Co., 1907–8.

———. *Atlas of the City of New York, Borough of Manhattan*. Philadelphia: G. W. Bromley and Co., 1911.

Brooklyn Daily Eagle, June 17, 1904.

———, "General Slocum Disaster," June 23, 1904.

Burrows, Edwin G., and Mike Wallace. *Gotham: A History of New York City to 1898*. New York: Oxford University Press, 1999.

Caldwell, Wilber W. *The Courthouse and the Depot in Georgia, 1833–1910: The Architecture of Hope in an Age of Despair*. Macon, GA: Mercer University Press, 2001.

Caldwell Watchman (Columbia, LA), "Waterways Convention Held in Little Rock," September 27, 1912, p. 1.

Chace, James. *1912: Wilson, Roosevelt, Taft & Debs—the Election That Changed the Country*. New York: Simon & Schuster, 2004.

Charleston Evening Post, "Huck's Finished," November 25, 1969.

Charleston News and Courier, "Came to Charleston to Kill Roosevelt," October 16, 1912, p. 7.

Charleston, South Carolina. Charleston: Walker, Evans & Cogswell, ca. 1912.

Chattanooga Daily Times, "Chattanooga Will Give Ex-President Roosevelt Warm Welcome," September 29, 1912, p. 6.

———, "Leader of All Moose Arrives in Chattanooga in True Roosevelt Fashion," September 30, 1912, p. 1.

Chattanooga Encampment Association. *47th National Encampment, Grand Army of the Republic, Chattanooga, September 15–20, 1913.*

Chevalier, August, *The "Chevalier" Commercial, Pictorial, and Tourist Map of San Francisco...,* 1911.

Chicago Examiner, "Wilson Charges Untrue, Says Roosevelt," September 29, 1912, p. 7.

———, "Roosevelt Here at 9:30 A.M. To-Morrow," October 11, 1912, p. 4.

———, "Roosevelt Here To-Day; to Make Two Speeches," October 12, 1912, p. 4.

———, "Roosevelt's Voice Breaks; Stops Talk," October 14, 1912, p. 2.

———, "Mrs. Longworth Told of the Shooting of Her Father," October 15, 1912, p. 1.

———, "Colonel Wires Mrs. Roosevelt His Wound Is Trivial," October 15, 1912, p. 3.

———, "Roosevelt's Only Danger Is Blood Poisoning," October 16, 1912, p. 1.

———, "Martin Tells How He Stopped Second Shot," October 16, 1912, p. 2.

———, "Schrank Admits Guilt Before Court," October 16, 1912, p. 3.

———, "Wilson to Stop Speaking Till Rival Is Well," October 16, 1912, p. 4.

———, "Mrs. Roosevelt Guards Colonel from Visitors," October 17, 1912, p. 2.

———, "Colonel Resumes Charge of Campaign," October 18, 1912, p. 1.

———, "Threat to Kill Wilson Is Heard; Candidate Under Heavy Guard," October 18, 1912, p. 1.

———, "Roosevelt Now Plans to Leave Tuesday," October 19, 1912, p. 1.

———, "Colonel Suffers Setback," October 20, 1912, p. 1.

———, "Roosevelt and Heney Compare Bullet Wounds," October 20, 1912, p. 1.

———, "Roosevelt Tired After Trip, but Rests Well," October 23, 1912, p. 11.

Christiano, Gregory J. "The Five Points." Online article at urbanography.com.

Cleland, Max. "Mittie Bullock Met Future President in Famed Hall," *Rockmart Journal,* November 6, 1991, p. 9B. Note that the headline writer was confused on two counts—*Bulloch* is misspelled, and at Bulloch Hall Mittie didn't meet the president (her son) but his father, Theodore Sr.; the body of the article, however, written by Max Cleland, at the time Georgia Secretary of State, appears to be accurate.

Cooper, John Milton, Jr. *The Warrior and the Priest: Woodrow Wilson and Theodore Roosevelt.* Cambridge: The Belknap Press, 1983.

———. *Woodrow Wilson: A Biography.* New York: Random House, 2009.

Craig, Jeremy. "Celebrating a Century of Alumni Hall." Online article at Georgia State University website (gsu.edu).

Daily Picayune (New Orleans), "Winter Garden," October 23, 1910.

———, "Roosevelt Day in New Orleans, September 27, 1912, p. 1.

———, "Roosevelt's Speech at the Winter Garden," September 28, 1912, p. 7.

———, "Warm Reception by New Orleans," September 28, 1912.

Davidson, John Wells (editor). *A Crossroads of Freedom: The 1912 Campaign Speeches of Woodrow Wilson.* New Haven: Yale University Press, 1956.

Davis, Oscar King, "Roosevelt's Marvelous Escape from Death," *Munsey's Magazine,* January 1913, pp. 606-9.

———. *Released for Publication: Some Inside Political History of Theodore Roosevelt and His Times, 1898–1918.* Boston: Houghton Mifflin Company, 1925.

Davis, Paul. "Exchange Hotel Is Ending of an Era," *Tuscaloosa News,* September 14, 1973.

Day Book, The (Chicago, IL), September 28, 1912.

———, "Hear Punk Witnesses," September 30, 1912

———, February 19, 1914.

Donald, Aida D. *Lion in the White House: A Life of Theodore Roosevelt.* New York: Basic Books, 2007.

Duffy, Peter. "100 Years Ago, the Shot That Spurred New York's Gun-Control Law." Blog posted on *New York Times* website, January 23, 2011.

El Paso Herald, "Roosevelt Defends the Recall," September 23, 1912, p. 1.

———, "Roosevelt Quotes the Golden Rule," September 25, 1912.

———, "Roosevelt Locked Out in Thin Attire," October 1, 1912.

Ellis, Edward Robb. *The Epic of New York City: A Narrative History.* New York: Basic Books, 2004.

Encyclopedia Britannica 1911 edition (available online at 1911encyclopedia.org).

Evansville (IN) *Courier,* "Think Schrank Was at Sterling," October 17, 1912.

Evansville (IN) *Journal-News,* "Schrank Was Very Reticent; Always Feared Watchers While He Was at Hotel Here," October 17, 1912.

Fond du Lac (WI) *Reporter,* "John Schrank in City Today," November 25, 1912, p. 3.

Gable, John Allen. *The Bull Moose Years: Theodore Roosevelt and the Progressive Party.* Port Washington, NY: Kennikat Press, 1978.

Gardner, Joseph L. *Departing Glory: Theodore Roosevelt as Ex-President.* New York: Charles Scribner's Sons, 1973.

Gibson, Robert A. "The Negro Holocaust: Lynching and Race Riots in the United States, 1880–1950." Website of the Yale–New Haven Teachers Institute (Yale.edu).

Gompers, Samuel. Papers. Available at the University of Maryland website (www .history.umd.edu).

Gores, Stan, "The Attempted Assassination of Teddy Roosevelt." *The Wisconsin Magazine of History,* Summer 1970, pp. 269–77. Available on the website of the Wisconsin Historical Society (wisconsinhistory.org).

Gould, Lewis L. *The Modern American Presidency.* Lawrence: University Press of Kansas, 2003.

———. *Four Hats in the Ring: The 1912 Election and the Birth of Modern American Politics.* Lawrence: University Press of Kansas, 2008.

——— (editor). *Bull Moose on the Stump: The 1912 Campaign Speeches of Theodore Roosevelt.* Lawrence: University Press of Kansas, 2008.

Guardian, The "J. W. M'Grath, Former Private Secretary to Mr. Roosevelt, Dies," March 8, 1934, p. 4. Available online at the archive of *The Arkansas Catholic* (arc.stparchive .com).

Hahn, Harlan. "The Republican Party Convention of 1912 and the Role of Herbert S. Hadley in National Politics." *Missouri Historical Review,* 59:4 (July 1965), pp. 407–23.

Harbaugh, William Henry. *Power and Responsibility: The Life and Times of Theodore Roosevelt.* New York: Farrar, Straus and Cudahy, 1961.

Historical Statistics of the United States. New York: Cambridge University Press, 2006 (available online, for a fee, at hsus.cambridge.org).

Horton, Tom. "Touring Charleston Back in 1912." Posted on the *Moultrie News* website, June 1, 2011 (moultrienews.com).

Jeffers, H. Paul. *Commissioner Roosevelt: The Story of Theodore Roosevelt and the New York City Police, 1895–1897.* New York: John Wiley & Sons, 1994.

Johnson, Galen K. "The Pilgrim's Progress in the History of American Public Discourse." *LATCH,* Vol. 4 (2011), pp. 1-31 (available online at openlatch.com).

Kaufman, Burton, I. "New Orleans and the Panama Canal, 1900–1914," *Louisiana History,* Vol. 14, No. 4, Autumn 1973.

Kelly, Frank K. *The Fight for the White House: The Story of 1912.* New York: Thomas Y. Crowell Company, 1961.

Keowee Courier (Pickens Court House, SC), "Say Schrank Is Insane," November 26, 1912.

Lake Shore News (Evanston, IL), "Many at Church to See Roosevelt," October 17, 1912, p. 6.

Macoll, John D. "The Clapp Committee on Campaign Finance Corruption, 1912–13," in Bruns, Roger A., David L. Hostetter, and Raymond W. Smock (eds.). *Congress Investigates: A Critical and Documentary History.* New York: Facts On File, 2011, pp. 384–416.

Milkis, Sidney M. *Theodore Roosevelt, the Progressive Party, and the Transformation of American Democracy.* Lawrence: University Press of Kansas, 2009.

Millard, Candice. *The River of Doubt: Theodore Roosevelt's Darkest Journey.* New York: Doubleday, 2005.

Milledgeville (GA) *News,* "Roosevelt Headquarters Wire News of His Trip," September 27, 1912.

Miller, Nathan. *Theodore Roosevelt: A Life.* New York: William Morrow and Company, Inc., 1992.

Miller, Scott. *The President and the Assassin: McKinley, Terror, and Empire at the Dawn of the American Century.* New York: Random House, 2011.

Milwaukee Journal, "Doctors Decide to Leave Bullet in Roosevelt's Chest for the Present," October 15, 1912, p. 1.

———, "Delay Operation; Bullet in Chest," October 15, 1912, p. 2.

———, "Cheer Colonel at Auditorium," October 15, 1912, p. 3.

———, "Alienists Will Examine Schrank," October 16, 1912, p. 1.

———, "Roosevelt Is Doing Nicely," October 16, 1912, p. 1.

———, "Wilson Quits Stump," October 16, 1912, p. 2.

———, "Athletic Young Stenographer Who Prevented a Second Shot," October 16, 1912, p. 3.

———, "London Papers Marvel at Nerve Displayed by Col. Roosevelt," October 16, 1912, p. 4.

———, "Colonel's Chauffeur Tells What He Saw of Shooting," October 17, 1912, p. 1.

———, "Wants to Get Back in Fight," October 17, 1912, p. 1.

———, "Claims Bullet Belongs to Him," October 18, 1912, p. 1.

———, "Move Roosevelt to Oyster Bay Next Tuesday," October 18, 1912, p. 1.

———, "Put Ahead Plan to Move Colonel," October 19, 1912, p. 1.

———, "Roosevelt Off for Oyster Bay," October 21, 1912, p. 2.

———, "'Schrank Is Sane,'" October 22, 1912, p. 1.

———, "Roosevelt Home; Must Take Rest," October 22, 1912, p. 1.

———, "'Model Prisoner' Pleases Schrank," November 25, 1912, p. 1.

———, "Assailant Who Wounded 'Teddy' Roosevelt Dies," September 16, 1943, p. 1.

Montague, James, "Roosevelt Surgeons Awaiting Crisis," *Chicago Examiner*, October 17, 1912, p. 1.

Morris, Edmund. *The Rise of Theodore Roosevelt*. New York: Coward, McCann & Geoghan, Inc., 1979.

———. *Theodore Rex*. New York: Random House, 2001.

———. *Colonel Roosevelt*. New York: Random House, 2010.

New York State Penal Code, Article 400; available online at law.onecle.com.

New York Sun, "Col. Roosevelt in Utah Scolds Senator Smoot," September 14, 1912, p. 4.

———, "Roosevelt Spends Day of Rest at Emporia," September 23, 1912, p. 5.

———, "Roosevelt Now Ready to Enter 'Solid South,'" September 24, 1912, p. 7.

———, "T.R. Urges Canal Force to Deepen Mississippi," September 26, 1912, p. 7.

———, "T.R. in New Orleans, Says He'll Stop Flood," September 28, 1912, p. 10.

———, "Roosevelt Ending Tour of 10,000 Miles," September 30, 1912, p. 7.

———, "Debs Ridicules Roosevelt," October 7, 1912, p. 6.

———, "Edison Declares for TR," October 7, 1912, p. 6.

———, "I'm a Natural Born Bull Moose—Edison," October 7, 1912, p. 6.

———, "Roosevelt Assails Gov. Deneen Bitterly," October 13, 1912, p. 15.

———, "Schrank Writes Memoirs," January 19, 1913, p. 5.

———, "Roosevelt's Secretary Gets 30 Days in Jail," March 29, 1916, p. 1.

New York Times, "Steamship *Comanche* to Be Launched," August 21, 1895.

———, "Clyde Line's New Steamship," December 1, 1895.

———, "President McKinley's Coffin," September 15, 1901.

———, "Roosevelt Unsafe, Taft Tells Ohioans," May 14, 1912.

———, "Roosevelt's Own Creed Set Forth," August 7, 1912.

———, "Threat to Kill Roosevelt," September 15, 1912, p. 1.

———, "Roosevelt Scorns Wilson's Philosophy." September 15, 1912.

———, "Armed Automobiles Guard Roosevelt," September 17, 1912.

———, "Roosevelt Has Lost Hope," September 21, 1912.

———, "Roosevelt Jokes on Defeat," September 22, 1912.

———, "Mr. Roosevelt's Testimony," October 6, 1912.

———, "Roosevelt Attacks Deneen and Wilson," October 13, 1912.

———, "Mrs. Roosevelt Left Theatre in Tears," October 15, 1912.

———, "Progressives Here Had Great Fright," October 15, 1912.

———, "Would-Be Assassin Is John Schrank, Once Saloonkeeper Here," October 15, 1912.

———, "Mrs. Roosevelt Goes to Join Her Husband," October 16, 1912.

———, "Schrank Brooded But Seemed Sane," October 16, 1912.

———, "Schrank Owns Guilt, Callous, Then Sorry," October 16, 1912.

———, "Taft Wires Regret to Col. Roosevelt," October 16, 1912.

———, Untitled article on Elbert Martin, October 16, 1912.

———, "Roosevelt Gains, Bullet Located, Lodged in Rib," October 17, 1912, p. 1.

———, "Attacks on Colonel Banned in Campaign," October 17, 1912.

———, "She's Boss," October 18, 1912, p. 1.

———, "Wilson to Be Urged to Stay on Stump," October 19, 1912, p. 1.

———, "Schrank Bequeaths Bullet," October 19, 1912.

———, "Political Talks Tire Roosevelt," October 20, 1912, p. 1.

———, "Cheering Crowd Storms Wilson," October 20, 1912.

———, "Roosevelt Off for Home To-Day," October 21, 1912, p. 1.

———, "Murders Increase Despite Pistol Law," October 21, 1912.

———, "Avoids Crowds in Chicago," October 22, 1912.

———, "Roosevelt Stills Garden Tumult; Grave in Speech," October 31, 1912, p. 1.

———, "Speculators Got Control of Tickets," October 31, 1912.

———, "Garden Crowd Wild for Wilson," November 1, 1912, p. 1.

———, "Roosevelt Ready to Talk Tonight," November 1, 1912.

———, "Hopes Roosevelt Will Pity," November 2, 1912.

———, "Last Words from the Candidates," November 3, 1912.

———, "Cheering Thousands Jam Times Square," November 6, 1912.

———, "Taft, Owning Defeat, Calls to Deserters," November 6, 1912, p. 5.

———, "Crowds Throng Theaters," November 6, 1912.

———, "The Great Wilson Victory," November 6, 1912.

———, "Roosevelt Meets Defeat Buoyantly," November 6, 1912.

———, "Sanity Board Named to Examine Schrank," November 13, 1912.

———, "Schrank to Asylum, Declares He Is Sane" November 23, 1912.

———, "Schrank Causes Odd Real Estate Tangle," August 8, 1913.

———, "Schrank Worse; Cannot Be Tried," July 25, 1914.

———, "Augustus Van Wyck, Jurist, Dies at 71," June 9, 1922.

———, "Taft Gained Peaks in Unusual Career," March 9, 1930.

———, "Schrank, Who Shot T. Roosevelt, Dies," September 17, 1943.

New York Tribune, "Bull Moose Attacks Both Smoot and Borah," September 14, 1912, p. 4.

———, "Wilson's Doctrines 'Outworn,' Says TR," September 15, 1912, p. 4.

———, "Bosses Drubbed by Colonel in Nebraska," September 21, 1912.

———, "Dent in the South Colonel's Only Hope," September 26, 1912, p. 5.

———, "Colonel Sheds All Blame for Trust Gifts," October 5, 1912, p. 1.

———, "'Dodging Truth Tellers,'" October 7, 1912.

———, "Roosevelt Pleads for 'Human Welfare,'" October 9, 1912, p. 5.

———, "Roosevelt Angry When Charged with Untruth," October 10, 1912, p. 4.

———, "T.R. Exposes Wilson's Views on Immigration," October 11, 1912, p. 4.

———, "Third Party to Spend $350,000, Says Colonel," October 12, 1912.

———, "Roosevelt Defends His Trust Record,'" October 13, 1912, p. 4.

New York World, "Fighting Students Silence Roosevelt; He Has a Bad Day," October 1, 1912, p. 1.

———, "Taft to Practice Law in Cincinnati; Is Not Depressed," November 6, 1912, p. 1.

Office of the Sheriff, Milwaukee County, Wisconsin: Millennium History Book 1835–2000. Paducah, KY: Turner Publishing Company, 2000.

Ogden (UT) *Evening Standard,* "Roosevelt Talks to Great Crowd," September 14, 1912.

———, "Big Crowds Greet Teddy," September 24, 1912, p. 1.

———, "Long Tour Is Finished," October 2, 1912, p. 14.

O'Toole, Patricia. *When Trumpets Call: Theodore Roosevelt after the White House.* New York: Simon & Schuster, 2005.

Pacyga, Dominic A. *Chicago: A Biography.* Chicago: University of Chicago Press, 2009.

Post, Robert C. "Judicial Management: The Achievements of Chief Justice William Howard Taft." Yale Law School Faculty Scholarship Series. Paper 194, 1998. Available online at http://digitalcommons.law.yale.edu/fss_papers/194.

Pratt, John B. "Roosevelt Says Bosses Stole Clark Vote." *Chicago Examiner,* September 24, 1912, p. 4.

———. "Roosevelt on Tour Through South." *Salt Lake Tribune,* September 26, 1912, p. 2.

———. "Colonel Hurls Shot at Wilson," *Washington Herald,* October 12, 1912, p. 1.

———. "'Would Rather Die with My Boots On,' Declares Colonel," *Chicago Examiner,* October 16, 1912, p. 1.

———. "Schrank Thinks Colonel Dead; Tells of Trailing and Almost 'Getting' Him in Chattanooga," October 17, 1912, p. 3.

Pringle, Henry Fowles. *Theodore Roosevelt: A Biography.* New York: The Cornwall Press, Inc., 1931.

Rand McNally New Commercial Atlas of New Orleans. Chicago: Rand McNally and Company, 1912; available online from the University of Alabama (alabamamaps .ua.edu).

Rauchway, Eric. *Murdering McKinley: The Making of Theodore Roosevelt's America.* New York: Hill & Wang, 2003.

Reitano, Joanne. *The Restless City: A Short History of New York from Colonial Times to the Present.* New York: Routledge, 2010.

Remey, Oliver, E., Henry F. Cochems, and Wheeler P. Bloodgood. *The Attempted Assassination of Ex-President Theodore Roosevelt.* Second edition. Milwaukee: The Progressive Publishing Company, 1912. Available online free of charge.

Richmond Times Dispatch. "Colonel Trying to Capture South," September 28, 1912, p. 1.

———, "Middling Lively Time for Colonel," October 1, 1912, p. 7.

———, "Still Battling at Armageddon," October 2, 1912, p. 1.

———, "Deneen Is Latest in Ananias Club," October 13, 1912, p. 1.

Rock Hill (SC) *Evening Herald,* "Roosevelt Getting Along Nicely; Physicians Say Crisis Will Come by Friday," October 16, 1912.

Roosevelt, Theodore. *An Autobiography.* New York: Macmillan Publishing, 1913. Available online from Google Books (books.google.com) and elsewhere.

———. *Through the Brazilian Wilderness.* New York: Charles Scribner's Sons, 1914.

———. *The Letters of Theodore Roosevelt. Volume VII, The Days of Armageddon, 1909–1914.* Cambridge: Harvard University Press, 1954.

St. Paul Appeal, "To Get Schrank's Weapon," April 25, 1914.

Salvatore, Nick. *Eugene V. Debs: Citizen and Socialist.* Urbana: University of Illinois Press, 1982.

Salt Lake Tribune, "Thousands Greet Wilson in Chicago," October 11, 1912, p. 2.
San Francisco Call, "Colonel Urges People of West to Beat Bosses," September 14, 1912, p. 13.
———, "Bull Moose Chief Shakes City's Dust," September 16, 1912, p. 2.
———, "Colonel Makes Wilson Oracle of Trust Evil," September 17, 1912.
———, "Roosevelt Kicks Up Desert Waste," September 18, 1912.
———, "Pueblo Indians See Big Moose," September 19, 1912.
———, "President Declines Debate," September 21, 1912, p. 1.
———, "Colonel Defends Political Flop," September 21, 1912, p. 11.
———, "Colonel Enjoys Rest in Kansas," September 23, 1912, p. 2.
———, "Politics Drives Mooser Insane," September 24, 1912, p. 1.
———, "T.R. Has Regular Wall Street Day," September 26, 1912, p. 4.
———, "Colonel Reaches 'Darkest South,'" September 28, 1912, p. 11.
———, "Colonel Faces Riotous Crowd in Southland," October 1, 1912, p. 3.
———, "'Trust Money Was Legal'—Roosevelt," October 5, 1912, p. 10.
———, "Colonel Snaps Out Invective," October 5, 1912, p. 10.
———, "Chicago Gives Big Ovation to Wilson," October 11, 1912, p. 3.
———, "Chicagoans Snub Chief Bull Moose," October 13, 1912.
———, "Colonel Lyon Sees Assassin," October 16, 1912, p. 2.
———, "Schrank Wants Pistol Returned," April 26, 1913.
Sanborn Map Company. "Augusta, Richmond County, Georgia, 1904." Available from the University of Georgia Libraries Map Collection, Athens, Ga., presented in the Digital Library of Georgia (dlg.galileo.usg.edu/sanborn/id:Augusta1904).
———. "Chattanooga, Tennessee, 1917." (I was not able to locate an online version of this map.)
———. "Milwaukee, 1910." Available online at the University of Wisconsin-Milwaukee website (http://collections.lib.uwm.edu/cdm/landingpage/collection/san/).
Schneider, Dorothee. *Trade Unions and Community: The German Working Class in New York City, 1870–1900*. Champaign: University of Illinois Press, 1994.
Schneiderman, Rose. "A Cap Maker's Story: Rose Schneiderman." Available on Digital History website (digitalhistory.uh.edu).
Senate Historical Office, "Russell Senate Office Building: The First Century, 1909–2009" (available online at senate.gov).
Shearer, John. "Hotel Patten Completed One Hundred Years Ago, Officials Planning Centennial Celebration." *The Chattanoogan*, June 8, 2008 (available online at chattanoogan.com).
Sooy, Harry O. "Memoirs of My Career at Victor Talking Machine Company." Available online at the David Sarnoff Library (davidsarnoff.org).
Stern, M. R. "Map of the City of Chattanooga, Tenn," 1911.
Tacoma Times, "Roosevelt in Reno Scores Big Hit," September 14, 1912.
———, "National Campaign," September 23, 1912, p. 1.
———, "Crank Tries to See Teddy," September 30, 1912, p. 7.
———, "Debs Closes," November 2, 1912, p. 1.
Thomasville (GA) *Daily Times Enterprise*, "His Itinerary Announced," September 23, 1912, p. 1.

————, "Attend Waterways Convention," September 25, 1912.

————, "South Must Be Broken," September 27, 1912.

————, "Roosevelt in Alabama," September 28, 1912, p. 1.

Thompson, Charles Willis. *Presidents I've Known and Two Near Presidents.* Manchester, NH: Ayer Company Publishers, Inc., 1929.

Tiller, Theodore. "Crowds Cheer Col. Roosevelt in Golden Gate," *Washington Times,* September 15, 1912, p. 2.

————, "Woman Chorus Greets Colonel with 'America,'" *Washington Times,* September 16, 1912, p. 2.

————, "Roosevelt in Bryan's State with Answers." *Washington Times,* September 20, 1912, p. 1.

————, "Colonel Slaps Bosses, Kansas Men Applaud." *Washington Times,* September 21, 1912, p. 2.

————, "Colonel Rests by Speaking in Big Phonograph," *Washington Times,* September 22, 1912, p. 1.

————, "Bull Moose to Show Missouri His Principles," *Washington Times,* September 23, 1912, p. 2.

————, "Colonel Urges 'Americanism' in the South," *Washington Times,* September 25, 1912, p. 4.

————, "T.R. Declares for Waterways and Levee Plan," *Washington Times,* September 26, 1912, p. 3.

————, "Colonel Urges Solid South to Enter Fold," *Washington Times,* September 27, 1912, p. 7.

————, "Colonel Finds Bull Moosers in Alabama," *Washington Times,* September 28, 1912; p. 1.

————, "Roosevelt Makes Pilgrimage to His Mother's Old Home," *Washington Times,* September 29, 1912, p. 10.

————, "Colonel Back in Tennessee Urging Issues," *Washington Times,* September 30, 1912, p. 3.

————, "Colonel Hopes to Split South in Two States," *Washington Times,* October 1, 1912.

————, "Col. Roosevelt Is Headed for Home and Brief Rest," *Washington Times,* October 2, 1912, p. 7.

————, "Roosevelt Arrives Ready to Testify Before Committee," *Washington Times,* October 4, 1912, p. 20.

Van Smith, George A. "Thousands at Coliseum Give Evidence of Their Faith in Head Mooser." *San Francisco Call,* September 15, 1912, p. 1.

Walsh, Peter. "The Strange Birth of NY's Gun Laws," *New York Post,* January 15, 2012.

Washington Herald, "Teddy Attacks Governor Wilson," September 15, 1912, p. 3.

————, "Clark's Name Brings Cheers," September 24, 1912, p. 3.

————, "Wilson Men Howl Down TR," September 29, 1912, p. 4.

————, "Colonel Raps Favorite Son of Tennessee," October 1, 1912, p. 1.

————, "T.R. to Make Another Tour," October 7, 1912, p. 3.

————, "Colonel Starts on Long Tour," October 8, 1912, p. 3.

————, "Big Ovation for T.R. in Michigan," October 9, 1912, p. 3.

————, "T.R. Throws Hot Shot at Deneen," October 13, 1912, p. 3.

Washington Times, "Utah Mormons Give Colonel Great Welcome," September 14, 1912.

————, "T.R. Pledges New Laws for Working Man," September 17, 1912.

————, "President Makes Bitter Attack on Col. Roosevelt," October 6, 1912, p. 2.

————, "Roosevelt Leaves Today for West," October 7, 1912, p. 1.

————, "Factories Closed to Permit Workers to Hear Roosevelt," October 8, 1912, p. 1.

————, "Roosevelt Ready for Attack Upon La Follette Today," October 11, 1912, p. 3.

————, "Wilson Is Flayed by Col Roosevelt for Tariff Stand," October 12, 1912, p. 1.

————, "Colonel Flays Wilson Record on Trust Issue," October 13, 1912, p. 1.

————, "Man Who Shot T.R. Is Close Student of War Progress," June 28, 1918, p. 10.

White, William Allen. *The Autobiography of William Allen White*. New York: The Macmillan Company, 1946.

Yockelson, Mitchell, "'I Am Entitled to the Medal of Honor and I Want It': Theodore Roosevelt and His Quest for Glory." *Prologue Magazine*, Spring 1998, Vol. 30, No. 1. Available on the National Archives website, www.archives.gov.

INDEX

About the Author

Gerard Helferich is the author of the widely praised *Stone of Kings: In Search of the Lost Jade of the Maya* (Lyons Press), *Humboldt's Cosmos: Alexander von Humboldt and the Latin American Journey That Changed the Way We See the World*, and *High Cotton: Four Seasons in the Mississippi Delta*, which received the Mississippi Library Association's Authors Award for nonfiction. A member of the National Book Critics Circle, he publishes reviews in the *Wall Street Journal* and has contributed to the Fodor's travel guides to Mexico and Guatemala. For the past decade, he has been on the faculty of the Columbia Publishing Course at the Columbia Graduate School of Journalism and has presented nonfiction workshops at the San Miguel Writers Conference. Before turning to writing in 2002, he was an editor and publisher for twenty-five years at companies such as Doubleday, Simon & Schuster, and John Wiley & Sons. He lives in Yazoo City, Mississippi, and San Miguel de Allende, Mexico, with his wife, the writer Teresa Nicholas.